CANNIBAL

CANNIBAL

The History of the People-Eaters

Daniel Korn, Mark Radice & Charlie Hawes

First published in March 2001 by Channel 4 Books
This edition published 2002 by Channel 4 Books, an imprint of Pan Macmillan Ltd
Pan Macmillan, 20 New Wharf Road, London N1 9RR, Basingstoke and Oxford.

Associated companies throughout the world

www.panmacmillan.com

ISBN 0 7522 6196 7

9 8 7 6 5 4 3 2

A CIP catalogue record for this book is available from the British Library.

Design and colour reproduction by Ben Cracknell Studios
Typeset by seagulls
Printed by Mackays of Chatham plc

Picture credits: *page 1* – (top) Mary Evans Picture Library, (below) Mary Evans Picture
Library; *page 2* – (top) Paola Villa, (centre) Paola Villa, (below) *The Last Supper* by Vicente
Juan Macip (Juan de Juanes) (c. 1510–79) Prado, Madrid, Spain/Bridgeman Art Library;
page 3 – (top) Nadezhda Zapiantsev, (below) Mark Radice; *page 4* – (top left) Russian
State Archive of Film and Photographic Documents, Krasnogorsk,(top right) Siege Museum
of Leningrad, (below) Siege Museum of Leningrad; *page 5* – (top) Art Book Co. Ltd,
Taiwan, (below) *The Raft of the Medusa*, 1819 by Theodore Gericault (1791–1824) Louvre,
Paris, France/Bridgeman Art Library; *page 6* – (top) Topham Picturepoint, (below) Corbis-
Sygma; *page 7* – (top left) Richard Lourie, (top right) *Democrat and Chronicle*, Rochester
NY, (below left) Popperfoto/Reuter, (below right) Popperfoto; *page 8* – (top) Adrian Raine,
(below) Adrian Raine.

The publishers have made every effort to trace the owners of these photographs, and
apologise for any omissions.

Contents

Acknowledgements

Daniel Korn, Mark Radice and Charlie Hawes would like to thank everyone involved in the production of the 3BM Television series *Cannibal* for Channel 4 Television: Dan Chambers at Channel 4; 3BM Television executive producer Simon Berthon; programme directors Katharine English, Alex Marengo and Peter Nicholson; and all who advised and assisted with the production, especially Dr Timothy Taylor, Stephen Hallett, Beth Millward, Steve Bergson, Annalisa d'Innella, Julie Kleeman, Sarah Jackson, Beth Salt, Elena Batuyeva, Adam Levy, Yukiko Shimahara. Our thanks also to Gillian Christie at Channel 4 Books.

In addition, we would like to thank the contributors to each of the three programmes:

Programme One, 'The Real Hannibal Lecters': Dr Fred Berlin, Professor Colin Blakemore, Lionel Dahmer, Dr Joel Fort, Dr Robert Hare, Dr Steve Hucker, Jim Jackson, Detective Pat Kennedy, Dr Richard Kraus, Dr Dorothy Otnow Lewis, Dr Richard Lourie, Dr Donald Lunde, Moira Martingale, Brian Masters, Dr Declan

Murphy, Captain Dennis Murphy, Professor Susuma Oda, Jack Olsen, Dr Jonathan Pincus, Dr Adrian Raine, Dr Kenneth Smail, Ryu Suzuki, Professor Andrei Tkachenko, and Colin Wilson;

Programme Two, 'Bones of Contention': Professor Margaret Cox, Fergus Clunie, the late Chief Mosese Tuisawau, Sekove Bigitibau, David DeGusta, Dr Yolanda Fernandez-Jalvo, Dr Shannon Novak, Irene O'Sullivan, Richard Lloyd Parry, Professor Marshall Sahlins, Professor Chris Stringer, Dr Christina Toren, Dr Paola Villa, Dr Allen Abramson, Professor Paul Sillitoe, Professor Tim D. White, Dr Tim G. Allen, Dr Tarisi Vunidilo, Ratu Jone Naucabalavu and Paul Geraghty;

Programme Three, 'Man Meat': Dr John Barber, Professor Orlando Figes, Bishop Alexander Bykovetz, Dr Nadezhda Cherepenina, Professor Andrei Dzeniskevich, Mikhail Tarasov, Alexander Zotov, Jasper Becker, Liu Binyan, Chip Tsao, Zheng Yi, Professor Christine Yu, Stephen Ellis, Robin Hallett, Piers Paul Read, Fernando Parrado, Carlitos Paez, Dr Mike Stroud, Scott Cookman, and Dr James Thompson.

Finally, we would like to thank anyone else who assisted with the making of the series and writing of this book, whose name has been unintentionally omitted.

ONE

Encountering the Cannibal

In the 1970s, Australian anthropologist Alfred Gell was conducting fieldwork alone among the Umeda people of the West Sepik district of Papua New Guinea. Memorably and shockingly, he encountered a cannibal:

> I happened once, during my fieldwork, to be peeling a stick of sugar cane together with some companions from Umeda village. Clumsily, I allowed my knife to slip and it embedded itself in my finger. Unhurriedly, but still unthinkingly, I deposited the offending kitchen knife and the still unpeeled stick of sugar cane and raised my bleeding finger to my lips. The external world ceased momentarily to exist for me, conscious only of the familiar saltwater taste on my tongue... [this] lapse of consciousness was a lapse indeed, as the shocked countenances and expressions of disgust evinced by my Umeda companions told me soon enough, just as soon as I recovered my wits and looked about me.

Gell had never conceived of himself as a cannibal – yet the instinctive reaction of plunging a cut finger into his mouth transformed him into one for the Umeda. Other auto-cannibalistic habits the Umeda strenuously avoided included nail-biting and swallowing nasal mucus. The Umeda, rather like Westerners, expressed a total contempt for cannibalism, even though it featured prominently in their stories and myths. But from a Umedan point of view Westerners have probably all been guilty of cannibalism at one time or another.

Gell's embarrassment among the Papuans is a nice cautionary tale. It highlights one of those convenient blind spots (placenta-eating is another) that Westerners seem to develop when cannibalism goes on back home. More important, it serves to remind us that the way in which modern Westerners imagine and define cannibalism isn't the only legitimate means of doing so – a lesson well worth bearing in mind. Nevertheless, as we shall see, the practice and extent of cannibalism has never been simply restricted to nail-biting.

Cannibalism is an exotic and frightening concept that looms large in our legends and childhood stories. It is certainly the strongest of all taboos, a practice we find so repellent and horrific that it becomes quite literally unimaginable. Throughout recorded history and from many different societies, 'cannibal' has always been a charge used to dehumanize opponents and rivals, or a boast made to terrify them. The term has undoubtedly been used to justify genocide, conquest and rule by Europeans in the past, but conversely often also becomes a slur used by the oppressed against the powerful (as in parts of Africa and Papua New Guinea).

Over the last twenty years some scholars have questioned if cannibalism has even existed. They argue that cannibalism is a myth turned into reality by credulous (or racist) missionaries and explorers and perpetuated into modern times by historians and ethnographers all too willing to believe in this uniquely monstrous concept. In short, the history of the cannibal has been intensely sensational, controversial and riven with dispute ever since Columbus returned in 1492 claiming to have encountered man-eaters in the New World.

These first chapters of *Cannibal* will investigate the evidence that suggests that cannibalism has been widespread through human prehistory and history. We will survey the history of our knowledge of cannibalism and the arguments that have always raged about it before exploring the new osteological evidence that is finally starting to bring the subject into the realm of proper study. Finally, we will look at what cannibalism meant in one society where for thousands of years it was indisputably an important and vital aspect of religious and political life – the Fiji islands in the Pacific.

The type of cannibalism discussed here is distinct from that covered in the remainder of the book. Everyone acknowledges that in times of famine, or when groups of people are stranded away from food, cannibalism can be a desperate survival strategy. Similarly, it is clear that rare individuals, like Jeffrey Dahmer, develop some form of sexual psychopathy that (among other things) makes them like to eat parts of their victims. On the other hand, what has been in dispute, and what the first chapters of this book will explore, is the existence of cannibalism as an act of choice existing as a generally accepted custom within a society. In fact, as we shall see, the evidence for this kind of cannibalism, usually called customary or ritual cannibalism, is very strong, although its prevalence and practice has certainly been exaggerated and distorted by Europeans (and everyone else) in the past.

For most anthropologists and among archaeologists who study human bones, the question of whether or not cannibalism existed is now long since answered by an abundance of convincing and rigorous evidence. Clearly, cannibalism has been of greater significance in the past than it is today. Nevertheless, cannibalism remains a very distinctive kind of human behaviour and as such merits sober curiosity and proper analysis.

Our inherent fears and ideas about the cannibal are what made the term itself. 'Cannibalism' is a relatively new word, introduced into the English language by Christopher Columbus, who first used it in his journal of 23 November 1492. The noun 'cannibal' comes from the Arawak 'caniba', which is a corruption of 'cariba', meaning 'bold'. This was the term the Caribbean Indians of the Lesser Antilles used to describe themselves, but when the word was used by their neighbours, the peace-loving Arawak, it became an insult indicating extreme barbarity. Columbus picked up the word from the Arawak on his first voyage and used their meaning of it in his journal.

Columbus misinterpreted the term as 'Khan-iba' and associated it with the Great Khan of the Mongols he was expecting to encounter on his voyage. He also associated the word with the Latin for 'dog' – 'canis'. The great classical author Pliny had populated the fringes of the world with man-eating Cyclopean and dog-headed tribes, so when the Arawak began talking about man-eaters Columbus put the two together. Columbus could never accurately determine which of the monstrous men of antiquity he had encountered on his first voyage. On 11 December 1492 he wrote: 'I therefore repeat what I have said several times already: that the Caniba are none other than the people of the Great Khan, who must be neighbours to these. They have ships, they come and capture these people, and as those who are taken never return, the others believe that they have been eaten.'

On his second voyage, in 1493, Columbus actually encountered the Caribs on the island of Guadeloupe. The discovery of dismembered body parts and a severed head in an abandoned Carib village seemed to vindicate the accusations of the Arawak, and it was this event that seared European consciousness with the idea of cannibal tribes in newly discovered lands.

Before the term 'cannibalism' was coined, a different, more neutral word had been used to describe man-eating: 'anthropophagy'. Used by the Greek historian Herodotus in the fifth century BC, this was a combination of the Greek words 'anthropos' ('man') and 'phagein' ('to eat'). It's a more descriptive word than 'cannibalism' and is still much in use, preferred by anthropologists and historians. The people Herodotus identified as man-eaters were the androphagi, who had 'the most savage customs of all men'. Herodotus located the androphagi somewhere beyond the Scythians, on the far north-eastern fringes of the known world.

Thus, the shift from the anthropophagous androphagi of the classical writers to the sixteenth-century cannibals of the Age of Discovery was seamless. The latter were widely publicized by Peter Martyr's chronicles of Columbus's great discoveries, *De Orbe Novo*, in 1511: 'The wylde and mysterious people called Canibales or Caribes, which were accustomed to eat mannes flesshe (and called of the olde writers Anthropophagi)... Vexed with the incursions of these manhuntying Canibales.'

It is, as we shall see, highly significant that our modern word for the practice of people-eating originates in a descriptive term for a warlike enemy, but this doesn't necessarily mean that all modern languages create their words for man-eating in a similar way. The etymology of the term in the language of a people among whom cannibalism was an accepted part of life is, of course, very different. In the Fijian dialect, the word meaning 'cannibalism' is the far less politically charged *veikanikani* – literally, 'eating one another'.

Why and how cannibalism happened (and happens) varies extraordinarily between different peoples, although it is possible to come up with some general guidelines. As the *Encyclopedia Britannica* states: 'There is no one satisfactory and all inclusive explanation for cannibalism. Different peoples have practised it for different reasons, and a group may practise cannibalism in one context and view it with horror in another.'

At one end of the scale of customary cannibalism are societies like the Aztecs or Old Fiji, where man-eating was practised on a large scale as one aspect of a spectacular ritual and had important and highly elaborate religious meaning. Towards the other extreme might be a society like the Yanomami of Amazonia, where cannibalism is a less common, highly private and intimate affair, practised by the kin of the deceased as part of the mourning ceremony. Another alternative could be nineteenth-century Europe or China, where cannibalism was practised as a medical remedy. Cannibalism can, of course, be purely symbolic, as in the core ritual of Christianity. Transubstantiation is the doctrine whereby the wine and bread that Christian worshippers accept during Communion become the blood and flesh of Christ.

The key characteristic of customary cannibalism that all such groups share is the choice individuals can explicitly make under particular circumstances not dictated by basic survival, and that the behaviour is comprehensible to the wider group, though comprehensibility doesn't automatically mean that it is encouraged. Any modern Westerner can envisage the torture of an enemy captured in warfare, although we certainly don't condone it. Killing and then eating an enemy, however, is not something we can imagine doing under any circumstances, yet it seems that doing so has been a deliberate act for many people under conditions of conflict throughout human history and prehistory. In Britain today, the act of torture is, of course, illegal, while the act of cannibalism is not. So what's significant is that not only do we not practise cannibalism, but we can't even imagine it as something we could possibly do – hence the tendency of Westerners to sensationalize and disbelieve accounts of the practice elsewhere.

So, if cannibalism has occurred for a wide variety of reasons, how can we even begin to define this diverse and complex human behaviour? Anthropologists and archaeologists have tended to categorize cannibalism broadly into two general types according to who is eating whom: exo-cannibalism and endo-cannibalism.

Exo-cannibalism is defined as one group or society killing and eating members of another group, almost always enemies. This is man-eating as the ultimate revenge. What can be more terrifying than the thought of being consumed by your enemy, or a more satisfactory means of expressing total victory and domination over a hated and defeated foe than defecating their digested remains? Exo-cannibals often also believe that eating their dead enemies gives them an additional spiritual victory, either by incorporating coveted powers of the eaten or by annihilating their souls in some fashion. This is cannibalism as an aspect of conflict, slaughter and revenge, and certainly the kind we tend to associate with the practice in the West. The Maoris of New Zealand were the archetypal exo-cannibals of the eighteenth century, and in the sixteenth century the Tupinamba of Brazil were infamous for eating enemies captured in battle.

Endo-cannibalism, on the other hand, generally means the eating of your own dead, typically relatives or kin. This generally indicates cannibalism as part of a reverential funerary ritual, a way of incorporating the substance of recently deceased kin back into their living relatives in a supreme act of veneration. Numerous peoples in South America and Papua New Guinea have practised endo-cannibalism in the twentieth century, and ancient writers reported the practice in European tribes.

This distinction is supported by evidence suggesting two different practices. As archaeologist Dr Timothy Taylor states:

Different sorts of cannibalism leave different types of traces, or perhaps no trace at all, in the archaeological record. If we look at the funerary cannibalistic rites of the Yanomami Indians of Central Amazonia, when a child dies they consume it so thoroughly, even pulverizing the bones and drinking them down in plantain soup, that there is nothing left.

Archaeologically, the sorts of signatures we have for cannibalism tend to be signatures of a different type showing aggressive exo-cannibalism that may not be closely related to reverencing the dead and much more connected to conflict and manhunting.

Much of the following chapters will be focused on osteological evidence believed to be the result of some kind of aggressive exo-cannibalism. The people whose bones are studied today were killed and eaten first and foremost because they were somebody's enemies. Generally, cannibalism that has actually been observed or reported by anthropologists in the twentieth century has been in the reverential endo-cannibalistic funerary tradition – such as that in Amazonia or Papua New Guinea. So the kind of recent cannibalism we have archaeological evidence for is not the kind we are most immediately familiar with.

Myth or Reality?

In 1979 the American anthropologist Dr William Arens called into question the very existence of cannibalism, and his book, *The Man-Eating Myth: Anthropology and Anthropophagy*, proved to be enormously popular and influential. It has become required reading for anthropology undergraduates and made the subsequent academic debates about cannibalism headline news.

The Man-Eating Myth is really about anthropology. Arens was interested in why anthropologists (and everyone else) have been so willing to believe in the widespread existence of cannibalism. Arens claimed to have been able to find no reliable eyewitness accounts of the practice, either in the historical record or among his peers in anthropology. Cannibalism, according to Arens, was little more than a racist legend. Even worse, its existence has been used as propaganda to justify European colonialism – most famously in the Spanish conquest of the New World in the sixteenth century.

Arens was undoubtedly correct to question the extent of the practice of cannibalism and to draw attention to its use as propaganda. In the long run the book has had the intended positive effect of stimulating debate about man-eating and generally raising the standards of proof used by archaeologists and anthropologists whenever cannibalism is discussed. Most of Arens's colleagues, however, thought that he overstated the case against cannibalism by claiming no proof existed for it. It is also hard to assume, as he does, that all conquistadors, explorers, missionaries, traders and colonizers – as well as many anthropologists, historians and journalists – have embellished or fabricated what they reported. Worse, by lumping all such people together and characterizing them as prejudiced and credulous (or just dishonest), wasn't Arens engaging in exactly the exercise he condemned in others?

Arens also seemed to have been unusually selective in the use of evidence to back up his argument, and he didn't discuss Polynesia in any real depth at all. Finally, he didn't seem to be able to conceive of a situation in which cannibalism not only existed but was also used as a justification for conquest and 'civilization' by Europeans. As he stated it, cannibalism was either real or it was propaganda, but could never be both at once. So what kind of ethnographic evidence is there for the existence of cannibalism? Here, published in the 1970s, is an anthropologist's eyewitness description of mortuary cannibalism among the Guiaca, a village people of the upper Orinoco River in South America:

> We have observed several instances of the cremation of the deceased in the village plaza on the day of his death, the careful collection of the half-carbonized bones from the ashes, and the grinding of these bones in a wooden mortar. The resulting powder was poured into little calabashes and given to the dead person's closest relatives, who kept them near the roof of their hut. On ceremonial occasions... the relatives would put some of this powder into a large calabash half full of plantain soup and drink the mixture accompanied by lamentations. The family was very careful not to spill any of it.

How have explorers and travellers characterized cannibalism over the years? Of course, it's impossible to catalogue every reaction, and many travellers did exaggerate, embellish and lie when they told tales of cannibalism back home. But to state that all such people did so fails to capture the historical reality of what some of their attitudes really were, and what was actually reported in particular cases.

Captain James Cook's three journeys of exploration in the eighteenth century present an interesting example. In 1770, during his first voyage on the *Endeavour*, Cook was accompanied by the young natural scientist Joseph Banks. Sir Joseph Banks later became known as the greatest botanist of his day, founded Kew Gardens and remains among the most influential scientists in British history. Like many rational scientists of the time, Banks was also highly dubious about the practice of cannibalism, until he encountered evidence for it himself among the Maoris of New Zealand.

New Zealand (or Totara-Nui as it was known by the people who lived there) had been 'discovered' in 1642 by the Dutch explorer Tasman, who weighed anchor fairly rapidly after four of his crew were attacked and killed by some hostile Maoris. Cook's ship, the *Endeavour*, carrying a Tahitian chief named Tupia who acted as interpreter, arrived off the North Island of New Zealand in the winter of 1769. The following story of Cook's encounter with Maori cannibalism was definitively documented by New Zealand anthropologist Professor Dame Anne Salmond in her book *Two Worlds: First Meetings Between Maori and Europeans 1642–1772*. It should be noted that this passage doesn't include an analysis of what Maori cannibalism meant to the Maoris, although it was similar in many ways to Fijian cannibalism, which will be explored in depth later in the book. The passage does, however, illustrate how complex the response of European explorers encountering cannibalism could be.

The *Endeavour* had been in New Zealand for several months at various locations before Cook and Banks found anything like hard evidence of cannibalism. They had gone ashore one evening in January 1770, with Tupia, to a cove about a mile from the ship. On the way they had passed a body of a woman floating in the water. Banks knew by now that some Maoris disposed of their dead kin by weighing the bodies down at sea, and clearly this was one corpse whose stone ballast had slipped off. Coming ashore, they met a group of Maoris and discovered that the woman was a friend of theirs. Banks related in his journal what happened:

The family was employed when we came ashore in dressing their provisions... near [were] many provision baskets. Looking carelessly upon one of these we by accident observed two bones, pretty clean picked, which as appeared upon examination were undoubtedly human bones. Tho' we had from the first of our arrival on the coast constantly heard the Indians acknowledge the custom of eating their enemies we had never before had a proof of it, but this amounted almost to demonstration: the bones were clearly human, upon them were evident marks of their having been dressed on the fire, the meat was not intirely picked off from them and on the grisly ends which were knawed were evident marks of teeth, and these were accidentally found in a provision basket. On asking the people what bones are these? they answered, The bones of a man. – And have you eat the flesh? – Yes. – Have you none of it left? – No. – Why did you not eat the woman who we saw today in the water? – She was our relation. And who then is it that you do eat? – Those who are killd in war. – And who was the man whose bones these are? – Five days ago a boat of our enemies came into this bay and of them we killed seven, of whom the owner of these bones was one. – The horrour that appeared in the countenances of the seamen on hearing this discourse which was immediately translated for the good of the company is better conceivd than describd.

Banks was convinced by this encounter, but both he and Cook caused a sensation, and were widely disbelieved, when they returned to Europe and reported cannibalism among the New Zealanders. Luckily for Banks's scientific reputation, Cook's second visit to New Zealand, in 1773, during his next voyage on the *Resolution*, provided a more conclusive event. The shipboard scientist on the return trip was an empirically minded British astronomer named William Wales. As described by Professor Salmond, the course they took was different this time around, with the *Resolution* calling at New Zealand twice in one voyage. As they departed after the first visit towards the Pacific islands of Tahiti and Tonga, Wales reflected on the Maoris' reputation for violence and cannibalism:

Before going to leave this island of Canibals, as it is generally thought to be, it may be expected that I should record what bloody massacres I have been a witness of; how many human Carcases I have seen roasted and eaten; or at least relate such facts as have fallen within the Compass of my Observation tending to confirm the Opinion, now almost universally believed, that the New Zeelanders are guilty of this most detestable Practice. Truth, notwithstanding, obliges me to declare, however unpopular it may be, that I have not seen the least signs of any such custom being amongst them... the real state of the Case is this.

They first began with shewing us how they handled their Weapons, how they defyed the Enemy to Battle, how they killed him; they then proceeded to cut off his head, legs & arms; they afterwards took out his bowels and threw them away, and lastly shewed us that they went to eating. But it ought by all means to be remarked that all this was shewn by signs which everyone will allow are easily misunderstood, and for any thing that I know to the contrary they might mean they Eat the man they had just killed; but is it not as likely that after the Engagement they refreshed themselves with some other Victuals which they might have had with them?

Wales was an exacting and scrupulous scientist who would not accept as fact anything he had not actually witnessed, and he was instinctively distrustful of the seamen's accounts of Maori man-eating. But Wales had not seen actual Maori warfare, or its aftermath. On the *Resolution*'s return to New Zealand in November 1773, the ship's company did brush up against some local conflict. On 21 November some of the local men embarked on a plundering raid against their enemies to the west in order to acquire new objects to barter with the *Resolution*'s crew. After their triumphant return, and the subsequent exchange of goods, Cook and Wales went ashore to check some of the gardens planted by the men to supply vegetables for future voyages.

Meanwhile, one of the ship's officers, Pickersgill, and some of his shipmates went across to another area of the shoreline, where they found several women sitting together weeping and cutting their foreheads with sharp stones (*haehae* – a sign of grief). Close by, a group of warriors were cutting up the body of a young man whom they had killed in the raid. The warriors explained that they had killed several of their enemies, but some of their companions had been killed and they had only been able to bring one enemy body away. One of the warriors, no doubt teasing the Europeans, skewered the discarded lungs of the dead man on the end of his spear and 'with great gayety' raised them to Pickersgill's mouth. Pickersgill refused the offer, but he bartered for the severed head of the corpse as a souvenir that he took back to the *Resolution*.

On board the ship an officer named Charles Clerke cut a piece of flesh from the cheek of the head and took it to the galley, where he grilled it on a gridiron. He then offered the cooked meat to the Maoris then on the quarterdeck, one of whom ate it with pleasure 'suck[ing] his fingers half a dozen times over in raptures' (no doubt aware of and amused by the Europeans' reaction).

When Cook, Wales and Hitihiti (a young Polynesian from Borabora who had recently joined the ship) arrived back on board, Clerke repeated the demonstration for the captain, the 'experimental gentlemen' and the assembled crew. Some of the sailors laughed, while others vomited in disgust. Hitihiti was appalled, transfixed 'as if Metamorphosed into the Statue of Horror', while the local people laughed at him.

Charles Clerke had previously exhibited a delight in the strange and the marvellous, publishing a straight-faced account of 'giants' in Patagonia in the Royal Society's Philosophical Transactions in 1767, much to the delight of his shipmates. His improvised cannibal barbecue on the *Resolution* mocked both the cannibals and the Europeans, as well as the notion of scientific 'witnessing'. The sceptical William Wales was now convinced:

They do not, as I supposed might be the Case, eat them only on the spot whilst under the Impulse of that wild frenzy into which they have shewn us they can & do work themselves in their Engagements; but in cool Blood: For it was now many days since the battle could have happened... It cannot be through want of Annimal food; because they every day caught as much fish as served both themselves and us: they have moreover plenty of fine Dogs which they were at the same time selling us for mere trifles; nor is there any want of various sorts of fowl, which they can readily kill if they please... It seems therefore to follow of course, that their practice of this horrid Action is from Choice, and the liking which they have for this kind of Food; and this was but too visibly shewn in their eagerness for, and the satisfaction which they testified in eating, those inconsiderable scrapts, of the worst part on board the Ship.

The event also prompted Cook to muse on Maori cannibalism in a passage that is revealing about the attitudes of particular European observers towards 'savages' in general:

That the New Zealanders are Canibals can now no longer be doubted, the account I gave of it in my former voyage was partly founded on circumstances and was, as I afterwards found, discredited by many people... The New Zealanders are certainly in a state of civiliza-tion, their behaviour to us has been Manly and Mild, shewing allways a readiness to oblige us; they have some arts among them which they execute with great judgement and unweared patience; they are far less addicted to thieving than the other Islanders and I believe strictly honist among them-selves. This custom of eating their enemies slain in battle (for I firmly believe they eat the flesh of no others) has undoubt-edly been handed down to them from the earliest times and we know that it is not an easy matter to break a nation of its ancient customs...

In *The Man-Eating Myth*, Arens also criticizes travellers and missionaries as other Europeans responsible for spreading racist myths about cannibal tribes. Again, no doubt many people did brand societies as savage when they encountered cannibalism, and certainly many missionaries used the charge to justify their evangelical mission, but that doesn't mean they made it up, or that there are no reliable first-hand accounts of the practice.

The earliest detailed account of a society that practised cannibalism was published in the sixteenth century. Hans Staden's *The True History and description of a Country of Savages* related his experiences among the Tupinamba, a society who lived on the (now) Brazilian coast. He related in detail their exo-cannibalistic rituals with captured prisoners of war. Was Staden lying? How could Europeans have spoken the Tupi language? Were later writers who claimed to have visited the Tupinamba and witnessed cannibalism simply plagiarizing Staden? One of these subsequent writers was a Frenchman named Jean de Lery, who published his account of the Tupinamba in 1580, entitled *History of a Voyage to The Land of Brazil, Otherwise called America*. This is generally thought to be the first 'modern' ethno-graphic account of another society, a classic of its type in anthropological literature. The long and detailed chapter in which he discusses Tupinamban cannibalism is called 'How the

Americans Treat their Prisoners of War and the Ceremonies they observe both in Killing and in Eating Them'. De Lery, like Cook 200 years later in the Pacific, offered his opinion as to the basic motivation behind this practice of aggressive exo-cannibalism:

> Not, however (as far as one can judge), that they regard this as nourishment; for although all of them confess human flesh to be wonderfully good and delicate, none the less it is more out of vengeance than for the taste... their chief intention is that by pursuing the dead and gnawing them right down to the bone, they will strike fear and terror into the hearts of the living.

D.W. Forsyth, an American anthropologist, challenged the claim that such accounts of the Tupinamba are inherently flawed. He has analysed in detail the writings of the Jesuit monks who lived among the Tupinamba in the sixteenth century, noting that they spent much time in Indian villages, learned the language and attended to the Indians without charge (unlike the harsher treatment of the settlers). One of the Jesuits translated parts of the Bible, as well as chants and prayers, into the Tupi language; another wrote a grammar of the language which all Jesuits were required to learn. Some of the brothers had years of experience with the Tupinamba; one had been a slaver who spoke the language fluently and had abandoned his occupation to become a lay brother.

All this led Forsyth to accept many of the Jesuits' eyewitness accounts of cannibalism, to believe accounts that they confiscated bodies to stop them from being cannibalized, and that they had intervened successfully and prevented some prisoners from being killed and eaten. Why should the Jesuits have wasted their time in trying to stop cannibalism if the practice did not exist? He wrote:

> If the Tupinamba did not practice cannibalism, numerous experienced and knowledgeable Jesuits lie outright. They lied in their letters to friends and associates. They lied in their letters to superiors. They lied in reports to their order. They lied in their letters to one another. And they did so, consistently, without qualification or exception, over more than half a century.

If we accept many of the Jesuits' other observations about Tupinamban behaviour – that they maintained extended households, that descent was traced through the male line and that they slept in hammocks – why should we disbelieve their extensive reports about cannibalism? Forsyth admitted that there may be distortions because the ultimate goal of these Catholic missionaries was to convert the Indians. But Tupinamban society was observed in depth and at length. Cannibalism was seen as horrible, and attempts were constantly made to stop it. Europeans did eventually destroy their culture (and the culture of all other indigenous American peoples), but this does not mean that the day-to-day observations of the Jesuits among the Tupinamba were inaccurate.

The existence of societies where cannibalism was accepted as a norm, like the Tupinamba and the Maoris, continues to pose considerable philosophical and ethical difficulties for contemporary Europeans. But after some reflection on the state of their own societies, many writers have come to surprisingly similar conclusions, as summed up by Jean de Lery:

So let us henceforth no longer abhor so very greatly the cruelty of the anthropophagous – that is, man-eating – savages. For since there are some here in our midst even worse and more detestable than those who, as we have seen, attack only enemy nations, while the ones over here have plunged into the blood of their kinsmen, neighbours, and compatriots, one need not go beyond one's own country, nor as far as America, to see such monstrous and prodigious things.

The charge of 'cannibal' has, in our history, always been loaded with racist overtones towards the 'primitive' and the 'savage'. Reflecting on it risks bolstering centuries-old, unquestioned attitudes of discrimination, but new osteological evidence suggests that the practice has been prevalent in human prehistory throughout Europe and the rest of the world.

Moreover, whether we argue for or against the existence of customary cannibalism, we still tend to invest it with our own cultural baggage. Is it possible for such deeply held notions to change? In the last decade a new concept of how we can imagine the cannibal has emerged. Cannibalism is seen as just another option in the range of behavioural repertoire available to humans. Culture determines whether a society practises it or not, and what forms it can take. When we rehabilitate conscious, aggressive exo-cannibalism in this way and place it alongside, say, genocide and torture as practised by twentieth-century Europeans, how much worse does it become?

The famous sixteenth-century philosopher and writer Michel de Montaigne considered the ethical implications suggested by the Tupinamba's cannibalism, drawing a rational conclusion yet to be expressed more succinctly in his famous essay 'On Cannibals':

I am not sorry that we notice the barbarous horror of these [cannibalistic] acts, but I am heartily sorry that, judging their faults rightly, we should be so blind to our own. I think there is more barbarity in eating a man alive than eating him dead; and in tearing by tortures and the rack a body still full of feeling, in roasting a man bit by bit... than in roasting and eating him after he is dead.

TWO

Bones of Contention

Since the mid-nineteenth century, scientists have been claiming that some excavated human remains show evidence of cannibalism. Old social evolutionary theory equated primitive tribes with prehistoric man, so some prehistoric human remains were assumed to be the leftovers of cannibal feasts. Making casual claims of cannibalism in archaeology, as in anthropology and history, has a disreputable pedigree, and most of those original claims have since been discredited.

But over the last twenty years, a series of new finds, combined with advances in forensic analysis, have made archaeologists' claims of cannibalism more certain. Scientists have been confronted by compelling evidence in the form of excavations of unusually damaged human bones. These interpretations of cannibalism are not without their critics, but the evidence, as we shall see, remains highly convincing.

How is it possible to suggest that a particular discovery of human bones presents evidence of cannibalism?

Generally, when archaeologists discover human remains they find complete, undamaged skeletons buried in graves as part of a formal burial. None of the finds, or 'assemblages', of human bones discussed in this book resembles what we would consider a formally buried skeleton in a grave. These are bones that, from the very first glance, are clearly different – they are intensively smashed, cut and broken, with the skeletal remains of many individuals mingled together at one site.

These assemblages span human history and prehistory and come from sites all over the world, from northern Spain 800,000 years ago to nineteenth-century Fiji. What they all have in common are several key features that together form a pattern that archaeologists believe meets highly rigorous diagnostic criteria that allow the inference of cannibalism to be made.

No archaeologist, anthropologist or palaeontologist makes an interpretation of cannibalism lightly or without comprehensive analysis of the data. But recent advances in the analysis of human bones after death – human taphonomy – give much of this new work its real potency.

Taphonomy includes both analysis of the bone tissue itself and the position in which it is found in the ground. As explained by American anthropologist Christy Turner in his monumental book *Man Corn: Cannibalism and Violence in the Prehistoric American Southwest*, taphonomy constitutes the *death history* as opposed to the *life history* of an individual. The crucial advance in this field is the ability to be able to determine when damage to bone occurred in relation to the time of death of the individual – antemortem (prior to death), perimortem (immediately around the time of death) and postmortem (after death).

This is possible because living bone tissue is comparatively soft, and a fracture or break on it will follow particular patterns and then gradually heal over time – a process that can be observed on a cellular level with a scanning electron microscope. On the other hand, bone tissue after death eventually becomes dry and brittle, and any impact will break it into distinctive small fragments. But in the period immediately at or around the time of death, bone retains its softness but not the ability to heal damage. So fracture patterns, cuts and scrapes that occur during this perimortem phase look quite different. Clearly, it is the range of damage occurring just after death which is important for diagnosing the type of cuts, fractures and smashes that are now being associated with cannibalism.

Observing cut marks and the edges of smashes and fractures at a microscopic level, as well as seeing how the overall structure of the bone has responded to intense pressure, makes it possible to categorize any damaged human bone along these lines. It becomes easier, for example, for archaeologists to differentiate between human bones intentionally smashed by other humans right after death and weathered human bones lying in a cave accidentally smashed by a rock fall.

What is crucial to attempt this kind of analysis accurately is to know precisely where the bones were found, where they lie relative to other bones in the excavation, and what happened to them after excavation. Archaeologists use the word 'context' to describe this process.

The key point is that, overall, the way in which the bones have been cut and smashed by other humans follows a particular pattern, a pattern identical to the way in which animal bones are treated when a carcass is cut up for food. The skill of turning an animal carcass into meat for consumption is known as 'processing'. In the modern Western world, most of us never need to learn how to process animals for consumption; we go to a butcher or supermarket instead. But for our ancestors throughout most of human prehistory, processing must have been a ubiquitous and vital skill.

This became readily apparent to the Spanish palaeontologist Dr Yolanda Fernandez-Jalvo when in 1996 she made an intriguing discovery of early human remains. The fossils were found at a site called Gran Dolina in the Atapuerca Hills in north central Spain. Atapuerca is one of the most exciting archaeological sites in the world if you are interested in human origins and our deep past, the kind of place that archaeologists of an earlier generation might have expected to find only in Africa. More than three-quarters of all human remains dating between 100,000 and 1.5 million years ago have been discovered there. Within recent years some scientists think a new kind of early human ancestor has been found at Gran Dolina. They call this hominid *Homo antecessor* – 'man the pioneer'.

The fossils Yolanda discovered were 800,000 years old. The bones have what scientists call negative polarity, and it is this that enables them to be dated. The Earth's magnetic field pointed south, not north, until 780,000 years ago, and the point when the field reversed to its present north-facing orientation is used as a convenient time-marker by archaeologists and palaeoanthropologists excavating material from our deep past. Yolanda's fossils came from just below the negative polarity boundary.

The remains were in ninety-two separate pieces and belonged to at least six individuals. The remains were interesting because of their extreme age and the excellent state of fossilized preservation. But there was more, as Yolanda explained:

> Well, when the first remains were discovered, it wasn't expected that we would find cut marks. The first thing that we found was a fragment that represents the back of a skull. It was covered by cut marks.

As the excavation continued,

...we were recovering more and more bones, not only humans but also animals. We were seeing that there were frequent cut marks... most of them related to butchery, also related to dismembering, some of them to filleting.

John Lord, an archaeologist and expert on flint tools, processed a deer carcass with flint tools for us, similar to the ones used by the hominids at Gran Dolina, to demonstrate how cut marks are made:

When we come into contact with bone... green bone marks very easily, so every time you hear [a] sort of scraping sound we are making real cut marks and they would show up very very well. Some would be microscopic.

Scanning electron microscope images of cut marks can, by allowing the micro-morphology of the cut to be examined, indicate an incredible level of detail, such as whether a stone or metal blade was responsible, how the blade was sharpened and whether the cut was a slicing one or the result of a sawing action. The location and pattern of the cut marks are also important. Cuts can be made on bone when the cutter is dismembering the carcass, or de-fleshing, scraping or skinning it. Scraping marks, for example, were evident on many of the bones and had been made on the marrow-rich bones before they had been smashed. The most revealing cut marks are the ones left by the process of cutting away the ligaments and muscles – the nutritious meat found on the limbs and alongside areas of the spine. Cut marks on their own, however, are not enough to indicate that cannibalism has occurred. They are crucial indicators of human modification of bones after death, but there are other clues to take into account.

Another characteristic damage associated with processing bodies for food is the smashing of the long bones to extract marrow. Marrow is the soft and protein-rich tissue found inside living bone, and it is extremely nutritious. Smashing was very prevalent at Gran Dolina, explains Dr Fernandez-Jalvo:

> We found remains like [a] tiny femur fragment, which shows percussion marks that indicate the actual femur was held against the stone like an anvil and was hammered on the surface to break the bone and extract the marrow.

These percussion point marks left on the bone are diagnostic of the use of a stone hammer-like tool, the impact of which leaves a very distinctive type of crushing pattern at each point where the blow lands. This act of smashing the bone also leaves scrape marks on its reverse side where it lies against a hard surface; these are known as anvil abrasions.

Some of the thinner bones displayed another kind of damage that could have happened only when the bone was soft. 'One interesting thing we found was that the human remains show a kind of breakage, which is a peeling kind of breakage – holding the bone in the hands and bending it.' Peeling is rather like bending a green twig in your hands until it breaks along one side. This damage was evident only in the kind of animal and human bones that could be broken by hand, with the larger bones smashed by crude stone hammers leaving percussion marks.

Finally, the human and animal remains were mixed together, which to Yolanda could indicate only one thing:

The fact that the human remains have been found in the site in a very random way, mixed with the animals and the stone tools, with not a specific distribution, actually indicates they are the discard of food, and they are actually the food remains of other people. The evidence is clear: the cannibalistic practice is actually nutritional.

So the evidence at Gran Dolina was very convincing. But these were early types of human 800,000 years ago. This is before the generally accepted date for the invention of any kind of ritual behaviour or culture. It is uncertain how close the behaviour of these early hominids is to us, whether they were more ape-like or human-like.

Cannibalism is found in modern non-human primates in the wild, but only cannibalism of infants by males. It is a reproductive strategy on the part of the male, who stands to gain when the mother of the dead infant becomes sexually receptive again following the death of her offspring. The killing of the infant – infanticide – comes first; cannibalism is an afterthought that is more likely to occur the more carnivorous the primate species is, and the frequency with which that primate species preys on other mammals. Cannibalism is considered to be a rare event among non-human primates in the wild, except in the case of chimpanzees, among whom it is surprisingly common. Chimpanzees, of course, are the apes that are most carnivorous and are most like us.

So from modern observations in the wild you could argue that the more carnivorous the primate and the more it habitually attacks other mammals for food, the more likely it is to cannibalize. As a result, we would expect the incredibly carnivorous hominids at Gran Dolina, with their killing of large game animals and their use of stone tools, to be more likely to cannibalize –

and they were, consuming other adults (not only infants) of their own species. This is what the evidence at Gran Dolina shows – an early human ancestor engaged in cannibalism in an area already rich in other prey. It seems as if these hominids were able to treat their own kind as food.

So what about modern *Homo sapiens*? What is the evidence for cannibalism in our more recent prehistoric past among anatomically modern human beings?

Yolanda has also analysed another prehistoric processed bone assemblage, this time a more recent find from England. In Gough's Cave at Cheddar Gorge in Somerset, unusually damaged human remains have been found which are only 12,000 years old.

The bones are from five people: two adults, two teenagers and a young child aged about three. Like Gran Dolina, Gough's Cave is part of a cave system that was used as shelter by animals and also habitation by people. Its use extends back at least 30,000 years. The human bones are dated to the very end of the Upper Palaeolithic (40,000 to 11,000 years ago), and Gough's Cave has produced more faunal remains and artefacts from this period than any other Upper Palaeolithic site in Britain.

Stable isotope analysis of the human bones from Cheddar has shown that the people who lived there 12,000 years ago were primarily hunting red deer and wild cattle, though horses were also part of their diet. They were probably nomadic herdsmen who moved around the country seasonally.

Yolanda worked on the bones with Professor Chris Stringer of the Natural History Museum in London. Chris, a world expert in hominid evolution and human origins, had been involved in the Cheddar excavation after an initial find by a dedicated archaeologist named Roger Jacobi. Chris explained: 'As soon as we were excavating material, in fact in 1987, we started to find human material where as soon as we washed off the sediment we could see cut marks on the bones.'

One skull in particular was very revealing:

> We've got a pretty consistent pattern of, if you like, butchery or dismemberment... But in particular there is a pattern of marks across [a] part of the skull, and these cut marks would have been applied if you were separating the jaw from the skull, and the preservation of the cut marks is so good that we can even tell the direction... a right-handed individual was cutting upwards with a flint tool to actually remove the flesh from this skull.

Other clues pointed towards a processing explanation:

> The preservation of the material was interesting. We were finding fairly complete ribs, which are fairly delicate bones, and yet we were finding very little evidence of, for example, leg bones and arm bones. These seemed to be in very small fragments, as though they'd been broken with considerable force... So we had an unusual pattern there of differential preservation.

The human remains, just as in Gran Dolina, were mixed in with animal bone food refuse. One horse vertebra was found right on top of a human skull. The two kinds of remains had also been processed in an identical way:

> And what's particularly interesting is if we take, for example, this mandible of a deer, we can see the cut marks along the jawbone, and some of these marks have

certainly been made to remove the tongue. When we look at some of the human material – and here is an adult jawbone – there are a series of vertical cut marks inside the jawbone, which again seem to have been applied to remove the tongue.

Chris Stringer feels certain that this fine detail of the processing, so similar when you compare the animal and human remains, clinches the case for cannibalism at Gough's Cave. The evidence cannot say why this was going on, though there are several options: 'We don't, of course, know whether they were eating members of their own group because they have died naturally, but that's certainly a possibility.'

But equally there is the other possibility that these humans were systematically killed and eaten by another group. One can argue that these individuals were killed in the cave by another group who then ate them. Alternatively, you can argue that the bodies were brought into the cave from somewhere else and butchered.

One of the individuals does seem to have been beheaded. Cut marks on neck vertebrae indicate that the individual was beheaded, probably when he (or she) was lying face down, but again we don't know how much violence was involved in the death.

Was cannibalism the only plausible explanation for human bones damaged in this way? Another site provided perhaps the best evidence for an explanation of prehistoric cannibalism in Europe, and it has become the focus for a debate about whether a conclusion of cannibalism can be inferred from these kinds of processed human bone assemblages.

In 1986 Italian archaeologist Paola Villa excavated an assemblage of prehistoric human bones in Fontbregoua Cave in south-east France. They were the remains of six individuals who lived 7,000 years ago: two children, one adolescent, two young adults and one older adult. At the time, the cave was used as a temporary residential camp by nomadic pastoralists who also hunted wild animals. They grew some domestic cereal crops and had pottery and personal ornaments. The most common mode of burial in south-east France during this period was primary burial, or inhumation.

Inside the cave were discrete clusters of butchered human and animal bones. Both had been butchered in similar ways, and the state of preservation was excellent. One interesting difference was that the domestic animals had been killed one at a time, while the wild animals had been butchered in groups. The people had been butchered like the wild animals.

The frequency of cut marks was high – 41.7 and 40.8 per cent of the human and animal humeri (upper arm bones) respectively. Their location on the bones was also similar; 70 per cent of the cut mark varieties on the human bones could be matched to similar marks on corresponding animal bones. The cut marks and other damage, as at Gran Dolina and Cheddar, were not due to carnivore gnawing, trampling, sediment pressure or excavation tools.

Some similar cut marks were found on the tops of the human, deer and marten skulls. As Paola explains: 'This is a way of opening the skin of the head, and then you can pull it down. It's a way of skinning which we also find on animals.' Paola concluded that the clusters of bones were discarded food refuse. There was no difference in the location of the clusters, which were scattered throughout the cave. Also, the kinds of bones missing from human and animal clusters were the same – both humans and animals had been selectively butchered and anatomical segments of high food value had been removed. None of the bones showed evidence of cooking, but de-fleshed meat may have been cooked once it had been removed from the bone.

Paola's theory is that the butchering was done on animal skins inside the cave, the most nutritious parts removed to be consumed outside, while the remaining detritus of the carcass was tidily bundled up in the skin and left to one side. This would explain the discrete clusters, why all the broken bones were found so close to one another, and why fine sifting of the sediment around the larger bones revealed many tiny splinter fragments caused by the original smashing.

The preservation of the bones was also so excellent that Paola was able to conclude that all the people were processed as part of a single event. All had been killed and butchered at once, and this would prove to be a highly significant clue:

> The people that were cannibalized might have been a
> family or an extended family, and so I think this is quite
> interesting because often when archaeologists excavate
> human remains they don't know the relation of one bone
> to another. But in this case we were able say that six or
> seven individuals were butchered all at the same time.

But should we always assume that human bones, cut and smashed in a processing event identical to nearby animal bones and dumped among other food refuse, can be inferred as the product of cannibalism?

Australian archaeologist Michael Pickering disagreed with the cannibalism hypothesis at Fontbregoua. Human beings dispose of their dead in an extraordinary variety of ways. Pickering had researched eyewitness accounts of mortuary practices among Australian Aborigines that resulted in bone damage apparently similar to the Fontbregoua (and other) assemblages. One common type of mortuary practice is called 'secondary burial'. This involves the burial of a body for a temporary period to allow the flesh to decompose before it is exhumed and the bones then treated ritually in some way. Often they might eventually be bundled together and reburied in a container: a hollow log, for example. Secondary burial was common among some of the American Indian societies who lived on the Great Plains. It is still practised today by some societies.

Reports in Australia told of such burial practices where bodies were skinned, the head removed, the legs cut off at the knees and the thighs, and the arms removed with the shoulder blades intact. The bodies were then de-fleshed – '... all scraping and cutting away the flesh from the bones' – and the flesh was later buried. Finally, 'the bones, when scraped, are distributed among the relatives and friends of the deceased... and again the bones are broken to get out the marrow'.

If such customs have been recorded in the ethno-historical record, then are there other, non-cannibalistic explanations for the bone assemblage at Fontbregoua and other sites?

Paola, Chris Stringer and other archaeologists argue convincingly that their conclusions withstand this type of critique. If the bones were the end product of a funerary ritual, then you must conclude 'that the Fontbregoua people hunted, herded and butchered – but did not eat – food animals and that they gave secondary burial to boars, deer, sheep, roe deer, badgers and marten'. Chris made the same point about the bones at Gough's Cave: 'If you argue for that, we've then got to argue that these animal bones were being treated ritually and buried in the same way. So I think the human bones were being processed in the same way as the animal bones for food. So we clearly have this cannibalism going on.'

Paola also argued that the age range of the people who died at Fontbregoua ('I mean, are we dealing with an epidemic of people that died all at the same time?') and the fact that they were all killed and butchered at once makes the funerary ritual hypothesis very implausible.

In addition, analysis of bones broken and cut for secondary burial when compared with bones broken and cut for food processing contradicts the assumption that the two processes leave analogous cut mark types and patterns.

Anthropologist and archaeologist Dr Carol Raemsch has examined the skeletal remains of approximately 300 individuals who had undergone this kind of secondary burial. The bones, from a site called Riviere aux Vase in Michigan in the United States, consisted of bundles containing various long bones and a skull.

She reported that although the bones showed evidence of de-fleshing and dismemberment, the location and frequency of the cut marks were different from processed human bone assemblages. She concluded:

> Specifically, cuts are not found in the specific areas affected by a butchering process. There is no evidence of hammerstone or anvil use on the skeletons; bones show fragmentation of different forms (those that commonly result from *in situ* crushing, transport, excavation etc.), and few skeletons show evidence of charring.

Paola argues that cannibalism is the simplest and best explanation for what happened to the bones at Fontbregoua. But what caused the cannibalism? What lay behind it? Paola considered the options:

> There is the hypothesis of starvation: OK, cannibalism done for starvation. This, I think, is equally implausible, and this has more to do with the context in which you have to place these kinds of episodes... These are people who have agriculture, these are people who have domestic animals, these are people who were hunting, these are people who were moving around the landscape very easily. Generally, when people are starving they go to another location... so I think the plausible explanation is that there was some form of aggressive cannibalism tied to conflicts.

It seems that the six people at Fontbregoua died in one violent attack and that afterwards the attackers ate their victims. The link between conflict, warfare and aggressive exo-cannibalism seems to be the strongest explanation for the Fontbregoua assemblage. Moreover, as Chris Stringer pointed out:

> But of course the fossil record is only a tiny sample of the people who lived in the past. If we are picking up butchery in this very sparse sample of humans and human behaviour in the past, then indeed it cannot have been a rare event. One has to say that.

So is there more evidence of a link between cannibalism and conflict in the archaeological record? In the American southwest just a thousand years ago it seems that what had happened in the cave at Fontbregoua was happening on a far wider scale.

American forensic anthropologist Dr Shannon Novak analysed a fragmented bone assemblage belonging to people of the Fremont Culture, a society that lived in what is now the American state of Utah between AD 400 and 1300. What particularly attracted her attention was that, in addition to being smashed into small pieces, the bones had flaked as a result of being exposed to heat – a process known as exfoliation.

The Fremont hunted and farmed, primarily cultivating maize. They were a fairly small-scale society but none the less had a unique pottery style, cloth and basket-weaving techniques and rock art. They lived in pit-house dwellings organized into small hamlets. Beyond these basic facts, the Fremont are something of a mystery, as Shannon explained:

> We know very little behaviourally about the belief systems of the Fremont. They have very simple items, very simple ceramics. They had some unique figurines that suggest something symbolic we can't quite inter- pret. There are signs of headhunting. Certainly, the rock art suggests some kind of symbolism we haven't quite figured out.

An excavation in the 1970s uncovered the skeletal remains of a group of people at an excavation site called Backhoe Village. The remains had been left strewn across the floor of a hamlet. At the time they were interpreted as being the result of secondary buri- als charred when the structure of the hamlet burned down around them. They were the remains of two children, two women and four males, and they had died about 1,100 years ago. Shannon was puzzled by the assemblage:

Piles of bones were found on the floor, which was unusual for the Fremont because they did bury their dead. They didn't de-flesh bodies – there is no evidence of that. There is no evidence of cremating bodies. So I got back into the collections and recognized that there was something very unusual about these bodies.

Of the 546 elements or fragments of bone, only 17 per cent were complete; the rest were in fragments. More than half were affected by heating (57 per cent), nearly 20 per cent by peeling and crushing, and 16 per cent by percussion marks. Only 11 per cent of the fragments had cut marks. Overall, Shannon thought, 'this pattern was very similar to what we see in large mammals at Fremont sites. Large game – deer, for example – are processed in a similar manner'.

But it was the heating that interested Shannon most of all, and the way in which it had (or hadn't) affected the other kinds of damage:

Almost all the individuals, as we started to reconstruct the heads, exhibited [a] unique roughened exfoliation on the tops of the heads. As we started looking closely at this exfoliation, you can see this grey smoking pattern, and when you look closer using a microscope you see very small, fine cut marks. Also interesting was [that] some of the trauma to the head occurred before the heating of the head. And you can see that very clearly on [a] young female; there are large blows on the forehead and on the top of the head that penetrate the thermal damage, suggesting that you have a process of scalping, heating and then breaking the head down further.

On the long bones, the areas where the heavier soft tissue deposits were located appeared to have been protected from the heat, while areas without much tissue on them, like the shins, were much more damaged and exfoliated. In addition, the percussion blows used to break open the long bones had been made after the heating. A sequence of events was starting to emerge. Could this have been part of a burial practice or were the victims being cooked? Shannon argued:

> Certainly, it's not the kind of heat a body would be exposed to with cremation – where you get a blackening and then blue. This is more of a lower temperature, where you still have flesh on a good part of the body and more of a roasting low heat.

Shannon has analysed human remains from a variety of times and places, but the Fremont assemblage at Backhoe was unlike anything she had ever seen before:

> Having worked with modern homicides and in mass graves with modern wars, this was different from what I'd seen with homicides, mass killings and even mutilation of the body. The labour intensity, the amount of time spent processing these bodies, is something unusual from what I'd seen both in a prehistoric context at this point, as well as any modern context, in working in forensic cases. In trying to weed out the other hypotheses, cannibalism seems to be the only one that sticks. It's what we see with very violent forms of warfare and intimidation. And that's what we are seeing in the archaeological record.

In fact, Shannon's conclusions fitted into a wider regional pattern that has emerged in recent times from the work of other American anthropologists and archaeologists. Professor of Anthropology Christy Turner had been arguing for many years that some bone assemblages from a larger and more complex society centred a hundred miles south of the Fremont – the Anasazi – showed evidence of cannibalism. He and Professor Tim White, an archaeologist working separately, had proposed rigorous criteria for recognizing cannibalism in the American Southwest – otherwise known as the Four Corners Region (the point at which the states of Utah, Arizona, Colorado and New Mexico meet).

The main difference between the older European assemblages and these sets of human remains from the Four Corners was that the American bones tended not to be mixed in with animal bone refuse, but they did display a clear processing pattern. American archaeologists have intensively studied the Anasazi, from whom modern Pueblo Indians are descended, for over a century, and occasional claims of cannibalism have been made throughout that time about particular sites.

Turner and his wife Jacqueline reviewed unusually damaged human assemblages from seventy-six sites, and in 1999 they published the results in their seminal work, *Man Corn: Cannibalism and Violence in the Prehistoric American Southwest*. As they wrote: 'The skeletal assemblages from the 76 sites reviewed are far from representative of Anasazi burials. The vast majority of all Southwestern burials, including those of the Anasazi, show abundant evidence of consideration and concern for the dead.' They concluded 'that at least 38 Southwestern episodes of cannibalism took place that involved the eating of at least 286 persons of all ages and both sexes'.

In an earlier inventory of Anasazi human remains totalling 870 individuals from 165 sites housed at the Museum of Northern Arizona, they concluded that 68, or about 8 per cent, appeared to have been cannibalized.

The majority of these events had occurred in a specific time frame of AD 900–1300. This period is recognized as the birth and expansion of the Chacoan Culture in American archaeology. Considerably more sophisticated architecture, agricultural techniques, pottery and extensive road networks all start appearing in the American Southwest in around AD 950.

A significant majority of the cannibalism sites were also clustered near the cultural centre of this society, in what is now called Chaco Canyon. The Turners argue that the cannibalism among the Anasazi was associated with Chaco. It was a form of terrorism and social control used as part of warfare to subjugate and terrify other groups. This cultural trait certainly came from Mesoamerica, and we will go on to look at the evidence for cannibalism as a part of warfare in the region.

THREE

The Riddle of the Iron Age

In April 2000, an archaeological excavation in Berkshire, at the construction site of an artificial lake for the rowing teams of Eton College, announced an extraordinary discovery. The team from the Oxford Archaeological Unit had been digging in what was once a channel of the Thames. They found that an ancient sandbank island had stood in the middle of the river, and in the dried-up channel around the island they had found skulls and bones belonging to fifteen individuals. The bones were dated to the late Bronze Age/early Iron Age – about 3,000 years ago.

The way the bones from the same skeletons were found *in situ* implied that the dead had been deposited in the water on purpose. Five of the long bones also had cut marks, which alone was very unusual for early Iron Age bones, but, in addition, some of the same bones had had their ends intentionally smashed. These two kinds of damage taken together, with their implication of food processing and thus cannibalism, are absolutely unprecedented for the British Iron Age. In consequence, the bones were quickly dispatched to a leading British forensic archaeologist, Professor Margaret Cox of Bournemouth University, for detailed analysis.

That wasn't all the Oxford team found. Alongside one island was a group of wooden stakes with pots buried near the stakes. Nearby, a wooden platform had been constructed over another island. As well as the human bones, the excavators found skulls from horses and cattle. By the edge of the stream a pair of quern-stones had been carefully placed, one above the other. A Bronze Age ard, or plough, was also found a couple of years ago in the middle of the channel.

Even without the smashed and cut long bones, this was a very exciting archaeological discovery. To understand why, you have to know a little about the great archaeological mystery of the British Iron Age. As expert Dr Timothy Taylor explains:

> The riddle of the British Iron Age is that the dead appear to have vanished. There was a large population, warlike tribes that the Romans had a lot of trouble subduing, and yet archaeologically we have something like 0.01 per cent of the bones that we ought to have. We just don't know where the bones have gone.

During the early and middle Bronze Age, ancient Britons left plenty of formal burials with grave goods for archaeologists to eventually find and mull over. But at some point in the early phase of the last millennium BC, burial practices in Britain changed. Most of the bodies or body parts which have been found from this later – early to middle Iron Age – period consist of isolated bones or disarticulated joints uncovered in pits, ditches, hillfort ramparts and the boundaries of settlements. There have also been some burials found, and there is some evidence of cremation happening in particular areas, but the vast majority of the dead just aren't there. No one has ever been able fully to understand why this is, or what form the new funerary rituals might have taken. But there are clues, and though the significance of the find at Eton College rowing lake is still being considered, it promises to be an excellent one.

Archaeologists study Iron Age societies mainly through excavation, but there are written accounts from ancient Greece and Rome that describe Celtic societies. There are also writings of Celtic mythology recorded in Wales and Ireland from early medieval times. Both describe cultural practices and beliefs that come from much later than 1000 BC and usually from other parts of Europe or the British Isles, but in some intriguing ways the archaeological evidence from the early to middle British Iron Age does tally with them. So it is possible to recognize some aspects of early Iron Age archaeology that match the known practices and beliefs of later Celtic groups in Europe.

What is certain about the religious rituals of Iron Age Britons is that water – lakes, rivers, swamps and pools – played a highly significant role and was undoubtedly sacred in places. Irish Celtic myths record that the Other World was located through special mounds, down wells or beneath lakes, pools or rivers. Many river names in Europe are derived from Celtic goddesses. The Clyde, for example, takes its name from the Celtic Clota. The Celts entered into contracts with their deities in the same way that they did with people, by making deals. Offerings would be made by leaving highly valued items in water that would bind the gods into making reciprocal gifts to mankind.

The very early Greek Stoic philosopher Poseidonios visited Mediterranean Gaul in 100 BC. He referred to sacred lakes as repositories for treasures among the Tectosages of Toulouse. Though he was writing about a particular people at one time, the custom seems to have been widespread throughout Atlantic

Europe, we know this for the simple reason that archaeologists have always found high-value metal items from the Iron Age preserved in the silt beneath watery places. Many of them are weapons, typically swords.

In the British Isles, several lakes have been interpreted as centres of this custom, including Llyn Cerrig Bach in Anglesey and Carlingwark in Scotland. The fens in East Anglia, the Rivers Thames and Witham, and also bogs in Ireland, Scotland and various parts of England have also yielded these metalwork offerings, or votive deposits as they are better known. A similar interpretation has been argued for the lake of La Tene in Switzerland, where thousands of weapons and tools and also some jewellery and coins were found. The weapons are often found bent or broken, 'killed' before being sacrificed in the water. The practice seems to have been less common on the Continent than it was in Britain, where almost all the Iron Age swords found have been recovered from water.

There is also some evidence that islands played a significant role in Celtic belief systems. Poseidonios very specifically describes an island in the mouth of the Loire served by a female cult. At a particular time each year when the temple was re-roofed, a member of the cult was sacrificed by the others, who attacked and killed her by tearing her to pieces. The Roman historian Tacitus associated the island of Anglesey with the druids and with women he likened to the Furies. In Britain there is archaeological evidence of an island sanctuary in the form of a wooden circular temple on Hayling Island. The natural water boundary around an island may well have been associated with sexual boundaries, since female priestesses are mentioned in each of the ancient references.

Close examination of the disarticulated and jumbled skeletal remains that have been found at other sites also indicates that the Iron Age Britons practised some form of secondary burial ritual, almost certainly excarnation. Excarnation involves exposing a corpse to the open air so that the flesh will decompose to the skeleton, sometime with the intentional assistance of animal scavengers. Bodies might be left outside on a raised scaffold, as was a custom among the Sioux and Cheyenne Indians of North America, or left in a hut, as did the Toradja of the central Celebes.

Once the decomposition process is quite far advanced, the skeleton begins to come apart following a regular sequence. It starts with the skull and limbs, then proceeds to the ribs, the limb bones and finally to the vertebral column. A significant amount of Iron Age skeletal remains that have been found were clearly allowed to go through this process. The bones are often scattered, some are weathered and many are incomplete skeletons. The smaller bones, like ribs, are often missing. All these are clues that indicate the bodies had been subject to a secondary burial process of some kind before being interred. In 1997 two archaeologists, Adam Gwilt and Colin Haselgrove, examined thirty-three British Iron Age sites and concluded that secondary burial was a good explanation for the state of much of the skeletal remains in a variety of different contexts. They did suggest that many of the assemblages they looked at needed to be re-analysed with modern osteological techniques, as many had been originally poorly excavated.

Human remains are sometimes found in association with the Iron Age swords and other metalwork. Some of the best known of these are forty-eight skulls found in the Walbrook, a former tributary of the Thames that now lies beneath the City of London, which were dated to the Iron Age. A recent study also counted 299 skulls from the Thames presently in museum collections. Their distribution tallies with major groups of Bronze and Iron

Age metalwork found on the same stretch of river, and each group seems to be dated to a particular period. The skulls were rarely, if ever, found with other human remains, and some of them have been dated to the later Iron Age. They had also originally been placed in the river as skulls.

This is interesting because we know that the Celts venerated the human head. In fact, they were headhunters, severing the heads of their enemies in battle and keeping them as trophies. The Greek chronicler Strabo refers to the Celtic custom of embalming in cedar oil the heads of their most distinguished enemies and displaying them as a sign of martial prowess. The literature of early Ireland is full of descriptions of heroes returning from battle with the heads of their enemies and impaling them around their homesteads. Some Celtic temples have been excavated in France that show features corroborating these descriptions of head veneration. A temple at Roquepertuse, dating probably to the fourth century BC, had a portico in which human skulls were set in special niches. All the skulls were male and, when analysed, none was over forty years of age, which fits with the notion of their being the prized heads of enemies.

Some evidence indicates that, in a more general sense, humans were commonly conceived of as ritual victims in Celtic systems of belief. Strabo, and other classical writers, claimed that the Celts sacrificed people to their gods. Caesar famously described people being burned alive in huge hollow wicker effigies. Strabo mentions impaling and arrows as two methods of sacrifice. The Greek historian Diodorus Siculus, after stressing that human sacrifice was unusual in Celtic Gaul, gave a very precise description of the manner of death when it did occur: 'When enquiring into matters of great import, they devote to death a human being and stab him in the region above the diaphragm.' Strabo also describes how the Germanic Cimbri cut the throats of sacrificial victims and collected the blood in cauldrons. Other classical authors refer to altars in sacred groves being drenched or sprinkled with human blood. Divinations were often made by the druids, who examined the viscera of the sacrificed victims.

The large-scale human sacrifice described by Caesar probably took place during the two major religious festivals of the year, in spring and autumn. Caesar also makes clear that criminals were the preferred victims, being more acceptable to the gods, but that innocent people could just as easily be used to make up the required number. Sacrifices could also be made on behalf of individuals to save them from disease or to grant success on the battlefield.

Some archaeologists have interpreted several of the well-preserved bog bodies of Northern Europe as sacrificial victims. The Graubelle man, who died in the Roman Iron Age, had suffered a wound to his throat that had almost severed his gullet. Four of the best-known bog bodies had ropes around their necks and exhibited signs of garroting. One of the bodies pulled out of Lindow Moss near Manchester had been knocked on the head, had his throat cut and then was strangled; another had de-fleshing cut marks on the skull. Others had ingested special meals of crushed hazelnuts before they died and showed other signs of good treatment. The careful placing of bodies showing signs of 'overkill' in sacred places is now generally interpreted as being part of a sacrificial ceremony.

Tacitus refers to drowning as part of the ritual associated with the earth-goddess Nerthus. Given the sacred nature of watery places throughout the Celtic world, it seems logical that violent religious ritual could have been associated with them.

So where do the cut-marked Eton College lake bones fit into this picture? They are five long bones: four leg bones and one from an arm. As well as being smashed, the bones also show signs of animal gnawing on the ends and on the shaft. It was the job of Professor Margaret Cox and her graduate student Irene O'Sullivan to try to determine what might have happened to the bones in the past.

As Margaret explained, the bones were certainly broken intentionally soon after death:

> The smashing of the bones couldn't have been done accidentally... in order to do this you would have to dismember a body. You would have to take the legs away from the hip joint, for example, and that doesn't happen very readily or very easily. It would take quite a long time if you buried somebody for the bones to fall apart enough for that to happen naturally. And by that time, if you were then to actually smash the bones, they would smash in a different way from the fracture patterns we are seeing here... If bone gets broken when it's old, when all the collagen has gone from it, it breaks in a completely different way.

The bones also had 'very fine cut marks, which were made by a very, very sharp blade'. The reasons for analysing them were clear:

> The really important thing about this group of bones is that they suggest to us that the people in the early Iron Age were doing things to the bones of their dead. They were not simply being buried or simply being cremated and then buried. They were being processed in some way,

and what we have to do here is to try to disentangle the evidence that their processing has left behind and try to understand why they were doing it.

Margaret and Irene looked at the bones using light microscopy, and some more details began to emerge.

So what we've got at the moment is very clearly two different types of cut marks, one where they're going right through the bone quite clearly, presumably to take the end off the bone or contribute in part to that end coming off, and also cut marks that are again presumably associated with de-fleshing... We are also seeing dog, or presumably dog, gnawing cut marks overlying cut marks, which again is giving us some idea of the sequence of events. So it looks as though, possibly, the human activity was modifying the bone and then somehow dogs were getting hold of them and chewing them. But why weren't the dogs allowed to finish eating the bones? Somehow these bones have been retrieved from the dogs before they've been put in the water environment. So we've got a very complex picture here.

Margaret believes that cannibalism could certainly be a viable explanation for the smashing and cut marks on the bones, though more osteological analysis would have to be done on other Iron Age skeletal remains before firmer conclusions could be reached.

It's quite clear that they were removing the flesh, the soft tissues, the muscles from these bones. There is a whole range of reasons why they might have been doing that. It could be to do with disposal of the dead, wanting nice clean skeletons to use in some sort of ritual behaviour, or it could be that they were actually taking the meat off the bones for the purpose of consumption and that they might have actually been eating it.

Dr Timothy Taylor also examined the bones in the lab and thinks that the evidence is highly significant:

> I think the Eton lake bones are what we've been waiting for. They're very exciting. The very fine striations look very similar to what we've seen at Cheddar and Fontbregoua, Gran Dolina and the Fremont. It looks like a cannibalism signature, and the ancient authors, people like Strabo, talk about the Iron Age Irish eating their dead.
>
> Some people might suggest that the Eton boating lake long bones are the residue of a mortuary ritual that has involved simply the dismemberment of human bodies and not eating human flesh per se, but when you look at the cut marks, the very fine striations, they are consistent with removing flesh in a very careful way... Somebody's holding a lower leg and they are stripping the meat from it.
>
> There are scuff marks. They've taken everything off that would be useful and good for eating – quite fleshy cuts of meat. We obviously can't photograph ancient Britons eating human flesh, so this is archaeologically probably the closest we'll get.
>
> Precisely what the Eton bones will turn out to be, whether we'll be able to distinguish the precise signa-

ture, is a question we can't answer right now, but I feel that they are the best evidence yet for cannibalism in Iron Age Britain.

We know that Celtic peoples practised violent religious rituals, including human sacrifice, and that their conceptions of the dead were utterly different from our own. They deliberately dismembered corpses of their own kin and customarily used body parts of their enemies as war trophies. They venerated watery places, and some islands were holy sanctuaries where bloody rituals were reported to have taken place. So the cut-marked early Iron Age Eton bones found in a river alongside an island are very significant when understood in this context. They were certainly part of some kind of ritual treatment of corpses, and the smashing of the ends of the bones is consistent with processing for food.

What is clear is that cannibalism must now be considered as a possible behaviour being practised in the early British Iron Age, and, given the evidence for the frequency of cannibalism both in humanity's deep prehistoric past and more recently, that shouldn't be dismissed as a sensational hypothesis.

Archaeological analysis of human skeletal remains can also be used to argue against taking ancient references to cannibalism at face value. In a recent paper, two archaeologists, Professor James Mallory and E.M. Murphy, argue that Herodotus's famous references to cannibal practices among ancient Iranian-speaking steppe peoples are a mistake. In its place they offer an intriguing new explanation as to what it was Herodotus thought he was reporting.

In his *Histories*, published in the fifth century BC, Herodotus describes the mortuary practice of the Issedones, one the peoples inhabiting the steppe lands in the southern Urals. He relates:

It is said to be the custom of the Issedones that whenever a man's father dies, all the nearest of kin bring beasts of the flock, and having killed these and cut up the flesh they cut up also the dead father of their host, and set out all the flesh mingled together for a feast.

Herodotus also describes a similar endo-cannibalistic ritual practised by the Massagetae of west central Asia:

When a man is very old, all his kin meet together and kill him, with beasts of the flock besides, they boil the flesh and feast on it. This is held to be the happiest death; when a man dies of sickness they do not eat him, but bury him in the earth, and lament that he would not live to be killed.

In addition, He associates cannibalism with two tribes living south of the Indus, the Kallatiai and the Padaioi. Herodotus came from a culture that abhorred this kind of reverential kineating. In another passage he describes how Darius, the king of Persia and a sworn enemy of ancient Greece, mockingly asked the Greeks what price would persuade them to eat their fathers' dead bodies. The Greeks replied firmly in the negative. In all his accounts of cannibalism, Herodotus combines the bodies of the deceased with those of butchered animals in a funerary feast.

But these descriptions are not simply some kind of slur. When discussing the Kallatiai, Herodotus digresses: 'If it were proposed to all nations to choose which seemed best of all customs, each, after examination made, would place its own first; so well is each persuaded that its own are by far the best.' He then contrasts the

Greeks' horror of endo-cannibalism with the Kallatiai's disgust at the Greek practice of cremation.

Mallory and Murphy were able to conduct the first in-depth osteological analysis of human skeletal remains from the Iron Age steppes in southern Siberia. At Aymyrlyg, an Iron Age cemetery of the Uyuk culture dating from 300 to 200 BC, are over 1,000 formal burials. A.M. Mandelshtam, the director of excavations, had originally noticed that some of the bodies had been disarticulated and buried as compact burials, and that in some cases leather bags or cloth sacks were associated with the bundles.

Mallory and Murphy did indeed find cut marks on twenty-nine disarticulated individuals in the cemetery. The bones were whole, not smashed, and the marks had clearly been made some time after death. The majority of the cut marks were on the ends of long bones where they originally attached to the trunk, indicating disarticulation. Less frequently they found de-fleshing marks, though these looked as if they were related to the process of taking the body apart rather than the removal of edible portions of muscle tissue. The pattern was not like the archaeological signature of cannibalism found at other sites, and seemed to be more related to a process of secondary burial of some kind.

Mandelshtam suggested that the remains have to be understood in the context of the semi-nomadic life of the Uyuk people. The tribal burial grounds at Aymyrlyg were part of a series of stopping points on a cyclical migratory route through the steppes that the Uyuk followed every year. Located in a river valley Aymyrlyg would have made excellent grazing grounds for cattle in the winter, the tribe having spent the spring and summer in the mountains. The occasional bundled, cut and disarticulated skeletons were probably people who had died earlier in the migratory route and whose remains needed to be transported, hygienically and safely, throughout the summer to the main tribal burial grounds. People who died in the winter would have been easily preserved in the snow and buried whole as soon as the spring thaw came.

Mallory and Murphy surmise that this Iranian-speaking nomadic people, very similar to the groups Herodotus describes, practised this secondary burial ritual because of these seasonal factors. The butchery involved in the custom could easily have been mistaken for part of a process involving cannibalism and so could have become embellished in the retelling, leading Herodotus to describe nomadic steppe peoples as cannibals.

The religious rituals and funerary rites of Iron Age Europe, violent or otherwise, can only be glimpsed by modern archaeologists and historians, and inference and intelligent speculation play a large part in any discussion of funerary rituals and religious beliefs. However, other societies, closer to us in time, practised violent religious ritual, including human sacrifice and cannibalism on a large scale. The best-known and among the best-documented of these are the Aztecs in Mesoamerica. Over the last decade throughout Mexico there have been some exciting archaeological excavations uncovering skeletal remains that shed new light on these customs.

Historical descriptions of Aztec sacrifice and cannibalism were all made or compiled by Europeans in the sixteenth century during and after the Spanish conquest of 1521. Despite some inevitable ethnocentric exaggeration and bias, the consensus academic view does grant the accounts a core of accuracy.

The longest, most reliable and most respected ethno-historical records for Aztec society in central Mexico were compiled by Fray Bernardino de Sahagún, a Franciscan priest who first arrived in Mexico in 1529. He learned the native language, Nahuatl, and spent the rest of his life compiling a kind of encyclopedia of Aztec culture called the *General History of the Things of New Spain*. His work covers virtually all aspects of Aztec society, including detailed accounts of religion, botany, folk medicine and economics. He collected descriptions in words and pictures from Nahuatl-speaking informants and translated them into Spanish.

In Sahagún's descriptions of the Aztecs' religious ceremonies over their eighteen-month year were many sacrificial rituals when victims were dedicated to the gods. During the second month:

> Captives were killed by scalping them, taking the scalp off the top of their head... When the masters of these captives took their slaves to the temple where they were to be killed, they dragged them by the hair. As they pulled them up the steps of the Cu [temple], some of these captives would faint, so their owners had to drag them by their hair as far as the block where they were to die... After thus having torn their hearts out, and after pouring their blood into a jacara [bowl], which was given to the master of the dead slave, the body was thrown down the temple steps. From there it was taken by certain old men called Quaquaquilti, and carried to their calpul [chapel] and cut to pieces, and distributed among them to be eaten. Before cutting them up they would flay the bodies of the captives; others would dress in their skins and fight sham battles with other men.

Human sacrifice occurred in slightly different forms in honour of several deities within the Aztec pantheon. Tlaloc, god of rain and fertility identified with mountaintop shrines, had children sacrificed to him at particular ceremonies in the year, as did the feathered serpent, Quetzalcoatl, god of winds and storms. As well as sacrifice, cannibalism featured in rituals in honour of Xipe Totec, god of seeds and crops, and Huitzilopochtli, god of war, to whom the two temples on top of the great pyramid in the Aztec capital of Tenochtitlan were dedicated.

A major purpose of Aztec warfare was the procurement of enemy prisoners who would be taken back to Tenochtitlan and sacrificed in the manner described by Sahagún. This could happen on a terrifyingly large scale. Another Nahuatl-speaking monk who came to Mexico shortly after the conquest began was Fray Diego Duran, and he discussed the scale of sacrifice and cannibalism:

> I am not exaggerating; there were days in which 2,000, 3,000, 5,000 or 8,000 men were sacrificed. Their flesh was eaten and a banquet was prepared with it after the hearts had been offered to the devil.

The pioneering Mexican archaeologist Carmen Maria Pijoan Aguade has examined a number of assemblages of damaged human skeletal remains excavated around temple complexes in Tenochtitlan, over which now stands Mexico City. She analysed a series of dismembered body parts of 153 individuals excavated in 1961 by Francisco Gonzalez Rul. The remains were found near a structure called Templo Redondo that had been built between 1400 and 1420 and the burial occurred between 1418 and 1427. The majority of the skeletons had their sternum bones cut in half above the heart so were clearly sacrificial victims of the kind described by Sahagún. The analysis of Pijoan and her colleagues showed a strong pattern of cut marks on the various elements.

The pattern indicated dismemberment and the removal of flesh. Young men, women and children had all been processed as part of this event. Pijoan concluded that large amounts of muscle tissue had been removed for consumption. Many of the same body parts from each skeleton were complete and showed no processing marks, which indicated that considerable amounts of tissue must have remained on some parts of the corpses. She showed that 10 to 25 per cent of the limb and girdle (shoulder and pelvic joint) bones were missing, and anthropologist Christy Turner surmises that 'wherever these bones went, there the cooking occurred'.

Duran also described a colossal rack of human skulls ('tzompantli') in the central square of Tenochtitlan, clearly a form of trophy display. In 1963 excavations by Gonzalez, to the north-west of the main pyramid of Tlatelolco in Tenochtitlan, found an orderly mass of 170 skulls in front of a low platform with west-facing stairs. In 1989 three Mexican archaeologists analysed a hundred of the skulls and found that only one of them didn't have either cut marks or holes on the side through which a rack pole would have been inserted. The rack holes were generally circular, having been punched through the bone by a sharp pointed punch or chisel. Their diameter varied from five to ten centimetres. The majority of the skulls had cut marks consistent with severing the head and then removing attached skin and muscle tissue.

Underpinning the Aztec treatment of their sacrificed dead is a concept of the body as a kind of resource. These victims provided hearts and blood to appease the gods, ceremonial flesh for ritual feasting and trophies to mount around temple complexes. This fundamental attitude is reflected in the discovery by archaeologist Federico Solorzano Barreto of at least 2,000 objects made from human bones. The objects, unlike other human remains discussed here, were recovered from graves in the western part of Mexico and their origin spans over a thousand years up to the arrival of the Spanish. Among the vast collection were weapons, barbed points and daggers, while other bones had been fashioned into musical instruments. Though there is no evidence that these objects were directly related to sacrificial rituals, their existence and production can clearly be understood as part of a conceptual framework that conceived of humans as edible.

Other lines of evidence also support the claims of the early writers concerning the violent rituals of the Aztecs and their attendant paraphernalia. Some of the Aztec codices, the indigenous religious and historical texts, have survived, and a number of them include drawings of body parts either being feasted on or jammed in cooking pots. One codex, currently housed in Florence, shows food offerings to a deity, which include a human arm, as well as a feasting scene that has various pots containing body parts.

After the conquest the Catholic Church had some difficulty in eradicating the indigenous customs of human sacrifice and cannibalism. On 23 June 1523 Spanish law prohibited, among other activities, 'comer carne humana, aunque sea de los prisioneros, y muertos en la guerra' ('to eat human meat, even if it be of prisoners and war dead'). The law was repeated in 1538 and again in 1551. The scholar Teresa Piossek Prebisch believes the fact that the law had to be repeated indicates the persistence of the problem through the first half of the sixteenth century. In 1537 the Bishop of Mexico, Don Juan de Zumarraga, wrote that everywhere he looked he saw 'heinous practices, at one time suppressed, coming back stronger than ever; human sacrifice and cannibalism were almost common again'.

Other ethno-historical accounts indicate that the link between cannibalism, human sacrifice and warfare was a common one throughout Mesoamerica. In 1932 the American anthropologist Ralph Beals published an ethno-historical study of northern Mexico before 1750 and surveyed the violent rituals associated with warfare in northern and central Mexico:

Human sacrifice rarely occurs in Mexico without an association of cannibalism. Cannibalism in much of our area [of northern Mexico] was ceremonial in nature, even where not associated with human sacrifice... In practically all cases it was connected with the celebration of war victories, and in many cases with the preservation of the bones and skulls of enemies. Among the Acaxee, where cannibalism was most highly developed in our area, the bones and skulls were presented to an idol or deity on certain occasions, and the first portion of human flesh prepared for eating was placed on the altar... [Among the Aztecs] the sacrifices were in most cases associated with ceremonial cannibalism, and the heart of the victim was usually 'fed' to the god. There exists, then, a roughly continuous series starting on the one hand with the human sacrifice of Mexico, with the heart and other foods fed to the gods (a rather direct manifestation of the widespread idea of food offerings to the supernatural), and cannibalism. Next is the ceremonial cannibalism of the Acaxee (the first portion given to the god, the second to the slayer of the enemy being eaten) and the preservation of bones and skulls. Finally there are the less specialized methods of the Sinaloans and the peoples of Nuevo Leon and else-

where, and the apparently simple ceremonial cannibalism of the Yavapai.

Certainly, the concept of sacrifice was central to Aztec cosmol-
ogy. The origin myth of the Aztec universe involved the self-
sacrifice of two gods who became reincarnated as the sun and
the moon. The sun was perceived as a primary source of life and
was associated with the warrior castes in Aztec society. It was
their special responsibility to secure sacrificial victims for the
sun, and only regular human sacrifices would ensure that the sun
continued to rise. Aztec religion stressed the role of the Aztec
kings in particular, who played a key role in guaranteeing the
smooth functioning of the whole universe through the regular
performance of the ritual of human sacrifice.

But many scholars see the large-scale and culturally high-
profile sacrifice and cannibalism of the Aztecs as also part of a
ruthless political strategy of this rapaciously expansive state.
These were bloody rituals designed to terrify opponents into
subordination and to create an obedient population at home.
They facilitated the relatively recent process of extending social
control over other peoples throughout central and southern
Mexico, which the Aztecs had been engaged in for two generations preceding the arrival of Cortez in 1519. The Aztec empire
was organized around tribute, and many of the peoples subject
to their rule were controlled through the threat of violent retribution and were bitterly resentful. This emphasis on coercive
over more cohesive political strategies backfired during and
after the conquest as the oppressed people within the empire
used the opportunity of Spanish intervention to rise up against
the Aztecs.

In 1991 the archaeologist Richard E.W. Adams offered a

memorable interpretation of the nature of the Aztec state as it had developed by the end of the fourteenth century:

> The Aztec state had become a mad world of bloody terrorism based on the cynical, psychopathic policies of the high imperial rulers. Coronation ceremonies of the later kings were accompanied by the offering of fantastic quantities of human victims to the gods. These victims were purchased slaves from Aztec society itself, and the collected captives from the constant foreign campaigns of the Aztec armies.

To describe the Aztec policy of expansion as inherently psychopathic is extremely controversial and certainly doesn't convey the complexity of the Aztecs' attitudes to warfare and sacrifice. But however you choose to judge what the Aztecs did, they stand out as the society within the historical record which practised sacrifice and cannibalism on the grandest scale and placed it closest to the core of highly elaborate religious beliefs.

FOUR

Different Gods

Feejee as we are told lies three days' sail from Tongabatoo in the direction north-west by west. It was described to us as a large, but very fruitful island; abounding with hogs, dogs, fowls and all kinds of fruits and roots... Feejee and Tongabatoo frequently make war upon each other. And it appeared from several circumstances that the inhabitants of the latter are much afraid of this enemy... And it is no wonder that they should be under dread; for these of Feejee are formidable on account of the dexterity with which they use their bows and slings, but much more so on account of the savage practice to which they are addicted... of eating their enemies whom they kill in battle. We were surprised that this was not a misrepresentation. For we met several Feejee people at Tongabatoo and, on inquiry of them, they did not deny the charge.

Captain Cook, October 1773

Captain Cook never visited the Fiji Islands in the South Pacific during his voyages of discovery. The Fijians he quizzed on Tonga, 770 kilometres to the east, were the only ones he met. However, it wasn't the stories of warfare and cannibalism that deterred him, but the treacherous reef system that surrounds the archipelago. Abel Tasman, the first European to sail through Fijian waters, had reported extensive shallow coral reefs in 1643 that kept European vessels away for the next 130 years. The first Europeans we know about who actually lived on Fiji were sailors whose ships had been wrecked there in the early nineteenth century.

The Fiji (Viti) island group consists of more than 300 islands spread over half a million square miles in the south-west Pacific, embedded in the great coral reefs that form the western flank of Polynesia. The main island, Vitu Levu, is a substantial (4,010 square miles) volcanic island with a mountainous interior; a second large island, Vanua Levu (2,137 square miles), is close by. The islands were first inhabited 3,500 years ago by seafaring Melanesians from the west. The core population of Fiji is a mixture of Melanesian and western Polynesian ancestral stock, but there is a core of highly distinctive central Fijian society.

Traditional Fiji was undergoing a period of unusual social dynamism, technological change and political turmoil when the first Europeans arrived. Politically, Fiji was a patchwork of large and small territories dominated by hereditary male chiefs who controlled the allocation of land and labour. Villages grouped themselves into broader alliances over larger areas – confederacies – which were overlooked by a paramount chief. By 1800, several of these confederacies were engaged in wars of expansion. Two in particular – rival coastal clans named Bau and Rewa – would become notoriously powerful and aggressive and fight a large-scale war in the 1840s. The first Europeans in Fiji were used by these clans to give an advantage on the battlefield and to assist in organizing the highly profitable but short-lived sandalwood and bêche-de-mer (sea slug) trade that was well under way by the early years of the nineteenth century.

Fiji rapidly became known to Europeans for the intelligence and technological sophistication of its people, for the high level of violence and warfare that made trading there particularly hazardous, and for some of the unusual customs of the Fijians, the most notorious of which gave the archipelago its nineteenth-century nickname: the Cannibal Isles.

In terms of understanding a society that practised customary cannibalism, Fiji presents an unusual opportunity, despite the fact that the custom ceased in the 1870s. Overall, an abundance of ethno-historical information is available about old Fiji, enough for anthropologists like Dr Christina Toren or Professor Marshall Sahlins to be able to understand how pre-Christian Fijian culture 'worked'. Fiji was also much less intensively and aggressively colonized than, say, New Zealand, and many of the indigenous social and political structures have remained more or less intact, which facilitates anthropological and historical study.

There is also archaeological evidence: smashed and broken skeletal assemblages of the kind found in Europe and the United States. Archaeologists in Fiji (and other parts of Polynesia) have been discovering such assemblages occasionally throughout the century, but only recently have some of those original finds undergone a modern taphonomic analysis. Other human bones associated with the practice of cannibalism in Fiji include human shinbones carved into sail needles, skulls kept and fashioned into sacred drinking vessels, and long bones kept as trophies.

So it is this convergence of different categories of evidence – ethno-historical, archaeological, linguistic – that makes Fiji so especially interesting. There probably isn't anywhere else quite like it in terms of understanding a society that practised a type of high-profile and elaborated aggressive exo-cannibalism.

Although the same kind of analysis can be made on the Aztecs, the ethno-historical material is much more scanty.

Most of the earliest accounts of Fijian society come from missionaries and seamen. Some are more impartial, detailed, honest and insightful than others. European witnesses may not always have understood what they saw and they often felt morally compelled to denounce and change Fijian customs. But they did surprisingly often write down what they witnessed in detail. Can we trust their writings? American anthropologist Gananeth Obeyesekere has called into question two of the eyewitness accounts of Fijian cannibalism in the nineteenth century, both written by seamen. He argues that, despite the fact that both are highly detailed, they are unreliable descriptions on which to base serious ethnography. We asked anthropologist Dr Christina Toren how she felt able to trust what was written about Fijians by Europeans in the nineteenth century:

As an anthropologist who works in Fiji, I feel confident of the written accounts, [although some] contain details that do sound... a little bit too sensational. Your confidence comes from not only a lot of archival material, from mission diaries and such like, but those diaries describe practices that all reference one another. Of course, it's the case that there are certain anthropologists who are entirely sceptical about cannibalism anywhere. But none of them so far as I know have actually worked anywhere where there has been a history of cannibalism. And I suppose that when I first went to Fiji, I was as sceptical as Europeans normally are about cannibalism... Had I not done field work in contemporary Fiji, I don't think I would have been able to understand the archival material.

Indeed, the more reflective and diligent missionaries and seamen in Fiji in the early to mid-nineteenth century compiled the only detailed, complete and multi-faceted descriptions of Fiji society at this time that exist. Overall, a very consistent, mutually reinforcing picture of a society emerges complete with its particular customs, beliefs and social organization.

Most of this chapter is limited to an investigation of just a few aspects of Fijian life and society in the past – warfare, religious belief and cannibalism ('veikanikani' in Fijian) – as they were encountered by Europeans in the first half of the nineteenth century. It is not intended to portray a fully rounded picture of this society, but will convey how cannibalism was part of an absolutely fundamental religious and social understanding of the world. To comprehend cannibalism in Fiji, you have to understand its people's ancient belief system, founded on the worship of ancestor spirits, which is antithetical to Judaeo-Christian notions of God and self, and was tragically destroyed by the advent of Christianity.

Europeans were shocked and disgusted when they witnessed cannibalism and other strange customs, such as elderly parents being voluntarily strangled by their offspring and widows being killed when their husbands died. But all these were part of an underlying cultural logic that was obscure to all but the most observant and persistent Westerners. Fijians were not the bloodthirsty savages celebrated in much generalized fiction about the South Seas, like Defoe's *Robinson Crusoe*. As William Lockerby, a Scottish seaman stranded in Fiji in 1808, wrote:

> In war they are fearless and savage to the utmost degree, but in peace their disposition is mild and generous towards their friends, and the affection they bear towards their relatives is seldom found among Europeans.

It is important to keep in mind that cannibalism was still a terrifying act for Fijians, albeit one that was a distinct part of their behavioural repertoire in a way unfamiliar to Europeans. That isn't to say there weren't many atrocities associated with Fijian warfare and cannibalism, because there were, just as there is with 'civilized' warfare in its various guises. But Fijian cannibalism itself was not an atrocity but a perfectly logical, religiously and socially sanctioned practice. As the missionary Thomas Williams, perhaps the most diligent of all the early observers of Fijian life, wrote:

> Cannibalism among this people is one of their institutions; it is interwoven in the elements of society; it forms one of their pursuits, and is regarded by the mass as a refinement.

Cannibalism was always a special event, and bodies were always eaten as part of a religious ceremony. Consumption of a body was the critical act in the process of human sacrifice. Generally, those eaten were enemies killed in war, but other categories of people (conquered peoples, slaves) could also be legitimately killed to acquire a bakola at any time. This was necessary because certain regular events required human sacrifice: the construction of temples, chiefs' houses and sacred canoes, or the installation rites of a chief, for example. The paramount chief had special assassins (sometimes Europeans) who would procure these victims, generally by ambush.

Europeans often found the religious basis hard to believe, considering the scale on which cannibalism occurred in Fiji. The missionary Reverend Hunt estimated that over a five-year period in the 1840s approximately five hundred people had been eaten within fifteen miles of his residence at Viwa. Massacres of more than three hundred people were known to follow successful attacks on large towns. Ra Udreudre of Rakiraki, an infamous chief, built a line of stones, each marking an eaten enemy. Reverend Lyth, shown them by Udreudre's son in 1848, counted a total of 872.

These may sound like exaggerated numbers, but warfare in old Fiji sometimes did occur on a grand scale. The Fijian double-hulled war canoe, or 'drua', was the envy of Polynesia, the best-designed ocean-going vessel in a region celebrated for its seafaring technology and skill. The drua, perfected in the late eighteenth century, was built in Fiji, mainly for Tongan chiefs, by Samoan craftsmen. At first, no one in Europe believed Captain Cook when he described these vessels in Tahiti travelling at twenty knots. The largest drua could carry over 250 warriors as well as crew and cargo. A Bauan war fleet in 1809, comprising 64 drua in a fleet of 136 canoes of various sizes and designs, carried approximately 2,700 men.

Moreover, Fiji was an exceptionally violent place in the first half of the nineteenth century. In oral tribal histories recorded in the twentieth century, as collected by Peter France in his 1969 book *The Charter of the Land*, 'periods of peace are specially mentioned as interludes between the intertribal warfare, in the words "sautu tale na vanua" ("the land prospered again"). When a tribe settled for any length of time in one place without fighting, the fact is recorded as worthy of note.'

Thus, European ships visiting Fiji had to be constantly on their guard. The precautions on the trading vessel *Glide* in 1829 were typical, as described by seaman W.D. Dix:

Heavy cannon, loaded with canister and grape shot, projected from the portholes on each side. In each top was a chest of arms and ammunition. On deck and below, weapons of defence were so arranged as to be available at short notice. Boarding nettings, eight or ten feet wide, were triced up around the ship by tackles and whipping lines suspended from the extremities of the lower yardarms.

The frequency of warfare was perhaps most apparent in the elaborate fortifications constructed near or around every town or village. Villages on flat land near the coast were surrounded by up to (in one case) four miles of trench works, and all had wooden palisades and moats. Settlements in the mountainous interior often had a fort the inhabitants could retreat to in times of conflict. Often natural features like caves or hilltops were adopted and defensively enhanced. Traces of these moats, ditches and earthworks are still visible in many parts of the islands, and archaeological excavations date their use in Fiji from AD 1200. Visiting Europeans were impressed, including the Reverend A.J. Webb:

Their villages were mostly perched on most inaccessible peaks and precipices... These eyries were skilfully fortified with palisades and galleries for sharpshooters, which, with their well-chosen strategic position, rendered some of them traditionally impregnable... I have seen fortified places on a plain so surrounded by moats, where the mud was armed with stakes and split bamboos, and so encompassed with clay ramparts and stout palisades, line by line, that the very taking of them in purely native warfare was a very tedious or very fatal undertaking. I saw one village, called Waini-makutu, where the stream had been most ingeniously diverted into the circular moat, in which it was swirling round the town on its onward progress... An officer in the English army, who had taken some of these forts of the hillmen, expressed to me his surprise at the skill and science of engineering they displayed. Covered galleries and lanes, and curious platforms for sentinels and marksmen, were also features in these works.

Europeans introduced muskets and metal blades into Fiji in the first decade of the nineteenth century, but even by 1870 most fighting still depended on the traditional weapons of the Fijian warrior: the heavy wooden two-handed war club, the smaller throwing or missile club, and the spear, bow and sling. Dozens of different varieties of these weapons, each with a particular name and design, were used.

The proficiency with which they were wielded, by men trained since boyhood, was enough to daunt many Europeans, despite their natural advantage of firearms. Dix describes a Macauta chief's spear-throwing prowess in a demonstration on board a visiting ship in 1831:

Santa Beeta's excellence in handling the spear was thus singularly illustrated. A coconut was placed upon the windlass, and this chief, standing near the tafferel [taffrail], at the distance of about sixty feet, bent back at a fearful angle with the deck, and firmly grasping the spear by its centre, drove it, after careful aim, directly through the middle of the nut. So assured felt F-, one of the crew, of Santa Beeta's skill and good faith, as to persist in standing to within two feet, at the side, of the nut.

Europeans armed with muskets underestimated these warriors at their peril. American seaman J.G. Clark, of the US Navy Exploring Expedition of 1840, survived a skirmish in which two of his shipmates were killed:

> He was within fifteen feet of us, and his spear was quivering in his hand; the next moment Mr Underwood would have been transfixed by it. As I raised my rifle to fire at him, an Indian sprang out with a musket from behind a tree, and I let the chief throw his spear, thinking I could parry it off with my rifle then shoot the man who had the musket. The chief again poised his spear and darted it. My ignorance of the force of these missiles very nearly cost me my life. It came like a flash of lightning, struck me full in the face, tearing my upper lip into three pieces, loosening my upper foreteeth and, glancing out of my mouth, passed through the left arm of Mr U. I shot him through the head, and attempted to reload my rifle, when a man ran up behind me and knocked me senseless.

The standard fighting tactics were to disable an opponent with a throwing club (thrown with great accuracy and force) before closing in to finish him off with a heavy war club, as described by Seaman Clark on the death of the unfortunate Mr Underwood on the beach at Malolo in 1840:

> When they attacked him, he fired both of his pistols in succession, each killing a native. He then retreated a few steps backwards, when he was knocked down by a small club thrown at him, and struck him on the back of the head and he fell in the water, which was about knee

deep. After falling, two of the natives rushed at him and put an end to his life in a very few seconds.

Muskets were introduced to Fiji after the American schooner *Argo* was wrecked near Oneata island in early 1800. Some of the survivors were taken to Bau along with salvaged gunpowder and weapons and taught the chiefs their use. The first of many diseases was also introduced in that year, such that by the early twentieth century indigenous population levels were under half of what they had been at contact.

Within a few years, trading ships were sending in highly paid crews to fight battles with muskets and cannon on behalf of particular chiefs in exchange for cargoes of sandalwood (used to make joss sticks and profitable at Canton). The first Europeans to live in Fiji were such people, mostly relatively unscrupulous men involved in the sandalwood trade. The wreck of an American brig in 1808 with a cargo of thousands of silver dollars just off Nairai didn't help matters, but it gave the early Europeans a name: 'beachcombers'.

One incidental consequence of Fijian warfare was that Fijians became the most proficient surgeons in Polynesia. In Tonga in the early nineteenth century, battle surgeons were either Fijian mercenaries or, if they were Tongan, had to have been trained in Fiji to the necessary qualifications before a Tongan would allow a surgeon to operate on him. The most pressing concern was to avoid developing tetanus from deep, puncturing arrow and spear wounds. Tetanus is an anaerobic bacterium and so dies when exposed to oxygen. Fijian battle surgeons were most adept at opening up deep wounds with shell or bamboo blades, exposing the whole wound to the air and removing arrowheads and other particles from inside before overseeing a successful healing process. These procedures were known as 'drusu' or 'bote-a-na tamata'.

Many visitors to the Fiji Islands, sceptical about tales of cannibalism, were in for a profound shock. In July 1840 the US Navy Exploring Expedition had what was literally an 'eyewitness' encounter with cannibalism off Vitu Levu in the aftermath of a local battle. Commodore Charles Wilkes recorded what happened in the official account of the four-year voyage:

> Shortly afterwards a canoe came alongside, bringing the skull yet warm from the fire, much scorched, and marked with the teeth of those who had eaten of it. The brain had been roasted and taken out, as well as the eyes and teeth. Another canoe came alongside with some roasted flesh in it.
>
> While Mr Spieden and others were agreeing with the natives for the purchase of the skull for a fathom of cloth, a native stood near him holding something in his right hand, which he soon applied to his mouth, and began to eat. To their utter astonishment they discovered it to be the eye of the dead man, which the native had plucked from the skull a few moments before. So revolting and unexpected a sight produced a feeling of sickness in many; this ocular proof of their cannibal propensities fully satisfied them. The native was eating it, and exclaiming at the same time, 'Vinaka, Vinaka' ('Good, Good'). Another was seen eating the last of the flesh from the thighbone. This was witnessed by several of the officers and men, who all testify to the same facts.
>
> Previous to this occurrence, no one in the squadron could say that he had been an eyewitness to cannibalism,

though few doubted its practice, but the above transaction placed it beyond all doubt, and we have now the very skull, which was bought from those who were picking and eating it, among our collections.

What we would call religion in traditional Fiji was based on ancestor veneration. There were considerable regional variations around a common theme. Chiefs were living gods who personified and represented the ancestor spirits of departed chiefs. These spirits – 'kalou' (literally 'the spirit of a dead leader') – resided in the spirit world of Bulu and came in different varieties and forms. As Fergus Clunie, once Director of the Fiji Museum and the world authority on the culture of old Fiji, explains:

Fijian chiefs were destined themselves, if they got through life and managed to get into the spirit world, which wasn't easy to do, to become deities. And so there's living contact all the time with these dead, with these spirits of your ancestors. And the different clans, basically when they were at war with one another, were being led by the souls of their own dead war chiefs. So there's great contact all the time, both in peace and war with your departed leaders.

'Kalouvu' were the foundation spirits whose origins were too ancient to recall and were recognized across different clans. 'Kalougata' were spirits of the dead and were courted when their activities in life were being pursued by the clan. A legendarily successful warrior, for example, might become a war god and be venerated after death during periods of warfare, his temple falling into disrepair in peacetime. More numerous than the kalougata were the 'kalouyalo'. These were the spirits of the recently deceased who could become kalougata over time. Each kalou was represented on earth by his own priest – 'bete' – and had a temple, or 'burekalou', that was built over the grave of the dead chief or at some other site that was strongly associated with him in life.

Kalou could be called on to advise their people in times of necessity by physically entering the body of the bete and talking through him as the bete entered a trembling, shaking convulsive fit. They were also constantly manifested in and represented by the living chief, whose relationship with his people was regulated by a whole series of strict rules, called 'tabus', that marked out his divine status. For example, ordinary people were not allowed to stand up in his presence, and he had to be fed by close female relatives, being unable to touch food himself.

The Fijian people were considered to be the substance of the land, living extensions of its energy and productivity. In pre-Christian Fiji people who fell off canoes and couldn't swim were not saved by other Fijians but left to die by drowning. Similarly, people who were ill, or who were badly wounded in an accident, were thought of as already 'dead', and no attempt was made to try to prevent their dying. In both cases, Europeans found such behaviour savage and incomprehensible. But to Fijians this illness or misfortune was merely the expression of the land indicating that individuals shouldn't go on living for whatever reason. Death was an inevitable process once it began (when you fell out of the canoe or initially fell ill), not something that should be interfered with. You could be 'dead' for weeks and still be walking, talking and eating.

A powerful, vigorous chief with plenty of 'mana' ('effectiveness') meant powerful kalou and a fertile, prosperous land and people. But conversely, in myth, the chiefs did not (unlike their people) themselves originally come from the land they ruled.

Fijians (and many other Austronesians) explained the natural authority of chiefs and their divine nature by reference to a common origin myth. Chiefly lineages were foreign – 'kai tani'— their forebears intrusive and dangerous immigrants, a nobility that arrived from the sea. They were different from the 'land people' or 'native owners' of the soil, 'kai vanua'.

Legends told how these first ferocious foreign chiefs (cannibals themselves) entered a kind of social contract with the land people, whereby instead of being destroyed by them or destroying them themselves they made a deal. In exchange for marrying the daughters of the chiefs of the land, 'consuming' them sexually, the foreign chief gave the indigenous people a divine object – whales' teeth – and agreed to 'feed' them in the sense of supplying human sacrifices for the kalou.

So, symbolically, the immigrant chief consumed the land people in the benign form of marrying their daughters and, instead of being eaten by them, he agreed to feed them on bodies of people like himself. During the actual rites of installation of a chief, he was symbolically poisoned by drinking a mildly narcotic drink called 'yaquona' and was reborn as a living god of the land people, embodying the natural power of the land. The human sacrifices to the kalou are then made to him and the bete.

It was, fundamentally, as anthropologist Marshall Sahlins has described, an exchange of raw women (indigenous virgins) for cooked men (human sacrifices to be eaten). A further twist is that the immigrant chief, having been domesticated by the land people, needed others to do his killing for him. So a third category of persons became necessary: the 'dangerous men' ('tamata rerevaki'), foreign warriors and assassins whose role it was to procure sacrificial victims from beyond the land. In traditional Fiji, fishermen often performed this role, but Europeans also fitted very neatly into it once they started to arrive on the scene. Hence the ease with which some of the early wrecked seamen became mercenaries to particular confederacies like Bau (unless they were eaten).

So the necessity of cannibalism was right at the heart of how the traditional Fijian religious and social universe was conceived in myth and also in practice. The song sung by the warriors at the installation of a chief was the same one they intoned over the body of a bakola. The origin of cannibalism was, in fact, the origin of culture.

Cannibalism and War

I am the god of war. I only am strong, and wise to fight. I can do as I please. War is that by which I amuse myself. I love it. I wish now to sport in war. War is the proper exercise of chiefs; it becomes them. There are two things worthy of gods and chiefs: war and feasting. Go on. Build your walls, erect your fences. War is good... All the towns are preparing for war; but none will prevail against Bau.

A war god speaking through a
Bauan priest, prior to an attack

In wartime, with neighbouring lands in direct conflict with one another, the kalou were also fighting and advising their respective peoples in and from the spirit world. The Fijians believed that the spirit of a body clung to the corpse for four days after death. Sacrificing and eating the body annihilated the spirit and prevented it from ascending to the spirit world and becoming a source of power and guidance to your enemies. If you could kill an enemy, especially a chief or great warrior, and eat him, then by annihilating his spirit you were scoring a tremendous additional blow against your opponents. As William Endicott, a mate on the ship *Glide*, reported:

> Little credit is given to the warrior who kills his enemies if he does not obtain their bodies; much more is thought of the savage who kills one man and carries him home than of the individual who may kill a hundred and let their dead bodies fall into the hand of the enemy. The chief glory consists not so much in killing as in eating their enemies.

Destroying a great chief meant the destruction of the power of his land. It was the worst fate that could befall a clan. As Sekove Bigitibau, a researcher at the Fijian Institute of Language and Culture, explained: 'Once a chief is held captive, then the people who are under the chief have really lost hope, they are really downhearted, they are really broken.' So in the historical accounts of Fijian warfare, the stories of vicious fights on the battlefield to determine which side would secure the body of a fallen chief or warrior make a great deal of sense. A kinsman eaten, particularly a chief, was a devastating blow.

Victorious warriors would consume some enemies on the battlefield but would always ensure that some bodies were taken back to their town or village. A specific ritual surrounded the consumption and the dedication of a bakola to the war god back at the burekalou. The bakolas would be transported sitting up in the prow of a canoe. As John Jackson wrote in 1840:

They were set up in quite formal array in two rows along the spacious decks, on their hindquarters with their knees cocked up and their hands lashed together over their knees so as to leave a space in the hind part of the bend of the same, to admit a long pole... each body supporting the other, as the whole row of bodies were in contact with each other.

Often this notion of having the bodies look as lifelike as possible would be carried further, and they would be painted and decorated as warriors looked in life. If the bakolas were being transported overland, they were, as Endicott described:

lashed on poles in a singular manner. They were bound... by bringing the upper and lower parts of the legs together and binding them to the body, and the arms in a similar manner by bringing the elbows to rest on the knees, and their hands tied upon each side of the neck. Their backs were confined to poles, which were about twelve feet long. One was lashed on each pole, with six men, three at each end, to carry it.

The warriors would announce their victorious return in a number of ways. If returning by canoe, a bark cloth pennant called a 'boca' would be hoisted as a signal for every captured body. If the raid had been particularly successful, 'manumanu-ni-laca' – living or dead enemy children – would be swung in baskets or hung by their heels from the sail yards of the returning canoes. 'Lali', or slit drums, would be beaten in celebration by the villagers and by drummers on the canoes. A special beat, known as the 'derua', was used specifically to accompany the celebrations associated with the bakola. The warriors would also dance a victory dance, called a 'cibi', again practised only on these occasions. The cibi still survives today, danced by Fijian rugby teams before matches to intimidate opponents, rather like the New Zealand haka.

On reaching the outskirts of town, the warriors and the bakola would be greeted by a group of women dancing the lewd 'dele' or 'wate' dance. The women, appearing nude in public only on this occasion, would praise the sexual prowess of their heroes and degrade and insult the now-naked bakolas. The bakolas would then be dragged to the burekalou while the warriors went ahead dancing the cibi, brandishing their clubs and throwing them in the air. Before the temple, the bodies would be flung at the feet of the paramount chief, and the priests would dedicate them to the war god.

The heads of the bodies would then be dashed open against the vatu ni mena mona – the braining stone column in the ground outside the temple – sacrificing the brain to the appetite of the god.

With these rituals concluded, the sanctified pit ovens, or 'lovo', in the temple compound were prepared and lit, and the bodies were taken away to be washed in the sea, in a stream or on a large flat dissecting stone, the 'i sava'.

The butchering and cooking process itself varied by region. Captain Richard Siddins, a sandalwood trader in Fiji in 1808 and 1809, described the treatment of the body of a chief of Navaika at Bua Bay:

> The multitude then went down to their dead enemy, and
> with pieces of wood or bamboo, made very sharp, cut off
> his hands at the wrists, his feet at the ankles, his legs
> at the knees, and his thighs near the middle... the head

was cut off very low towards the breast; and they placed it on some hot ashes that had previously been prepared in a hole dug out for the purpose; and when it had remained there a sufficient time, they rubbed off the hair with shells, and replaced it with the other parts of the body in the hole, surrounding it on all sides with stones that had been made very hot. They then covered it up till it was completely roasted.

The body was sometimes cut up into smaller pieces, as witnessed by Dr R.B. Lyth, himself a surgeon, in 1840. After being singed and scraped of hair, the body parts were 'further cut and divided into a great number of small parcels. The instrument employed was the bamboo, which was used with great dexterity, every now and then taking a fresh piece of bamboo, or tearing a piece with the teeth to have a new edge.' The meat, once cooked, was often then scraped off the bone and 'made into parcels using the banana leaf for a bag, one bakola making from seven to ten large bag-fulls. Then boiled or rebaked, produces a rich red gravy... keeps by recooking for five to ten days...'

Particular choice portions – 'i sigana' – were reserved for the chief and the bete. These were treated differently and consumed in the burekalou. Some were eaten by the chiefs and some by the kalou himself through the medium of the possessed bete. Particular types of implements, resembling peculiar wooden forks – 'culanibakola' – were used to place the meat in the mouth. They were designed in such a way as to prevent the meat from having to touch the mouth of the bete or the chief as it went in, as it became defiled if this happened. At such times the kalou was considered as being present physically inside the priest, who was its vehicle, or 'waqa', and could consume the flesh of the bakola directly. As Fergus Clunie explained:

> And it was then taken by the god within the priest and swallowed, consumed. And the soul of the person who had been killed was thus fed to the god and destroyed. You've got the physical cannibalism which most people don't see beyond because it's such a traumatic thing for most people to witness or think about in modern society. And beyond that you've got what's going on spiritually, which is actually the whole point of the exercise, where the god is fed the soul of the person involved.

So the supply of bakola to a town was, in a sense, the *raison d'être* of a chief. As Chief Mosese Tuisawau of Rewa, himself the great-grandson of a notoriously cannibalistic chief, told us:

> It's the driving force. It propels you forward, to do as much damage to your perceived enemies and at the same time destroy their physical being. And subject it to... you know, unspeakable horrors and insult, as to placate your ancestral gods. And when you put them in the oven you imagine that your ancestral gods are also with you to participate in the ritual of eating of the flesh, which becomes therefore the high point of your existence and justification to your tribes about your leadership.

When even the very basic sketch presented here of the cultural logic of Fijian cannibalism is considered, a whole series of observations made by horrified European witnesses about the practice suddenly make sense. For example: why bakolas always had to be obtained from outside the group (the gods couldn't eat their own people); why cruelty and cannibalistic excess was considered a virtue among chiefs (the more enemies annihilated, the better); and why sometimes putrescent bodies kept for days would still be eaten (the spirit still had to be destroyed).

Because the spirit of the bakola was annihilated, the Fijians' normal respect for their venerated dead didn't come into play. Body parts and bones from the bakola could be treated with unusual impunity. It was common, for example, for human shinbones to be carved into the long, slender 'saulaca', or sail needles, used in boat construction, which were usually carved out of whalebone. Some of these needles have survived, notably several given to Reverend R.B. Lyth, which are now on display in the Fiji Museum in Suva, the modern capital of the islands. In 1831 William Endicott commissioned a pair from a craftsman who specialized in making them. In the aftermath of a bakola feast, this man 'sat near the king, with four shinbones between his own, and feeling himself entitled by his peculiar occupation to those parts of the victim, never failed to have a share of the spoils... I engaged [him] to make a pair of sail needles, one from the limb of each of the devoured victims, promising him a good compensation for them. He gave them to me two or three days after, neatly wrought...'

Another common type of use of bakola bones was for trophies, particularly the long bones from the arm or leg, which were stuck in the forks of shaddock trees in sacred groves in and around the temple compound.

The traveller Colonel Smythe noted at Namosi in Vitu Levu in 1860 'the sight of a tree garnished with two thighbones, a jawbone, a shoulder blade, and several ribs. While looking at this ghastly spectacle, a chief of the town joined us, and obligingly volunteered a short biography of the original owner of the remains. He had been a famous warrior of a hostile tribe, and had often carried terror to Namosi, but had at last been killed and eaten.'

The bones would often gradually become incorporated into the bark of the shaddock tree as it grew. The fork of one of these trees from the celebrated sacred grove at Namosi, in the highlands of southern Vitilevu, was cut down in 1876 and preserved. It is now in the Fiji Musuem, and the cut marks on the bones were analysed by the Australian archaeologist Dr Dirk Spenning, primarily because 'there is no question about its place of origin, or of its being a cannibal relic'. The butchering pattern matched the sequence described in several of the historical accounts of bakolas being butchered.

But most of the remains of bakolas would have been discarded as waste food products in middens, of the kind found in prehistoric Europe. David DeGusta, a human taphonomist at the University of California in Berkeley, analysed an assemblage of intensively damaged bones from Navatu in Vitu Levu, a notoriously violent area in the nineteenth century and a landscape which was very much part of some of the oldest myths associated with ancestor spirit worship.

The bones had been originally excavated in 1947 by the pioneering American anthropologist Edward W. Gifford. He had concluded his study of the assemblage with a famous quote: 'Outside of fish, man was the most popular of vertebrates used for food.' David compared the smashed bones with the remains of formally buried Fijians from nearby Vunda and concluded that the Navatu assemblages, dating from 50 BC to AD 1900, provide rigorous taphonomic evidence of the cannibalism signature similar to that recorded in the American south-west and in Europe. As he said:

When I looked at the bones I saw much the same things that Gifford did, except in a little bit more detail. On the pig remains we find burning and cut marks, as well as on the turtles and the fish and the other animals. We also find the same things on the human remains at about the same frequency; they are also cut-marked, burned and broken in about the same manner.

So what we can infer from this is that these animals, human and non-human alike, were intensively processed. The bones were cooked, the meat was sliced off and the bones were broken up and then discarded.

From the bones I can be sure that the people represented by these fragmentary bones were consumed by other Fijians.

What do modern Fijians think about this custom of their ancestors? Sekove Bigitibau spoke for the general attitudes of Fijians, many of whom are dedicated Christians: 'Some parts of what was practised in the pre-Christian era are thought of as evil practices nowadays, and we don't want to talk about them, especially cannibalism.'

Chief Tuisawau mused on the differences between then and now:

Looking back at the kind of mentality people had back then, I think it's rather horrible to think of. But cruelty in the normal sense of what we think of in modern days was not then part of the thinking. Objectives had to be attained, and physical, physical forces had to be marshalled to achieve those objectives. I think it was just part of their life... [there was] no sense of pathos or empathy with all those people who were subjected to this kind of ritual cruelty. I think the most gruesome part is that no one questioned it... It's just something that had to be done, and they carried on with it ruthlessly.

How should we, in the modern West, view these customs? An excellent point was made to the English seaman John Jackson by a chief at Tau in 1840 in the aftermath of an attack on Male and the subsequent bakola feasting:

> I started back, pretending to be more afraid and disgusted, if possible, than I really was, telling him that I had gone beyond the bounds of an Englishman to be even a spectator of such a scene, and telling him that this kind of work was not always believed when spoken of in my country... At last I made him comprehend the disgust we had to these practices, but could not by any means instil into him the wickedness of them... I told him that his gods were all false, and that it was the wicked god (the devil) that put these things into their heads, because he was an enemy of the true God. I went on to explain to him these things, but he said: 'Different countries, different fashions, and, in like manner, different gods.'

FIVE

On the Trail of the Russian Cannibal

A thousand miles east of Moscow, across the desolate Ural Mountains, lies Chelyabinsk, one of the largest cities in Russia's industrial heartland and one of the most polluted places in the world. Every day, its swathe of iron and steel works – relics from Second World War armament production – belches out yet more poisonous emissions into the atmosphere. Though these factories survived the collapse of the USSR, unemployment rises each month and more of the city's population slips beneath the poverty line. The daily struggle to survive in Chelyabinsk brings social dislocation and a rising crime rate, especially in alcohol-related incidents. Out of work and with no prospects, more and more of the male population turn to the bottle to relieve their suffering.

In the midst of this hopelessness, one horrific episode encapsulates the desperation of the 'new Russia'. On New Year's Eve 1999, the residents of an apartment block in the city centre were treated to a rare feast of fresh meat. The meat was supplied by Alexander Zapiantsev, who told the residents that he had requisitioned a consignment of veal from a butcher friend and wanted his neighbours to share his good fortune. Hungry and impoverished residents, like Valodka Poptsov, were delighted to receive the fresh meat:

> I thought the meat was OK. We ground it all up in the mincing machine with onion and garlic and ate it to our hearts' content. We basically lived off burgers from New Year's Eve onwards. My kid even ate some.

A few weeks later, a certain Valdemar Suzik was reported missing in what was known as the city's Lenin District. Suzik's sister told the police that when she had last spoken to her brother he had said that he was going round to a friend's flat for a drink. The friend was Alexander Zapiantsev.

Zapiantsev – who already had a criminal record – was picked up immediately and questioned by the police. In the interrogation, he confessed that he and Suzik had got drunk together and started arguing. The row became physical and Suzik fell, hitting his head on the cooker. Zapiantsev claimed he then passed out and was unconscious for several hours. When he woke up, he discovered that Suzik was dead.

The police investigator in the Lenin District, Mikhail Tarasov, didn't buy Zapiantsev's story for a moment. He believed that an altogether different sequence of events had taken place in Zapiantsev's flat on the night in question. Gradually, he pieced together the various bits of evidence and came up with a scenario that, when the case went to trial, would shock all Russia.

The only part of Zapiantsev's story which Tarasov believed was that he and Suzik had indeed got drunk and had had a fight. Rather than an unfortunate accident, however, Tarasov believed that during the course of the struggle Zapiantsev had grabbed an axe and bludgeoned the hapless Suzik to death. To cover his tracks, Tarasov reasoned, Zapiantsev had then decided that he had to dismember the corpse and hide the various body parts. Tarasov confronted Zapiantsev with this version of events, and after persistent and sustained interrogation Zapiantsev caved in. He confessed to the murder of Suzik and described in graphic detail how he had disposed of the body parts. Tarasov recalled Zapiantsev's harrowing confession:

> He had filleted the corpse and put the bones, the fingers and internal organs in one bag and the heavier items – such as the skull and other large bones, the tibia and ribs, in another bag. The bag with the skull in he deposited on a nearby rubbish tip. The other bag he buried beneath the pipes of the city's heating system on Goncharenko Street.

Zapiantsev took the police to the place where he had concealed the body parts, where they began their grisly excavation. After breaking through the icy ground, they soon came upon the last remains of the unfortunate Suzik: the various internal organs, hands and feet and swaths of skin were dug out of the ice. The bag with the skull and big bones was also retrieved from the rubbish tip. There was only one vital ingredient missing. 'We had recovered the skull and the big bones and the skin and innards,' Tarasov recalled, 'but we still didn't know what had happened to all Suzik's flesh.'

In a flash of inspiration, Tarasov remembered seeing a large amount of fresh meat in Zapiantsev's fridge, a sight that – amid the poverty of the surrounding apartments – was noteworthy enough for him to ask Zapiantsev how he had come by it.

Zapiantsev answered that he killed stray dogs, flayed them and cut them up for food. He was shifty and unconvincing in his response, and the terrible truth at last began to dawn. Tarasov and his colleagues again subjected their prisoner to a barrage of persistent questioning about Suzik's fate. Eventually, they broke through:

> ... at first he denied it all, claiming he had thrown Suzik's flesh away, in the same place where we had found the head. We knew he was lying, and when we pointed out the inconsistencies in his story he began to cave in. After a while he saw that the situation was hopeless and admitted that the meat in his fridge was Suzik's flesh. He also admitted that to dispose of much of the flesh he had taken it round to the hostel, where some of his friends lived, and he had treated them all, all those present, to this meat, without letting on where it had come from.

The hostel's hungry inhabitants had not questioned Zapiantsev too closely. They rarely had an opportunity to eat fresh meat and accepted their surprise benefactor's claim that it was veal. Many of them carefully divided the meat into portions so that it would sustain them for several weeks.

Even after giving much of the meat away, Zapiantsev found he had enough left over to sell and make a tidy profit. He cultivated the friendship of the unsuspecting Valodka Poptsov so that he would help him carry out his diabolical scheme. He confided in his new comrade that the meat was not veal, but dog meat.

Poptsov knew that meat could be exchanged for vodka at the farmers' market and that, such was the demand, they might even get a little cash as well. In evidence that was later crucial to the investigation, Poptsov recalled how Zapiantsev took him up to his flat to help fetch the meat:

> I was in his flat and all the doors were shut. When we went to get the meat, only the door to the kitchen was open. And all the doors were locked. He said his daughter had locked them. He got the meat from the balcony. It was in a metal box, which was, in fact, a metal drum from a washing machine. He kept the meat in there so it wouldn't spoil – it was winter and frozen. He told me to stand by the door so I wouldn't see what was going on. I asked if I could use the toilet, but he said it wasn't working. I later found out that he had carved up the body in the bathroom, which was why he wouldn't allow me to use it. We took the meat – of which there was probably about fifteen to twenty kilogrammes – to the market, where it sold very quickly. We had plenty of vodka to drink to celebrate our success. The next day he said I should have the last slithers of meat and the bones as a reward for my services. He told me I should take them home and boil them up for my son. I did as he suggested, but, as hungry as we were, the bones looked so unappetizing we decided to give them to a neighbour's dog. Even the dog turned his nose up at them.

It was now clear to Tarasov that the meat in Zapiantsev's fridge – the meat that the unwitting Poptsov and his son had eaten and which they had helped Zapiantsev to sell at market – was the flesh of the unfortunate Suzik. Tarasov confronted Zapiantsev with his suspicions and, to his surprise, Zapiantsev admitted calmly that he had carved up Suzik's body, had sold the flesh and had even eaten some of it himself. He tried to claim that he was mentally disturbed, but psychiatric tests proved that he was in perfectly sound mind.

At his trial, Zapiantsev was sentenced to twenty-four years in solitary confinement in the remote Yamalo-Nenets region, a thousand miles from Chelyabinsk. Even his own daughter – who continues to live in the flat where Zapiantsev had killed and cannibalized Suzik – has now disowned him: 'I feel revulsion, revulsion at my own father. And shame, probably. I feel no pity for him whatsoever. Not the tiniest bit. For me it is as though he doesn't exist.'

For Tarasov, the most difficult task was to inform the inhabitants of the hostel who had eaten the human flesh, believing it to be veal, that they were in effect cannibals:

> Well, Poptsov was uneasy and clearly perturbed when I told him, but he was relatively calm. He had evidently guessed that this was some sort of strange meat – not dog meat, and certainly not beef. It was the women in the hostel who suffered the most. Not that they were physically sick, you understand, but it was clear that they were out of sorts and agitated for some time at the thought that they had eaten the flesh of another human being.

The last link in the chain to fully understand the motives for Zapiantsev's actions would have been to interview the man himself. This we tried to do, and we had, indeed, received initial verbal consent from the Russian prison authorities. At the last minute, however, this was countermanded by the FSB (the modern equivalent of the KGB).

At a time when the 'new' Russia is trying desperately to woo the West after disgracing itself in Chechnya and over the Kursk tragedy, such antisocial activities are not considered suitable for public airing. What in particular the Russian authorities are eager to cover up is the fact that with homelessness on the increase – there are now believed to be in excess of four million people living on the streets of Russian cities – cannibalism is becoming more and more common.

Colonel Anatoly Khairov of the serious crimes division of the Russian Interior Ministry told us that in 1998 he was aware of over thirty victims of cannibalism. 'We have information about cases where human flesh is sold in street markets; also when homeless people kill each other and sell the flesh. Every month we find corpses with missing body parts.' Many of these follow a strikingly similar pattern to the Zapiantsev case.

In another case, in 1997, in the unlikely setting of the quiet Volga town of Manturovo, Valentina Dolbilina, a mother of a four-year-old boy, and Vitaly Bezrodnov, a factory worker, were accused of killing their drinking partner and cooking his flesh. In a scene eerily reminiscent of the Chelyabinsk hostel, a group of neighbours had got together for a vodka drinking session, following which Bezrodnov had announced that he was hungry and 'would like some meat'. He and Dolbilina inspected one of their comatose drinking companions but decided that he was too skinny and packed him off home. Their gluttonous eyes then fell on a fourth member of their party, who was better fleshed. Propelling him into their tiny kitchen, they decapitated him with an axe and sliced large chunks of flesh from his body. As Dolbilina held a tray, some fifteen pounds of meat were cut from the thighs and rump and a quantity put in the frying pan.

Awakened by the unusual smell of cooking meat, Dolbilina's flatmate, Boris Komarov, came into her room and asked to join the feast. Assured that the meat was from a stray dog, Komarov began to gnaw on a piece of leg straight from the pan. Little did he realize the full ghastliness of the situation: the dead man was his own brother, Leonid, who had joined him that morning for a few bottles of vodka. When eventually arrested and confronted with the awfulness of her crime, Dolbilina could only say in her defence that she was depressed and had been disorientated through alcohol and lack of sleep.

Like Zapiantsev, Dolbilina and Bezrodnov are now contemplating their folly from the confines of a maximum-security prison. But even in Russian prisons, cannibalism is not unknown. In a 1996 case in Barnaul, in a far-flung corner of Siberia, Andrei Maslich, twenty-five, decided that he did not like sharing his prison cell with another inmate. He strangled the man and then proceeded to cut out his liver with a shard of broken glass and a sharpened rod. He put the organ in a mug with water and boiled it up on a fire made from his bedding. Standing in the defendant's cage in the courtroom, Maslich admitted to drinking the loathsome soup. Part of the shrunken liver was found in his mug.

So widespread has cannibalism now become in Russia that there is private concern among Interior Ministry officials that it could reach epidemic proportions. Even as we left Chelyabinsk, we were told that another major cannibalism trial was about to open in a city called Ivanovo, a couple of hundred miles northwest of Moscow. Several people admitted in court that they had dug up recently buried bodies and had eaten human flesh. Unlike Zapiantsev, they did not even try to claim that they were mad but instead confessed simply to being starving and to not knowing how to get food to survive.

The Zapiantsev case and others like it beg the question of what has caused this recent outbreak of cannibalism. Certainly, the unleashing of market forces has led to widespread social dislocation, poverty and degradation. But there are many other countries in the world where the plight of the people is just as bad and yet which have not turned to cannibalism. What is it in the collective consciousness of the Russian people which makes them prone to an extraordinary, macabre outbreak of this kind?

In order to try to find out, we searched the annals of Russian twentieth-century history for other cannibalistic episodes. Our starting point was the famine of 1921–22 in the Volga region, caused by the requisitioning of grain by the Bolsheviks from 1918 onwards for their bitter civil war against General Denikin's White Army. This was one of the most brutal and vicious periods in Russian history – more brutal even than the terrors of Ivan the Terrible in the sixteenth century. Captured communists were given short shrift by the peasantry for whom the overthrown tsar still represented the nation's 'little father'.

In his epistle 'On the Russian', the writer Maxim Gorky described the more horrific treatment meted out to the captured communists:

They would open a prisoner's belly, take out the small intestine and, nailing it to a tree or telegraph pole, they drove the man around the tree with blows, watching the intestine unwind through the wound. Stripping a captured officer naked, they tore strips of skin from his shoulders in the form of shoulder straps and knocked in nails in place of pips; they would pull off the skin along the lines of the sword belt and trouser stripes – this operation became known as 'to dress in uniform'.

Amid this brutality, it was little wonder that the norms and taboos of society were set aside. By the time famine visited the region, the thin veneer of civilization in peasant society had been stripped away, exposing the bestial savagery beneath. People had started to become indifferent to the horrors of death and had even begun, in some cases, to enjoy the smell of blood.

The famine gripped the Volga region like a vice, slowly squeezing the lifeblood out of it. The Bolsheviks had been taking grain for the best part of four years – not just surpluses, but essential seed, foodstuffs for the livestock, basic stores from the household barns. When successive harvests failed in 1920 and 1921, there was nothing for the people to live on. The region's entire population of five million was destined to perish. Hunger quickly turned people to cannibalism, which became a much more common phenomenon than anyone has yet acknowledged. In the Bashkir region and on the steppes around Pugachev and Buzuluk, where the famine crisis was at its worst, thousands of cases were reported. It was also clear that much of the cannibalism went unreported.

The phenomenon really started to take off with the onset of winter in around November 1921, when the first snows covered the last remaining food on the ground and there was nothing else to eat. In their desperation to feed their children, mothers cut off limbs from corpses and boiled the flesh in pots. People ate their own relatives, often their young children, who were usually the first to die and whose flesh, according to folklore, was particularly sweet.

In some villages the peasants refused to bury their dead but stored the corpses, like so much meat, in their barns and stables. They often begged relief workers not to take away the corpses but to let them eat them instead. In the village of Ivanovka, near

Pugachev, a woman was caught with her child eating her dead husband. When the police tried to take away his remains, she shouted: 'We will not give him up. We need him for food. He is our own family, and no one has the right to take him away from us.' The stealing of corpses from cemeteries became so common that in many regions armed guards had to be posted on the gates.

The acknowledged expert on the Volga famine is Orlando Figes, whose book *A People's Tragedy: The Russian Revolution 1891–1924* was a worldwide best-seller. During the research for his book, Figes discovered dramatic and poignant written accounts buried deep in the Russian state archives of the last days of those who had perished in the famine. One of these was from a peasant called Muhin, who recorded how his plight had driven him and his neighbours to cannibalism:

> January 1922. There has been no grain in the village since Easter of last year. We have tried eating everything: grass, tree bark. Cats and dogs went long ago. Yesterday, I stumbled on the body of a young boy, no more than six or seven years old. I took it home, carved off the flesh and began to eat. It was the best meal I'd had all year.

When Muhin was later arrested by officials of the local Soviet, he wrote in bemusement: 'I don't understand why they have arrested me and not my wife or the other members of my family. We all ate human meat. Everybody in our village eats human flesh. If you go to the cafeteria, there's nothing else to eat.'

The authorities tried to cover up the existence of the famine, let alone the cannibalism that was breaking out as a result of it. But the scale of the crisis led prominent figures such as Maxim

Gorky to appeal to the West for aid. A huge operation was mounted under US President Herbert Hoover, known as the American Relief Administration (ARA). Several doctors from the ARA were sent to the Volga region to help the starving masses and recorded regular and disturbing sightings of cannibalism. They saw frozen bodies left by the roadside and by barns with chunks taken out of them, very obviously for food. Concerned about its effects on morale, the central Soviet authorities asked Lenin's feared secret police – the Cheka – to look into the problem. A commission was duly set up to prevent the spread of cannibalism. Some of its weekly reports have also recently come to light in the archives. These reports reveal not only the resentment of villagers forced to part with the dead bodies of friends and relatives on whom they were feeding but also an even more horrific and ghoulish by-product of the outbreak of cannibalism: a burgeoning trade in human flesh. Orlando Figes has helped to uncover the crucial documentary evidence of this trade:

> There were gangs who went around the towns capturing children, murdering them and selling the human flesh as horse meat or beef. Also, one must bear in mind that the Volga area was an area of considerable banditry. It was on the steppe. There were bands that would rustle cattle and sell that meat to the local Soviet administration. And I think one has to bear in mind that this really did take off because the local Soviet food agencies, which were notoriously corrupt in any case, were under pressure from Moscow or from provincial centres to get food into local cafeterias, factory kitchens and so on. In a situation of shortage that the central authorities didn't even begin to appreciate, you could see, well, if a gang came along and

said we've got some meat and don't ask too many questions about it, they would agree a price and put it into the cafeterias, so it's hard to estimate, but I'm sure that a considerable proportion of the meat in Soviet factories in the Volga area – and, who knows? Maybe it went all the way up to the Kremlin – was human flesh.

It is perhaps impossible for anyone who has not gone through the agonies of famine to imagine how the taboos of human civilization could so easily and frequently be broken to allow cannibalism. But reading the accounts of people living through the terror, chaos and confusion of a slow death by starvation makes it easier to comprehend.

Even more powerful and affecting are the testimonies of first-hand witnesses. Bishop Alexander Bykovetz now presides over a small but committed Ukrainian Orthodox community in Detroit, USA. Seventy years ago, however, he was one among many millions fighting for their lives in Stalin's so-called 'terror famine' of the early 1930s: 'I remember well the events of 1932–33 even though I was only a small boy... I have information first-hand from my grandfather, who came to us begging for help and then describing in detail the terrible problems in the villages.'

In the 1930s Stalin's forced collectivization of agriculture ravaged the resources of the Ukraine. His merciless raids on 'the breadbasket' of Europe were not intended merely as a means of acquiring food supplies for the rest of the Soviet Union but also to break the growing spirit of independence in the country, especially among its farmers. The resulting famine decimated the population, killing up to ten million people. It was a genocide that bears comparison with the Nazi Holocaust against the Jews. With grain being taken from their stores and even the half-eaten food on their tables being removed, the Ukrainian villagers resorted to whatever they could find to survive, as Bishop Bykovetz remembers:

> People started to eat their animals, then pets like cats and dogs. They were wandering around the vicinity of the village looking for dead horses and cows and consuming them raw. And when all this was exhausted, they started to die in their hundreds, and in some instances, when there was nothing to eat and no one to turn to for help, the mothers, being already in a hunger fever and out of their mind, even started to eat their own babies.

As in the Volga famine of ten years earlier, human flesh became a valuable commodity and a black market trade in body parts began to flourish, as Bykovetz explains: 'Children were kept inside. Their parents wouldn't allow them to play outside, and especially after dusk they couldn't walk on the street because there was the fear that they would be taken away and maybe next day sold at market.' Though the secret police were clamping down on the meat traders, the availability of human flesh at market was an open and acknowledged secret. People were glad of any kind of meat. There was no other means to survive.

Lest cannibalism be seen as largely the hunger-induced madness of primitive and ill-educated peasantry, the best-documented case in Russia comes from one of the most urbanized and civilized cities in the world – the jewel in the crown of imperial Russia and one of Europe's cultural centres, St Petersburg.

In September 1941 St Petersburg – or Leningrad as it was then known – was encircled by three advancing German armies.

Nearly three million people were trapped inside the city as the siege, which was to last 900 days, began. By the time it was over, nearly half the population – 1.5 million people – would have perished. As the siege continued in the teeth of the Russian winter of 1941, a group of Leningrad doctors determined that they would document the suffering of the people in a unique medical research programme of a community starving to death. They observed and examined the bodies of 'Leningraders' who had collapsed and died even as they walked along a street or sat on a park bench. They compiled a detailed survey of how the human body reacts to starvation and the order in which the various organs shut down if deprived of food for any length of time.

All this information would have been on record in the Siege Museum, set up after the war had ended, was it not for Stalin's strict censorship regulations. To preserve the myths of the great Soviet victory, Stalin was determined that no record should survive intact which cast the suffering of the Soviet people in anything less than a glorious light. The in-depth medical analysis that the Leningrad doctors had painstakingly documented was considered an unhelpful diversion from the triumph of the human spirit. As a result, these invaluable records were impounded for over half a century.

Now, however, they have been discovered in the St Petersburg archives by a research team led by Dr John Barber of King's College, Cambridge. During a three-year project funded by The Wellcome Trust, Barber and his colleagues unearthed a series of vital medical documents that reveal at first hand what it was like to endure the terrors of death by starvation. The documents tell a horrific tale, including descriptions of some of the most graphic and widespread episodes of cannibalism recorded. Barber is understandably excited about the nature of this evidence:

We now have official reports as to what happened, produced at the time or very shortly afterwards, which leave no doubt that cannibalism existed and that it took place on a far from insignificant scale. In addition to that, we have access to records, diaries, reminiscences that were produced by people who lived through the siege in which they quite explicitly and as a matter of fact talk about cannibalism as a part of everyday life.

The majority of the accounts come from the period when the city was worst hit, during the winter of 1941–42. Temperatures fell to below -30°C – one of the coldest winters on record – and almost no food was getting into the city. There was no public heating, light or water supply. The transport system had failed, and some 600,000 people died in only a few months. The records describe in detail the extent of the human misery:

There were corpses in people's houses, in the streets, in the rivers, in the squares and at the cemeteries themselves, where the personnel just couldn't cope with the influx of corpses; there would be hundreds and thousands of unburied corpses just lying there. At the largest cemetery, the Piskarovskaya, in February 1942, it's recorded that on some days there were up to 20,000 or 25,000 unburied bodies. So there was the opportunity for people who were in a desperate state to have access to human meat, and in many diaries and other records of the time we find people noting almost as a matter of course that they are walking along a street and they see a corpse which has had, as is written, the tender parts carved off. And quite often someone will look out of a window and see the body of a person who had fallen dead there the previous evening chopped up with only parts of it remaining.

Extracts from letters written by a starving Leningrader in January 1942 make similarly grim reading: 'The city has become a morgue – the streets have become avenues of the dead. In every basement of every house there is a heap of dead bodies. There are processions of bodies through the streets, and there are piles of them in the hospitals.'

In their desperation, people began to eat anything they could find – the paraffin glue used by the city's carpenters was melted down and became a local delicacy dubbed, with gallows humour, 'meat in aspic'. Grass and plants were uprooted from the frozen earth, and bark was stripped from the trees. People began to die in their thousands. As the body count rose, the attitude of the starving Leningraders towards their dead changed gradually from sorrow to ambivalence and, finally, to cannibalistic craving. This transition, which occurred from the winter of 1941–42 onwards, is graphically illustrated by the inability of the city's funeral services to deal with the mass of bodies. A 1943 report from the Leningrad funeral service has been recovered from the archives by John Barber's research team and reads as follows:

People began to steal parts of chopped-up bodies, particularly those of children. In one unburied coffin, the head and feet were left but all the remaining parts of the body had been carried away. At the Serafamofski cemetery, the director and the local police inspector discovered a corpse's head that had been cut off. Tracks led to a wooden house on the boundary of the cemetery, where they discovered the inhabitants cooking human flesh. The caretaker of the Bogoslovski cemetery stopped a woman who was carrying something out of the cemetery on a toboggan. In her bag were discovered the bodies of five children.

A report written by the military procurator of Leningrad in February 1942 and marked 'Absolutely Secret' describes in detail the scale of the problem and the arrests made of people who had committed cannibalism. In December 1941, for example, twenty-six people were arrested for cannibalism. In January 1942, 366 people were arrested for cannibalism, and in the first half of the following month 494 people were arrested. By mid-1942 the rate of arrests for cannibalism was running at about 1,000 per month.

These figures tally with the Cheka's reports, which reveal that, by the summer of 1942, 2,000 people had been charged with cannibalism; almost all of them had been found guilty, and nearly 600 of them had been executed. What was also interesting about the report was that cannibalism cut across all social and gender boundaries – it was neither an exclusively male activity nor something to which only the lower echelons of society resorted. Doctors, teachers, soldiers, males and females in equal measure – all resorted to eating human flesh, as one elderly siege survivor, Zinaida Kuznetsova, recalled:

I know that my neighbours ate their son – at the end of the war they let it slip. The boy always went around in a gas mask, collecting horse dung to eat. Then all of a sudden he disappeared. They said he'd gone away to the countryside. Then it slipped out in conversation that they'd eaten him, and they were arrested and tried for it.

There was a woman in the bread queue who was always trying to get me to go with her to her house, saying that it was nice and warm where she lived, that everything was just like it was before the war, but I didn't believe her and I didn't go. It later turned out that she'd killed and eaten twenty-two children in this way.

By December 1943, as the Red Army began to push the German armies back beyond its frontiers, Leningrad began to emerge from its collective nightmare. Plans were discussed by the city council for a Museum of the Defence of Leningrad, to be opened once the war was officially won. This museum was to catalogue all the suffering of the siege – including cannibalism – and to pay tribute to the people who had had to eat their own dead to survive. A few years after it was opened, however, in 1949, the museum was closed on Stalin's orders and its curator, Major Rakov, was imprisoned. When the museum was reopened by Nikita Khrushchev in 1957, all references to cannibalism had been expunged from the historical record. Only now have we been able to reveal the full horrors of Leningrad.

These three tragic and shocking episodes in Soviet history – the Volga famine, the famine in the Ukraine and the siege of Leningrad – have all left indelible scars on the Russian and Ukrainian psyche. The question remains whether it is possible to deduce anything significant about the development of people and society under the yoke of Soviet Communism. Orlando Figes believes it is hard to generalize:

I'm reluctant to give any cultural explanation of canni- balism in Russia. It seems to me that in certain circum- stances it could happen probably anywhere. On the other hand there are one or two things about Russian pagan belief that suggest it might take root in Russia more easily than it might elsewhere. Firstly, the peasants of Russia seem to take a rather practical view of death. Turgenev, the nineteenth-century writer, wrote about Russian peasants who, knowing that they were going to die probably later that day, would spend their last hours sort of arranging the cow to be sold to the neighbour and so on. Not to say that they're not afraid of death; it's that they took a rather sort of practical view of it. The other thing is that they seem to conceive of the soul in a different way from normal Christian or other Christian civilizations and that they see it as a living thing which continues to live among the living and that therefore the body has no connection any more with the soul. So you could see that in certain situations that might lead them to see the dead body as having nothing to do any more with the person who lived in it because the person who lived in it is still floating around somewhere and therefore they can dispose of it as they wish.

Similarly, Professor Alexander Bukhanovsky, a psychiatrist from Rostov-on-Don, an expert on the grimmer recesses of the criminal mind, insists that Russians are no more predisposed to cannibalism than anyone else, except that the desperate conditions of life at the bottom of the heap mean that more succumb to the temptation: 'This problem has no historical or geographical boundaries. You cannot say it exists in Russia and not in Britain, although there maybe only once in five years. With us it is much more frequent.'

Aside from these nuances of religion and a certain natural

pragmatism, there is little to suggest that the cannibalistic instinct is any more ingrained in Russian culture and behaviour than in any other European society.

What does seem clear is that in any society in which famine and starvation become part of everyday life, in which the living and the dead coexist, and in which life becomes cheaper than an ounce of grain, cannibalism will almost inevitably play a part in determining who lives and who dies.

SIX

Slow Boat to China

Cannibalism in China is a forbidden subject – to talk about it openly is to invite immediate censure from the authorities. This would not be so surprising but for the fact that cannibalism has played a central role in Chinese life and culture for nearly four millennia. So integral was it that Chinese author Lu Xun in his famous short story *Diary of a Madman* wrote that '4,000 years of Chinese history is actually 4,000 years of cannibalism'. Yet today, in China, cannibalism is a dirty word. Only in the safety of exile can dissident academics such as Liu Binyan of Princeton University in America talk about how cannibalism evolved in Chinese culture:

> Firstly, it was of course related to natural disasters in China. During times of famine, people had no other way out, so they resorted to cannibalism. They would even use the phrase 'to exchange one's children to eat' ('yi zi er shi') and actually eat their own children. I heard about this when I was young. It was true. But starvation was only one reason for cannibalism. Another was vengeance between one race and another, or one faction and another. You can find this in the poetry of Yue Fei. 'Manjianghong' is one of his famous poems. It describes drinking the barbarians' blood and eating the barbarians'

flesh. That was a way of treating other races – or one's own. Another form was not an expression of hatred, but an expression of loyalty to an emperor, or filial piety to one's parents. People might cut off part of their flesh or even cut out their liver to give their parents. This used to happen quite a lot.

Ever since the third century BC, when Han Emperor Gao Zu issued an official edict permitting people to sell or eat their children to ward off starvation, cannibalism has emerged at frequent intervals in Chinese history.

During sieges of walled cities in the dynastic conflicts of the sixth century, when warring clans like the Chu and the Song were continually skirmishing for territory, the word would go out that it was permitted 'to exchange children to eat'. More often, in fact, children who couldn't be fed would be taken into town to be sold. From there, the fate of these poor unfortunates was in the lap of the gods. So ingrained was this idea on the Chinese psyche that the expression 'exchanging children to eat' worked its way into the language and is still used figuratively at times of great hunger.

Unlike in Russia, cannibalism in China was not practised merely to ward off starvation. It was also thought to have a medical and nutritional purpose. Dating back to the Tang Dynasty of the seventh to ninth centuries, the practice of Ko Ku was based on the powerful spiritual tradition of filial piety. It was when a faithful son or daughter cut off a portion of thigh or arm to serve to an ailing relative as the final medicinal resort.

American academic Professor Christine Yu Chun-Fang of Rutgers University, New Brunswick, New Jersey, heard about this notion of filial piety from her grandmother and set out to discover its origins. Of the many cases reported, most were of daughters-in-law seeking to help a parent after all other remedies had been exhausted and death was perhaps close at hand.

Typically, the devoted daughter-in-law would tie her thigh or her arm very tightly with a piece of clothing. She would then use a very sharp knife to quickly slice off a piece from her upper arm or upper thigh. The flesh would immediately be mixed in with soup or gruel, which had been heated in preparation, and this would then be offered to the dying mother-in-law or father-in-law. According to folklore, there would then follow without exception a miraculous recovery.

In an eerie echo of this ancient practice, a young Taiwanese woman, Li Xiujin, cut off a piece of her thigh and fed it to her unsuspecting mother and father as recently as 1987. Though she was later diagnosed as being mentally unstable, her action nevertheless appeared to be some kind of throwback to the filial piety of Ko Ku.

In a lifetime of study, Professor Yu has traced the origins of this particular form of cannibalism back to the ancient Chinese legend of Miao Chuang, a beautiful princess sent into exile by her father for refusing to obey his command to marry. As the legend has it, Miao Chuang was eventually contacted by a messenger from her father to say that he was near death and that, to live, he needed her hands and eyes. Without hesitation, she gouged out her own eyes and cut off her hands and sent them to her father. These were brought back to the king, ground up and made into medicine. The king recovered and made public homage to his daughter, who was thereafter transformed into the goddess Guan Yin, said to have a thousand arms and eyes that she donated to sick people on Earth.

This story has reappeared in various forms throughout Chinese history. More recently, Ko Ku has become Ko Kan – the donation of a human liver to assist the recovery of a relative. Professor Yu has uncovered countless accounts of the practice of Ko Kan, the latest as recently as the nineteenth century. Some of these accounts are horrific in their detail:

> After bathing and worshipping, he took up the knife and aimed at the place where his liver and lung were located. Blood gushed out after one cut. The ribcage was exposed after the second cut. After the third and fourth cuts there was a resounding sound, and after the sixth cut the heart leaped out. Following the heart he groped for the lung and after the lung he found the liver. By then he nearly fainted because of the extreme pain. After a moment's rest he called his wife and told her quickly to cook the liver to serve his mother [probably a piece of liver, although the text didn't indicate so]. Not knowing what it really was, the mother ate it happily and soon became well.

To find out whether this procedure really took place and whether it could have been as commonplace as the accounts suggest, Professor Yu contacted a Dr Thomas Chen, a professor of pathology at the New Jersey Medical School. His verdict was as follows:

> I think it probably did happen. I think there probably were attempts to remove the liver. The question is how many of them actually survived the procedure... Doing a self-hepatechtatomy [removing your own liver] is a very dangerous procedure. Not only would it have been extremely painful just to open up the ribcage and enter the abdomen, but also the liver is an organ that bleeds

very rapidly and profusely. I doubt many of them would have survived. Possibly their only hope was that the liver's regenerative powers would have kept them going. The regenerative powers of the liver are tremendous... in rats, for example, you could remove 70 per cent and it would still come back. You could probably do the same thing in humans.

Many of the stories of Ko Ku and Ko Kan can be dismissed as myth, but there is ample evidence both from local histories and from the preponderance of references in literature that actual cases did take place. The number of government edicts at various times banning the practice also points to its practical application.

Though Ko Ku and Ko Kan may seem surgically primitive by modern Western standards, they are entirely consistent with early transplant medicine in the West. Liver, kidney and heart transplants are now a relatively common procedure, as are blood transfusions. Placentas, in particular, are cherished in both the West and the East for their nutritional properties and have even been sold by UK hospitals to French pharmaceutical companies for the extraction of albumin, glucocerebrosidase and gamma globulin for enzyme replacement therapy. One can see the origins of this utilitarian attitude towards the human body in the development of Chinese culture.

From its origins in Ko Ku and Ko Kan, the tradition of cannibalism in Chinese medicine evolved into an even more diverse and varied practice. In 1578 Chinese scholar Li Shizhen published the *Ben Cao Gang Mu*, a compendium of Chinese medicines, advising the curative qualities not only of herbs and animal body parts of every conceivable kind, but also of human body parts. In all, thirty-five body parts are recommended in the treatment of various ailments.

Again, Dr Chen was consulted on the viability of such body parts for medicinal purposes. He commented:

> There was a wide range of human body products that were used, such as nail, hair, skin, milk, urine, urine sediments, gall, placenta and even flesh. The most recent studies of the medicinal properties of these products have concluded that they were only effective in about 20 per cent of the conditions for which they were prescribed.

This lack of hard evidence for the medical benefits of human body parts has not deterred the cannibalistic traditions in Chinese medical practice over several centuries. They continue even to the present day. In Hong Kong in 1995, an underground market in human foetuses was exposed by undercover journalists posing as patients in mainland hospitals.

With the 'one child' rule rigorously enforced in China, there is no shortage of available foetuses, and traders claimed not only all sorts of medical benefits for the foetuses – from rejuvenation to a cure for asthma – but also a price tag of up to $300 apiece. The then editor of the *Eastern Express*, Chip Tsao, heard about the trade from a friend:

> A friend of mine had been receiving some kind of special treatment in the Citron province by regular injection of foetal essence, and he'd been doing that for two or three years. I knew him very well, and he came back to tell me he was a different person now. He'd even married his

Filipino maid, and he lived very happily until two or three months ago this poor guy found that he'd got a later stage of liver cancer – and he died shortly afterwards.

Reports of foetuses for sale in Hong Kong scandalized legitimate doctors and the general public alike. Paradoxically, there is now a strong taboo about cannibalism in China, despite its recurrence throughout history. Even though it has recurred throughout history and has been described in graphic detail in ancient texts, people are very shocked if they hear of cannibalism. It is now regarded as almost as great a taboo in China as it is in the West.

Some speculate that this contradiction can be explained by the lack of a strongly religious moral system in China. Authority in the country has always been secular – the ultimate power was vested in an earthly emperor before the revolution and thereafter in the Communist Party. Ideas of the sanctity of humankind, made in the image of an otherworldly god are alien. The quasi-spirituality of the pre-communist age – with competing Confucian, Buddhist and Christian ideals – provided as diffuse and uncertain a moral framework as the totalitarian regime that followed.

Others have suggested that it has as much to do with what is considered edible in a country which – like Russia – has always struggled to feed herself, as Liu Binyan explains:

Chinese cuisine is among the best in the world. Chinese restaurants keep many millions of Chinese in business around the world. We should either thank or blame our ancestors for this. Because eating has also caused many problems, including environmental destruction, poverty-induced eating of everything edible or inedible. When it comes to cannibalism, we have discussed famine and other reasons for it. But I think another reason is this: why, in history, did a minister kill his son, cook him and give him to his emperor? Surely it must have tasted good? Isn't that right? At first I didn't know, but I'm told that human flesh tastes good. The emperor would eat it because it was delicious. Human eating is to do with man and nature – whether you eat, how much you eat. But this then related to the relations between people. People became something that could be eaten. This desire can grow and grow. This is a problem in China now. People want to eat everything, whether or not it should be eaten. This is a problem very peculiar to China... Otherwise why do people still eat people? Twenty years later there are still occasionally people in Beijing and the south who eat human flesh. I suspect that they might have had this experience in the past and have never forgotten the good taste. They are also probably deranged, so they carry on eating human flesh.

But one of the main reasons for today's reticence about cannibalism in China can be put down neither to a broad moral ambivalence nor to gastronomic adventurism, but to the consequences of her tragic and bloodstained revolutionary history. First there was the great famine of 1958–60. As in Stalin's Russia, Mao forced the rapid collectivization of farms in the Great Leap Forward. Grain levies were based on hugely inflated boasts of production. More was demanded than had actually been produced, and the people in the countryside were left starving. Jasper Becker, author of a major study of the famine entitled *Hungry Ghosts*, who has perhaps read more accounts of the suffering of the Chinese at the time than any other specialist on modern China, has commented:

> Officials went around the countryside searching people's homes and collecting all possible grain. And if they couldn't find grain they took livestock and anything as a substitute. And by the end of the winter of 1958 in many places in China, people were left with nothing to eat, although the granaries were actually full and there was plenty of food. People began to starve and there were protests. A number of senior leaders began to protest about this, but Mao refused to believe it. He thought the protests signified the remnant of the capitalist spirit, and that the peasants were being dishonest. So they renewed the great quotas. This went on for three years, by which time thirty million, forty million, nobody is quite sure, a great, great many people had died in the countryside in China. Later on they claimed that this was a result of natural disasters. But there were no particular natural disasters during those years, and in fact the weather in most parts of the country was unusually good. This was a purely man-made famine.

Figures for the numbers of dead in the great famine range from twenty million to forty million. It was a period when the phrase 'to exchange one's children to eat' ('yi zi er shi') once again entered the Chinese vernacular. Jasper Becker believes that this was far from a simple turn of phrase or gallows humour:

> Some of the children were reportedly eaten. It was also claimed that people went out at night and cut the flesh

off corpses that were lying in their huts or in the fields and consumed that. And in doing this they said they fell back on the traditions of surviving famines which been part of their heritage for several thousand years. When I heard these stories I was rather sceptical. It's rather hard to believe that in the middle of the twentieth century, in a country basically at peace, where there was no real reason for there to be a famine, that such things could happen. And I went to the countryside in Hunan and I stopped peasants by the side of the road and I eventually asked them straight out if they had resorted to cannibalism. And people frankly admitted that they had, they themselves had taken part in this...

In the party archives in An Hui province, official documents specifically described cases of cannibalism, of people being arrested and shot, of the government issuing public notices forbidding cannibalism. So you have this documentary evidence in addition to the fact that the local people frankly admitted what they had done. And, you know, because there's not such a specific moral or religious taboo about this, they don't really feel particularly ashamed of it.

The Communist Party has never acknowledged that a major famine existed, let alone revealed accurate figures for the numbers of dead. Even now, ordinary people and officials alike refer to that period as 'The Three Years of Natural Disaster' or 'The Three Years of Difficulties'.

But there was an even greater shame than refusing to acknowledge the millions who died in the famine. In one particular period of Chinese history, respect for human dignity broke down altogether. The brutality of Mao Zedong's Cultural Revolution in the late 1960s has long been known, but only recently has it come to light that in extreme cases cannibalism became an act of revenge against the class enemy.

At great risk to his own life, the writer and former Red Guard Zheng Yi smuggled into America evidence and official documents about the atrocities committed during the militant phase of the Cultural Revolution from 1966 to 1968. For giving away the secrets of the 'revolution' he is now in permanent exile and can never again set foot in China. He, like Liu Binyan, pursues his writing and research at Princeton University.

One of the most appalling events about which he collected evidence is believed to be the most prolific episode of aggressive cannibalism in post-war history – an episode in which up to 10,000 people are believed to have taken part and over 100 people are believed to have been eaten. Zheng Yi not only procured official documents on this horror but also compiled the results of his own private investigation into the incident, conducted before he made his escape from the mainland. He interviewed the ringleaders and secretly took photographs that reveal an extraordinary and terrifying story.

The beautiful landscape of the province of Guangxi belies the barbaric fighting that took place here between rival factions of Red Guards during the Cultural Revolution. At the middle school in Wuxuan County, at the height of what is known as the militant phase of the Cultural Revolution, fanatical students turned on their own teachers.

It was, says Zheng Yi, a time when just killing the class enemy was not enough to express class hatred. Normal human notions of kindness and compassion – and indeed all ethical principles – were completely turned upside down. No moral or ethical obstacles were left to deter people from killing and even eating other people.

The revolutionary students denounced the Head of the Chinese Department, Wu Shufang, as a class enemy and beat him to death. But this was just the beginning of the horror story, as Zheng Yi discovered in one of the secret reports to which he gained access. As he says:

> They ordered the teachers, who were also considered to be class enemies, to carry his body to the bank of the river. Once they got there, one of them was forced to cut out his heart and liver with a knife. But one of the teachers – the person who later told me this story – picked up the knife and fainted. He just couldn't bring himself to do it. So the Red Guards forced one of the other teachers to take up the knife on pain of death. Completely terrified, this teacher cut open his colleague's stomach and pulled out his liver. A Red Guard then slung the liver from the end of his gun and went back to the school. After that, a group of students cut the liver into small strips and cooked it over a fire in the school yard. Later, the report said, and I quote: 'The school yard was full of the smell of students cooking their teachers.' It was a terrifying situation.

Zheng Yi's dogged investigations have made such internal Party reports public in the West. But in China they are still secret, and expulsion from the Party was the most serious penalty that even the most fanatical killers and cannibals were dealt out. They all claimed to be acting in Mao's name.

The killing and cannibalism in Guangxi should not be separated from the twenty years of history preceding it. Ever since

1949, Mao Zedong had been raising the level of class struggle and had harmed lots of people in the process. 'The Great Leader' had never said that people should love one another. In the Chinese language, in Mandarin, the word 'love' is usually applied to 'love of the Motherland', 'love of the Party' or 'love of the Leadership'.

The events in Guangxi were just a more modern, politically inspired outbreak of a kind of cannibalism seen since man's earliest incarnation across the globe. The Aztecs were perhaps the most famous proponents of killing your enemy and incorporating their strength into your own by devouring their internal organs (particularly the heart). But many other cultures – including the Fremont Indians of south-west America, the Fijians and even the ancient Britons – committed cannibalism based on a similar aggressive spirituality.

The Guangxi incident, however, presented an opportunity – albeit a dangerous one – to examine this type of cannibalism in a modern setting. Not content with smuggling the official top-secret documents on the episode and visiting the site, Zheng Yi took a step further into the lions' den – he confronted the killers themselves.

Although trying to talk to the perpetrators of these terrors was a potentially dangerous business, Zheng Yi discovered to his amazement that those he encountered were proud of what they had done. In one village, all the 'class enemies' had been wiped out. Still not satiated, the villagers remembered the son of a former landlord who lived nearby. Even though he had been living as a poor peasant for some years, the mob went to arrest him as a 'class enemy'. As soon as he saw them coming, the landlord's son knew the end had come and went to hang himself. The mob thwarted this attempt, tortured him half to death and dragged him down to the river bank lashed to a telegraph pole.

Then a poor peasant, Yi Wanshen, took a knife and cut open the man's stomach to take out his liver. They did this grisly deed at the water's edge because their victim's stomach was so hot that Wanshen couldn't put his hand inside. Water was poured into his chest cavity to cool it down. The liver of the landlord's son made a revolutionary feast for the villagers involved.

Eventually, Zheng Yi found a way of meeting the peasant Yi Wanshen face to face, and he secretly took photographs of him with a camera balanced on his knee. Zheng Yi describes that extraordinary meeting:

> I went to see the killer for myself. And I asked him if he was afraid of the revenge of ghosts. He patted his chest and said, 'I have a red heart!' (That's Communist parlance.) 'I'm not afraid of ghosts.' He seemed very brave and convinced that what he had done was right.

During the Cultural Revolution cannibalism was not only not considered a crime, but it was regarded as a positive expression of one's hatred for class enemies. It showed loyalty to Mao's teachings. Mao said, 'The class struggle is a matter of life and death. Dictatorship is the dictatorship of the masses.' Cruelty to the enemy was a sign of progressive thinking, so some of the cannibals of Guangxi actually did quite well: some entered the Party, got promotion and became rich.

China is by no means the only country that has seen cannibalistic atrocities on such a scale and rewarded in this manner. In the last couple of years, disturbing reports began to leak out about the vicious civil war in Liberia where, between 1989 and 1997, seven warlord-led factions slaughtered each other mercilessly in a bid to take control of the country. The most powerful of these, the National Patriot Front of Liberia (NPFL), eventually emerged victorious in 1997, and its leader, Charles Taylor, was elected president. Ever since, Taylor and his associates have battled to suppress the stories of sorcery, blood-drinking and cannibalism which have been brought to many European countries by Liberian exiles.

With a culture based on warrior initiation, secret societies and human sacrifice, it is not surprising that cannibalism rises periodically to the surface. In his book *The Mask of Anarchy* Stephen Ellis even alleged that Charles Taylor himself was a cannibal and had personally overseen the torture, dismemberment and consumption of enemy soldiers in the presidential palace. Incensed by this, Taylor sued Ellis and *The Times,* in which the book was serialized. *The Times* rigorously defended the action, and it seems unlikely that Taylor will come to the UK to press his claims (if he does, he will in all probability be arrested for human rights abuses).

The Liberian civil war was distinguished by recurring outbreaks of terrifying and gratuitous slaughter. Over 60,000 fighters of a total population of 2.5 million were under arms at any one time, and of these 60,000 about 10 per cent were women and a further 15 per cent were child soldiers (under 16 years of age). It is these child soldiers, and the way in which – like the Chinese Red Guards – they were seduced into acts of ritualism and spiritual violence, to whom Ellis pays special attention. As he argues:

> In the course of the war, children were turned into psychopathic fighters and cannibalism was rampant... human sacrifice and cannibalism had long been a part of Liberian ritual practice but under the control of tradi-

tional spiritual leaders, who limited it to special occasions. The authority of these spiritual leaders was destroyed during the war, and so cannibalism broke its traditional bounds. Young fighters, high on drugs and alcohol, tried to assimilate the power of the slain by eating parts of them.

Taylor's defenders have argued that Ellis has read too much into rumours of human sacrifice and blood-drinking initiation ceremonies practised by the secret Human Leopard Societies of the nineteenth century. According to an account from a British colonial commission of inquiry of the 1850s into the secret Leopard Societies of Liberia and Sierra Leone, these societies were formed of 'men of mature age, past their prime' who met in secret conclaves and regularly killed human victims in a form of sacrifice. They then ate the flesh of their victims with a view to 'increasing their virile powers [and] to secure human fat wherewith to anoint the Borfima [the name of the cult object kept by each society]'.

But whereas Taylor and his allies can claim that these Human Leopard Societies largely grew up as a reaction to the yoke of colonial rule and have since died out, they cannot make the same claims about the ritualistic belief system in the country, known as the Poro.

Poro was not just some tribal fad of a bygone era, but the most important and widespread of all religious institutions in the Liberian hinterland lasting several centuries – a spiritual belief system that informs even today's warrior rituals. To join the Poro, it is necessary to attend 'the bush school', in which boys and girls are initiated into adult society under the aegis of elders who control the rituals and other elements of their instruction and are strictly bound never to reveal details of their instruction to outsiders.

Poro is founded on the premise that the spirit world is real and that it may be entered by humans quite easily, and conversely that spirits may enter humans. The first time that this can happen is during the period of seclusion in the forest which all Poro initiates must endure. Boys who had been executed for offending the laws of the Poro society or who died of other causes during their period of seclusion during the Poro initiation would often have their vital organs eaten by others.

The veteran American missionary George Way Harley, probably the most knowledgeable of all foreign writers on Poro, observed that those initiated into this quasi-spiritualism 'lived in fear of death and no doubt felt that they were very close to the spirit world, perhaps actually in it'. According to Harley, the eating of human flesh became part of the Poro initiation as a means of offering a sacrifice to the all-powerful 'bush devil' and ensuring the continuity of the spirit of the victims, since their life essence or spirit was deemed to enter into those who ate their hearts and other organs. As Harley also noted, where transgressors of Poro law were killed, the victim might be thought of not as a wrongdoer but 'as a sacrifice to law and order'. Families of the victims would be told simply that the cannibalized had been eaten by the bush devil.

As with Aztec cannibalism rituals, Poro rituals articulate a view of power as a source of both life and death – the essence of life or strength of the victim sustained by the person who had consumed his flesh. Though dismissed by Taylor and others as a defunct belief system from a bygone era, Poro initiation ceremonies were still being carried out as recently as the 1960s, and it was precisely this quasi-spirituality which gave meaning to the cannibalism of the civil war period. In those territories where non-Poro militia forces, such as the Ulimo-K (who professed to be descendants of medieval Muslim immigrants), tried to drive the Poro society from the region, those forces were fiercely repelled by the villagers and farmers, for whom Poro was their only semblance of religious institution.

Several of the most graphic eyewitness accounts of cannibalism emerged from the bloodiest episode of the war – the 1996 battle for Monrovia, the capital of Liberia, in which the spectre of the Poro loomed large. In April 1996, during a particularly intense battle, a Liberian newspaper reported that 'our reporters on both sides saw fighters engaged in cannibalism and sorcery. In some instances, fighters would kill and butcher the chest and extract the heart and later eat it.' Quoting from a 1997 document, *Liberia Country Report on Human Rights Practices for 1996*, Ellis noted: 'Even the usually cautious US State Department was moved to observe that "Fighters [of all factions] targeted their enemies, fighters and civilians alike, removed their victims' body parts and ate them in front of civilians"'.

One refugee, Sensi Momoh, relived the horror when his village in north-west Monrovia was overrun by soldiers:

> They were young, some no more than teenagers, and heavily armed. They fired at random and ransacked the huts. They killed my brother. They opened up his heart and cooked it in palm butter. Then they ate it. I've never seen such a thing. It was unbelievable.

Nor was it only teenage fighters who engaged in such practices. Tom Wocwiyi, who had been NPFL defence minister and who described himself as Charles Taylor's right-hand man, alleged that Taylor himself was the founder member of 'a group of canni-bals called Top 20'. The group, claimed Wocwiyi, met in Taylor's house and carried out human sacrifices under the direction of Taylor's uncle, Jensen Taylor. A group of sixteen NPFL generals and fourteen Special Forces commandos made allegations so similar that it could not have been mere coincidence.

Dozens of Liberian refugees have described acts of canni-balism, believed to endow those who partook with supernatural powers. Such acts were by no means limited to Charles Taylor's NPFL troops but occurred with sickening frequency among all tribal factions. One woman said she saw young warriors of warlord Alhaji G.V. Kromah's United Liberation Movement (Ulimo-K) extract the heart and private parts of five boys and eat them.

While his youthful supporters – crazed by the combination of *dagga*, a narcotic form of hemp, and easy access to the spoils of war – terrorized the countryside, Kromah postured alongside his warlord rivals at the UN-inspired Council of State in Monrovia, paying lip-service to the international community's doomed efforts to bring peace to the anarchic state. As the talks proceeded throughout 1996, the battles and atrocities continued in the country unabated. Ruled by young soldiers of misfortune, with their red scarves, dark glasses and AK-47s, for the populace looting became the main source of survival. One of the UN observers estimated that with around 60,000 combatants, each with at least three dependants, about 200,000 people in Liberia subsisted on looted goods.

The best analysis of the mentality of these young volunteer fighters is provided by Dr Edward Snoh Grant, Liberia's only prac-tising psychiatrist. Of the adult fighter, he wrote:

He is someone between sixteen and thirty-six years of age who may have decided to become a combatant for several reasons: to get food for survival, to stop other fighters killing his family and friends, press-ganged into it on pain of death, sheer adventurism etc. He initially has little admiration for the leader of the faction enlisting him in a fighting force. He is rag-tagged, semi-literate or illiterate. Comes from the lowest socio-economic class of society, impoverished or disadvantaged. He is dehumanized. Exhibits no remorse or conscience. Has sunk so low as to be a human heart (he calls it 'the engine') eater. Rapist, plunderer and ill-tempered. Irrational, impervious to reason and has been programmed to obey and carry out orders from 'paper' generals and COs. He is now deeply hurt because he has been told he fought for freedom and not money and has been left with nothing to take home from the bush to his family.

In the same article, published in the Liberian journal *New Democrat* in October 1995, Dr Grant gave an equally disturbing picture of a typical child soldier:

He is fifteen years old and maybe as young as nine. He carries a gun that is sometimes greater than his body weight... He is very deadly. He is too immature to differentiate what is good from evil. He has been catapulted from childhood to adulthood. He has been taught to get anything he desires by force. Patience, perseverance, respect for elders are not part of his thinking faculty. He is the one that will address you as 'papa' and at the same time order you 'to bring your ass here'. He enjoys the cracking of a gun and the sound of a gun going off, the menacing noise of a rocket-propelled grenade, while oblivious to the destruction and the taking away of life this may cause. He is loved for his savagery and maybe made a general as young as twelve years old.

The civil war petered out in 1997 when all factions finally agreed to turn themselves into political parties and elections were held. Charles Taylor won a massive 75 per cent of the vote and was inaugurated as 'President of Liberia'. Like his unfortunate predecessor, Samuel Doe (murdered in 1990), Taylor claimed he had been anointed by God. Armed with a popular mandate, he has consolidated power in a familiar manner, ostracizing opponents and favouring cronies. The spiritual and moral anarchy of the country, however, remains, as Ellis points out, 'so deep as hardly to be touched by even the most dedicated work of peace'.

The sustained outbreaks of cannibalism in Liberia and China confound the notion advanced by cannibal deniers such as William Arens and others that 'the eating of human flesh as a pattern of cultural behaviour has never existed in human society'. Cannibalism of this nature has a dynamic force that can be sustained only through a basis in cultural tradition or firmly established quasi-spiritual conviction.

Respect for human life and dignity may have suffered in China and Liberia over the centuries, but even in societies based on a strong, unshakable faith, with all the comforts and privilege that wealth and Western civilization can provide, cannibalism can still emerge in dramatic fashion.

SEVEN

Surviving
In the Andes

On 12 October 1972, an amateur rugby team made up of old boys from an affluent Uruguayan Catholic school departed from Montevideo in a chartered plane bound for Santiago, Chile. Reports of bad weather in the Andes brought the plane down briefly in Mendoza, Argentina, before the journey was resumed the following day. Spirits were high on the flight, as the team members – ranging in age from nineteen to twenty-five – had brought along family and friends, bringing the total number of those on board (including crew) to forty-five.

Between 3.15pm and 3.30pm on 13 October, the pilot reported in to air-traffic control in Santiago three times, to record his progress over the Andes. On the last occasion, at 3.30pm, he reported his height as 15,000 feet. But when the Santiago control tower tried to check in with the aircraft a minute later, there was no response. The plane was never heard from again.

For eight days, separate groups of Chileans, Argentinians and Uruguayans trawled the mountain range in perilous conditions in a desperate effort to find the plane. Despite the commitment and courage of the would-be rescuers, the search proved fruitless. The pilot had evidently become disorientated by the heavy cloud cover and snowy landscape and had plummeted into the mountains.

The combination of high winds and heavy snowfall meant that there was little chance of finding the wreck. In any case, the freezing and treacherous conditions gave little chance of survival to the crew and passengers, even if they had managed to survive the initial impact. The forty-five men and women were missing, presumed dead...

The most extraordinary and compelling story of human endurance of recent times was how sixteen young Uruguayan rugby players managed to survive in the Andes for almost three months in 1972. On their return to Montevideo, these men claimed that they had been able to survive for so long by keeping themselves regularly hydrated and by stretching out their meagre rations for as long as possible. After a few days, however – and under pressure from mounting media speculation – they admitted that the only way in which they had survived was by conquering one of man's oldest taboos and forced themselves to eat the flesh of their dead colleagues.

At a press conference, one of the group, a trainee lawyer named Pancho Delgado, explained that they had drawn on religious inspiration to break the taboo. The image of the bread and wine of the Last Supper turning into Christ's flesh and blood had been at the forefront of their minds. They were absolved by the Archbishop of Montevideo and became national celebrities. Ever since, they have been feted for their extraordinary courage, and one of them, Roberto Canessa, has even run for president of Uruguay.

What is particularly fascinating about this group is that they came from one of the most privileged and affluent backgrounds imaginable. They were all pupils at the exclusive Christian

Brothers (Los Christianos) public school and all lived within a few minutes of one another in one of the most prosperous suburbs in Montevideo. And yet – when it came to a choice between death from starvation or life by doing the unimaginable – they were able to cast aside their cosseted upbringing and life of privilege to break a taboo that had lasted for several centuries.

It is evident that some – like medical student Roberto Canessa and would-be playboy Fernando Parrado – were better equipped to deal with the realities of cannibalism than those, like Roy Harley, who were unable to dissociate the flesh that sustained them from the memory of their dead comrades from whose bodies the flesh was cut. Canessa and Parrado were the ones who ultimately made the death-defying journey across the Andes to get help, whereas Harley had shrunk to a mere five and a half stone by the time he was rescued.

Though the story of the Andes survivors has been told in the film *Alive!* and in the book of the same name by Piers Paul Read, we believed we needed, for the purposes of this documentary series, to find out at first-hand how this group had been able to break the taboo of cannibalism. The Andes survivors are among the very few known groups of cannibals on the planet. Hearing about their experience was highly significant to our thesis that man is and always has been a cannibal but has merely suppressed this urge under the artificial construct of 'civilization'.

Finding the survivors was not a difficult task, as they still live in the same Montevideo suburb where they grew up. Getting them to speak about their experiences, however, was another matter. Pancho Delgado was understandably wary of discussing openly the religious justification for cannibalism – which many of the group have since admitted was something they came up with to help the relatives of the dead deal with their grief – and

Roberto Canessa, now a respected surgeon, was unwilling to meet unless he was sure that he would have some degree of control over the content of the film.

Only when we spoke to Fernando Parrado, a successful television producer, did we finally make some progress. Parrado was not only willing to contribute to what he recognized could be 'an important anthropological exercise', but he was also willing to help persuade another of the party, Carlos Paez – one of the first to eat human flesh, who has since conquered alcoholism and drug addiction – to talk to us.

Through these two men, and with the accompanying insight of experts such as Mike Stroud, who accompanied Sir Ranulph Fiennes in the first successful crossing of Antarctica on foot, and psychologist James Thompson, who was brought up in Uruguay, we discovered at first hand the desperate descent into cannibalism. This is the incredible story that Parrado and Paez revealed to us.

The journey to Chile on Friday 13 October 1972 should have taken an hour at the most. As it was, at the time the party of forty-five was meant to be starting its descent into Santiago – a little after 3.30pm – they were careering down an 11,500-foot valley, deep in the Andes mountain range.

Disorientated by the poor visibility and snow-covered landscape, the co-pilot had begun his descent too soon. As the cloud cover began to break up, he realized that he was flying directly into the heart of the most treacherous mountains. Despite his desperate efforts, there was no chance of avoiding them.

A wing and tail of the aircraft were sheared off on impact, but part of the fuselage remained intact and skidded to a halt on a snow-covered glacier. There were thirty-two survivors, stranded at 11,500 feet, where the temperature at night drops below

−30°C. Without shelter, they would have been dead within hours. The action taken by the few conscious and calm survivors in the party in the hours immediately following the crash saved the lives of the rest of the group.

The horrors inside the dimly lit fuselage after the plane had slewed to a halt on the mountainside are difficult to imagine. The handful of boys who had suffered only superficial injuries were scrabbling to remove the seats under which many of the wounded were trapped. The two medical students, Roberto Canessa and Gustavo Zerbino, were doing what they could to tend to the wounded.

One boy, Rafael Echvarren, had had the calf of his leg torn off, leaving the bone totally exposed. Another, Enrique Platero, was staring in bemusement at a steel tube protruding from his stomach. Zerbino bound Echvarren's leg in a white shirt before pulling the tube from Platero's stomach and finding that six inches of his intestine came out with it. The pilots, Ferradas and Lagurara, were pinioned to their seats by aeroplane instruments embedded in their chests. Ferradas was dead, but Lagurara was alive and begged to be given a revolver to put himself out of his misery. Amid this chaos and with the temperature dropping rapidly, the survivors built a barricade at the open end of the fuselage from seats and suitcases and bedded down for the night. But the wind was such that the makeshift barrier kept coming down, and each collapse brought yet more panic among the injured and dying.

The next day, the survivors surveyed the scene. At such a high altitude, and given the depth of snow, there were no trees, plants or animals. There was plenty of drinkable water and a crude filtration system was quickly devised, but provisions were in fairly short supply. They had wine, some liquor, odds and ends of food, such as chocolate and caramel bars, several pounds of cheese and some salted crackers. In addition, they had about 130 cartons of cigarettes (which had been put on board for sale on the black market and over which there would be continual controversy among the thirteen smokers) and a great deal of toothpaste.

The first two days were spent burying the dead, treating the injured and endlessly scouring the skies for rescuers. After two days in a coma, Fernando Parrado awoke to discover his mother dead and his sister dying. The few scraps of food salvaged from the cabin were about to run out, and the survivors were already in a state of panic and desperation. Looking back nearly thirty years later in the comfort of his beautiful Montevideo home, Parrado recalls their plight:

> I was knocked out on impact so I went into a complete and utter blackness immediately. When I began to come round, I thought for a moment that I was in my bed in my house... but I eventually woke up to the freezing cold of the high Andes. By the time I was fully conscious, there was barely any food left. The last thing I ate was a chocolate-covered peanut, and that chocolate-covered peanut lasted for three days. The first day I ate the cover of the chocolate-covered peanut. Then if you press with your teeth the peanut breaks in half... so I had the half for ten or twelve hours taking little slices of that peanut with my teeth, and the next day I ate the second half of the peanut.

To get some idea of the life expectancy of these stranded, desperate people, we spoke to Dr Mike Stroud, veteran of pioneering Arctic and Antarctic expeditions and author of *Survival of the Fittest*:

People, if they eat nothing, will survive for around fifty, sixty days, that sort of time in reasonably good conditions and deteriorating as they go. If you're talking about people who are stranded and they are in the cold, then the cold itself will demand extra energy, which will burn down your stores faster, and as you get thinner you become ever more vulnerable to it because you'll lose the fat that gives you insulation and that sort of defence. So I would imagine that survival times would come down really very markedly and, given shelter, you might survive – I don't know – twenty, perhaps thirty days at most.

But in addition to their own reserves of strength, the Uruguayans had one important advantage, as Parrado remembers:

It was very important that we were a team, a very united team. We had known each other for many years before the crash. Most of us had played rugby on the same team for ten years at least... In the first five minutes after the crash, the captain of the team, Marcello, realized that if we didn't keep the wind-chill factor from entering the fuselage we would be dead. So he made sure the barricades of luggage and seats around us were as secure as possible. At the same time, Canessa realized that the fabric covers of the seats could be used to bind injuries and provide extra clothing, so he stripped them off and distributed them among us. We would have died on the first night had we not begun to work as a team.

Carlos Paez was another of those who would eventually make it back to Montevideo. Like the others, he remains something of a

An early European representation of the cannibal tribes of the New World (1530).

Maori exo-cannibalism as imagined in nineteenth century Europe (c1840).

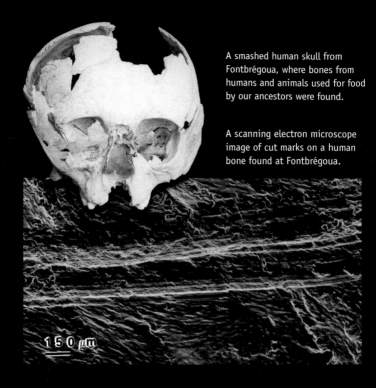

A smashed human skull from Fontbrégoua, where bones from humans and animals used for food by our ancestors were found.

A scanning electron microscope image of cut marks on a human bone found at Fontbrégoua.

150 μm

Below: The Last Supper (c1560), by Vicente Juan Macip.

Alexander Zapiantsev, who killed and butchered Valdemar Suzik, and served up the meat at a New Year's feast in Chelyabinsk, Russia.

Below: The kitchen where Zapiantsev murdered his friend Suzik.

Cannibals photographed with human remains during the 1921 famine in the Volga region of Russia.

A woman drags her dead child to the Piskarovskaya cemetery during the Siege of Leningrad.

A crowd gathers around a frozen corpse in Leningrad. Recently unearthed documents confirm cannibalism took place throughout the siege.

The hands of Princess Miao Chuang being offered to her sick father – an act of sacrifice which, according to Chinese legend, led to her deification.

The Raft of the Medusa (1819), by Théodore Géricault, inspired by one of the most famous cases of nineteenth century survival cannibalism.

Members of the 'Old Christians' rugby team minutes before their aeroplane crashed in the mountains in a remote part of the Andes in October 1972.

Survivors of the Andes crash shortly after rescuers reached them. They lived for twenty-two days by eating the flesh of their dead friends.

Andrei Chikatilo

Arthur Shawcross

Jeffrey Dahmer

Issei Sagawa

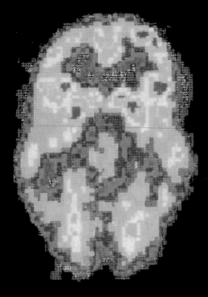

A Positron Emission Tomography (PET) brain scan of a normal individual. Warm colours (eg red and yellow) indicate areas of high brain activation; cold colours (eg blue and green) indicate low activation

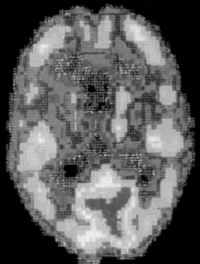

A PET brain scan of a murderer, illustrating the lack of activation in the prefrontal cortex (at the top of the image). Could modern brain scanning techniques explain why cannibal killers cannot control their violent impulses?

celebrity in Uruguay and currently hosts a popular radio show. After ten days on the mountain, five of those who survived the crash had died from their injuries. The twenty-seven who remained were losing weight rapidly: 'Even in the first ten days we lost a lot of weight. That was a real thing. I lost about seventeen kilos. It's a lot... You know, the cold was incredible, and I didn't think we would survive twenty days.'

Attempts to escape on foot through the deep snow proved hopeless. Air-force planes had been searching in the right area but had failed to spot the wreckage. The survivors were able to pick up radio broadcasts on a transistor radio, which had emerged intact from the plane. Ten days after the crash, they learned that the Chilean authorities had given up their rescue operations. They knew they were facing death by starvation, as Parrado recalls:

I knew after I regained consciousness, after I had seen my mother, my sister dead, what was going on. When we learned that they were not looking for us, I knew that the only way out was if we got out of there. In order to get out of there we had to get all the strength that we could, and I decided to transform myself into a survival machine, no thoughts, no feelings, nothing whatsoever. Not even to cry, not to waste energy or calories on tears or salt on tears. So I said, I am going to save all my energy, everything, in order that I can have calories and fatness in my body to attempt a final escape whenever it's needed. I knew then that I was turning into a survival machine and not a thinking human being.

It is this transformation into 'a survival machine' which is essential in such a crisis situation. The human brain – disorientated by cold and hunger – is capable of moving in one of two ways. It either descends into panic and anarchy, where the fear of impending death is so great that the capability for rational thought and decision-making simply shuts down, or – as in the case of Parrado and his colleagues – it kicks into survival mode. Collectively in this case, the group took definite steps and decisions in order to sustain life. Mike Stroud is an expert in the reactions of different people to adverse circumstances:

> Discovering that the search efforts had been called off must have been a decimating blow psychologically, and they must have realized immediately that they were going to die unless they did something about it. By ten days of not eating anything, they would have already been suffering; they would have been getting weaker. They'd have been feeling either apathetic or perhaps irritable or perhaps both, but certainly deteriorating rapidly physically and psychologically, and I think it's quite understandable in those circumstances that they now turn to thinking about quite desperate measures in order to survive. They don't want to die, and the survival instinct's incredibly strong. They've got to do something, and it's quite natural that they would turn to thinking about cannibalism. I think that most people in such a desperate situation would actively consider it and probably would succumb after a time.

If the survivors were going to stay alive, it would have to be through their own efforts. Gradually, it became clear that everyone was thinking the same thing, as Carlos Paez remembers: 'Everybody started with the same idea. The first one I hear it was from Nando. Nando told me, "Carlitos, there's nothing else in the supermarket." The supermarket was a little tiny chocolate. "... I will eat the pilot." That's what he told me.'

Again, it's significant with hindsight that Parrado suggested eating the pilot and not one of his dead friends. It was a classic response not only to shy away from consuming a loved one but to begin by eating someone who could be considered responsible for his plight. Half an hour later, all the survivors were discussing the same subject. They had to feed themselves and, as medical student Roberto Canessa pointed out, human flesh is rich in proteins and would be by far the most efficient way of sustaining themselves. But it was a ghastly prospect. It was not just eating human flesh; it was eating the flesh of dead friends and relatives.

Each member of the group was experiencing an agonizing roller coaster of emotions. Some were concerned for the feelings of their devoutly Catholic families back in Uruguay who were still praying for the safe return of their loved ones. Others were torn between the apparent sacrilege of eating human flesh, and the mortal sin of committing suicide by *not* eating, as defined by the Catholic Church. But the team had a starker choice – between life and death. And as, with each passing night, the realities of that choice became ever more apparent, so the other considerations and misgivings began to fall away. Parrado remembers the feeling of relief once they had finally made their decision:

> On the first night, when we decided what we had to do, we made like a pact between all the survivors, and we put our hands like you make when you're... very good friends, and we said OK, if I die please use me. Eat me because it might give you life, and there is nothing more beautiful than to give your life for the life of a friend.

It's very romantic, but it really happened, so I give it a
lot of credit, and it speaks a lot for the memories of our
friends who died. I can tell you that at the moment
nobody knew who would live and who would die, which
is a very important fact.

As their devoutly Catholic families prayed for them in Montevideo,
the survivors prepared to eat the flesh of their dead comrades.
The task of actually cutting meat from the bodies fell at first to
the medical students among the team, who had some
experience – however slight – of dissecting cadavers. Most of the
bodies were covered with snow, but the buttocks of one protruded
a few yards from the plane. Without a word, Roberto Canessa knelt
and, with a shard of broken glass, scraped twenty slivers from the
icy flesh. He brought them back to the others in the plane and
they waited until the flesh had thawed enough to eat.

Then came the critical moment of actually taking the fist
bite. Carlos Paez described to us what that extraordinary moment
was like:

> You need somebody to say, 'I'm the first', because you're
> going against all the general marketing of saying 'canni-
> bals are like this' or 'cannibals are...' you know, Indians
> or whatever. But if somebody breaks the taboo, then
> these things disappear... They went and cut some little
> pieces and I remember that they brought them to the
> plane. I was one of the first to eat because... I have no
> problem with raw meat, and so for me it was easy, and
> then I made a joke immediately... I said 'It's like ham
> from the market in Carrasco.' That's the place where we
> eat, and for me it was easy.

For many of the survivors, however, it was not so easy, and only through much prayer and soul-searching were they able to conquer the primitive and irrational taboo impressed on society by several centuries of civilization. The survivors couldn't make fires to cook the meat, so it was dried on the roof of the fuselage. One factor that may have made it slightly easier for the Uruguayans to suppress their revulsion was the fact that that they'd grown up in a carnivore culture, where eating meat was an assertion of masculinity as much as it was a gustatory experience. Psychologist at University College, London, James Thompson, has particular reason to believe that this would have made a difference to the survivors:

> I grew up in Uruguay, and it was a culture that assumed that one would have beef every day. People were used to going to butchers' shops where cows were cut up in front of you. We ate large quantities, and it was simply seen as your birthright. You had good-quality meat virtually every day and didn't bother with vegetables and salads unless you really had to.

One of the five women on the plane, Liliana Methol, resisted longest, but she, too, succumbed a few days later. She wanted to live to see her children again. For Methol and others, like Roy Harley, it was a constant struggle to eat the flesh of their friends. But for those who, like Fernando Parrado, had switched totally into 'survival mode', the act of cannibalism was relatively straightforward:

> It's absolutely incredible how you can adapt yourself to a situation, and I think that you can see it through the

lives of people who lived in concentration camps, how
they adapted themselves to very unreal and stressful and
very hard situations. And after the first and second day,
we got used to it... and every day it was easier and
easier. It was far more difficult for us to fight against
thirst and the cold than to eat human flesh because that
was our only chance to survive, the only one.

A week later an avalanche killed eight more of the survivors,
including Liliana Methol, and buried the original crash victims
deep in snow. Those who had just been killed were now the only
food available, and Carlos Paez recalls how he and his colleagues
made the most of their new supply of human flesh:

At the very beginning we started with the muscles and
those normal things and after that you say, Why not the
other things? We had to consume almost everything –
everything – because we were dying. We didn't have a
choice. So it's like... you eat different kinds of meat.
We're used in this country to eat different kinds of meat,
and it's just a different taste... It's like you justify it to
yourself: if God put this thing here, we must take all.

What was interesting, observed both Parrado and Paez, was the
craving for meat which beset even those who had had the gravest
reservations about eating their dead friends. So strong was this
craving that a system was devised for the disarticulation and de-
fleshing of the corpses. The Strauch brothers – Fito and
Eduardo – performed the grisly task of cutting large chunks of
flesh from the bodies. These would then be passed to another
team, which divided the bodies into smaller pieces for 'cooking'

(drying out on the roof). The 'cooking' was Paez's department, and he assiduously ensured that the meat was dried and made as appetizing as possible. Initially, he even wrapped it round chocolate to make it more palatable. The rations were then distributed at midday, under the watchful supervision of the Strauch brothers and their cousin Daniel Fernandez.

Paez began to realize that through their desperate circumstances he and his colleagues were beginning to view the dead bodies of their friends in a very different light from the corporeal reverence with which the dead are treated in the confines and comfort of 'civilization':

> You are looking at people, dead people, all around you, so you know what that's like – but you also get accustomed to being with dead people. If you say now, 'I will put dead people in your house', I will say no. But at that time we were sleeping with dead people... The reality was that after a while you knew where it was coming from, who was the meat, and it was much easier, the whole thing. It was like, 'Thank you, because of you we can live for three or four days.'

Though not a balanced diet, the fresh human meat gave the survivors new reserves of energy. The human body is quite a reasonable source of nutrition for a period. It's not ideal in terms of healthy living, because it doesn't have any carbohydrate or the benefits gained from eating fresh fruit and vegetables. Eating nothing but human flesh might – over a significant period – lead to vitamin deficiencies. But in terms of survival over a number of weeks in the freezing cold, human flesh has all the energy and protein necessary, and vital supplies of minerals and vitamins.

The liver, in particular, is rich in vitamins, and those with medical expertise encouraged their comrades to eat it. Having overcome their revulsion against eating that, it was easier for some members of the party to move on to the heart, kidneys and intestines. Like prehistoric antecedents, they all savoured the bone marrow and even managed to eat parts of the brains. Those who were more squeamish, however, confined themselves to the sheets of fat that had been cut from the bodies and quickly dried in the sun. Only the lungs, the skin, the head and the genitals of the corpses were discarded.

The survivors have never revealed details of which bodies were eaten when. But the food the bodies provided gave Fernando Parrado and Roberto Canessa the strength they needed for a death-defying ten-day trek over the Andes to get help. Before he left, Parrado told Paez that, should he fail to return and no help come, he – Paez – should eat his dead mother and sister. It showed just how far Parrado was committed to the survival of himself and his friends. All his emotions and efforts were focused not on the tragedy of the dead but on the survival of the living. Wearing seat cushions for snowshoes, scaling peaks of many thousands of feet with no equipment, carrying meat supplies with them in rugby socks, Parrado and Canessa were determined to prevail. After a perilous ten-day journey, the two bedraggled young men came across a farmer in a remote pasture who went off to fetch help. In their relief that they had finally made contact with the outside world, Parrado and Canessa fell into an exhausted sleep. When they awoke, they heard a noisy gaggle of people approaching. They imagined that it was inquisitive villagers. It was, in fact, the advance guard of the world's press – their first taste of media attention, which would last another three decades.

But this initial press interest was as nothing compared with the onslaught that followed when rumours of cannibalism began to surface. One of the members of the Andean Rescue Corps who went to pick up the other survivors divulged to the press that he suspected cannibalism. The sixteen young men who'd managed against all the odds to survive for seventy-two days in one of the world's most unforgiving mountain ranges were subjected to a worldwide media frenzy. Rather than being feted as heroes on their return, they were greeted by shock and revulsion from some quarters and – most hurtful of all – suspicion from some of the families of the dead.

Eventually, a press conference was held at which Pancho Delgado – a trainee lawyer who was also one of the more devout members of the group – was chosen to speak on behalf of the survivors. He read out the following statement to the hushed congregation at the assembly hall of the Christian Brothers school:

When one awakes in the morning amid the silence of the mountains and sees the snow-capped peaks all around, it is majestic, sensational, something frightening. One feels alone – alone in the world but for the presence of God... I can assure you that God is there. We all felt it inside ourselves, and not because we were the kind of pious youths who are always praying, even though we had a religious education. Not at all. But up there one feels the presence of God. One feels, above all, what is called the hand of God, and one allows oneself to be guided by it... And when the moment came when we did not have any more food, or anything of that kind, we thought to ourselves that if Jesus at His last supper had shared His flesh and blood with His apostles, then it was a sign to us that we should do the same – take the flesh and blood as an intimate communion between us all. It was this that helped us to survive, and now we do not want this [experience], which for us was something intimate, to be hackneyed, or touched, or anything like that. In a foreign country we tried to approach the subject in as elevated a spirit as possible, and now we tell it to you, our fellow countrymen, exactly as it was...

When Delgado finished, it was evident that the entire gathering was deeply moved by what they had heard, and when asked if they had any questions the journalists declined to probe the survivors – that could come later. Delgado's statement washed away any residual rancour provoked by the rumours; anger turned to sorrow as the community closed ranks to mourn its dead.

Thirty years on, however, Carlos Paez can reveal that the association of their cannibalism with the sacrament was more of a public relations exercise than a genuine deep-seated collective rationale:

I remember Pancho Delgado – when he came here, [he held] a big press conference and he [used the term] communion, giving his body to everybody, and he told us that we must do the same thing. For me, it wasn't like this. We were hungry, we were cold and we needed to live – these were the most important factors in our decision... I don't even think that Delgado himself believed [what he said] – it was just a very gentle way of saying things, and it was very diplomatic. All the families were waiting for answers, and it was a good thing to say, but it wasn't true. Really, it wasn't.

When the dust settled, the truth was apparent to both media and the families of the victims of the tragedy alike – had the survivors not cannibalized the dead, the crash would have claimed forty-five lives, not twenty-nine. As it was, although each survivor had lost thirty to eighty pounds apiece, the sixteen who made it home were found to be in reasonable health. When asked what they had last eaten, each described to the doctor in some detail the different parts of the human body they had consumed. The doctor later commented: 'Once they had decided to break that ancient taboo, they did it with great maturity and wisdom.' A young priest was then summoned to hear the confessions of those who felt the need to unburden themselves. Those who did not were assured that 'When it came to a question of survival, it is always necessary to eat whatever is at hand, in spite of the repugnance it may evoke'. This decision was later endorsed by the Archbishop of Montevideo.

Fernando Parrado certainly has no regrets about taking the steps he took in order to survive:

> I can say that we broke a taboo, and I can obviously put myself into the position of people who are reading or watching this interview or who have not done it. But if they put themselves in my position, they would have done it very, very easily. And this is hard to understand, but I'm sure they would have done it... I have a family now who would not exist if I hadn't done what I did.

Though he has battled against drugs and drink, Carlos Paez is now similarly untroubled by the memory of what they had to do:

This is a very important story, not only because of cannibalism but also because, for a while, I believe that we were very close to God. I felt the presence of God and believe He helped us to do what was necessary to survive... We must do what we must do. I think you would do the same thing. You would try to live. It's an obligation to live.

EIGHT

Cannibalism
In Extremis

What is extraordinary about the arguments of cannibal 'deniers' is that they ignore whole swathes of documented eyewitness accounts of cannibalism in the last three centuries. Though it might be reasonable to dismiss Herodotus's fifth-century BC encounter with the Androphagi – literally 'the eaters of men' – other graphic accounts, from Columbus and Captain Cook to the pre-eminent maritime explorers and Arctic adventurers of recent times, are simply too plentiful and detailed to ignore. Eating human flesh *in extremis* is the most easily understandable and straightforward of man's survival mechanisms.

Indeed, so prolific was this activity at one time that the accepted legal defence of cannibalism was one of necessity based on an appeal to the 'instinct for survival' – the principle of self-preservation that prompts people to save their own lives. The common defence is that it is better for some to have survived by sacrificing one or more lives than for all to die – although that defence has to be reconciled with a respect for the sanctity of human life.

An important qualification of the 'necessity' argument for cannibalism is the acknowledgement of the levels of stress that drive survivors to the brink of insanity, making them not responsible for their actions. Again, though this can happen in exceptional cases, it belies the fact that cannibalism *in extremis* is an entirely rational and clear-thinking reflex. It is only the taboo of cannibalism that means we try to invent myths of madness to justify it. As London University psychologist James Thompson observed:

> From a psychological point of view, instinct isn't much of an explanation, but if a loud bang goes off, we show a startled response and we quickly say we ought to concentrate on whatever that bang is. If we're in a situation of disaster where we're really up against survival issues, we do seem to go into a different state, but it could still be a rational state. We're doing things relatively sensibly in that particular context, and that, I suppose, is how in our ancient hominid past we survived so many different things and have prospered. So it's not primitive necessarily. It's functional, and it's different from the sorts of thoughts we can have in a well-fed, well provided for, civilized society.

In this chapter, we return to the eighteenth century, a time when maritime survival cannibalism was such a common and accepted practice that it was known as 'the custom of the sea' and was looked on with sympathy by the public and legal authorities alike. By gathering together historical episodes, it will show not only how prolific instances of cannibalism were even in the most 'civilized' of societies in the last three hundred years but also how attitudes have altered and the taboo has evolved.

Some of the best-documented examples of eighteenth-century maritime cannibalism come from America and the United

Kingdom. Late in the year 1710, the clipper *Nottingham Galley* left Boston for London with a cargo of butter and cheese and a crew of fourteen. On 11 December, the ship was sucked into a heavy swell and struck a rock. To save themselves, the crew went over the side and, amid heavy seas, headed for the rock. Remarkably, they all managed to reach it and hung on for dear life as the seas raged around them. By morning, all that was left of the ship was some planks, timbers, sails and canvas, as well as a few morsels of cheese washed up among the seaweed. Tantalizingly, the mainland was only twelve miles away, but conditions being what they were an ocean might as well have surrounded the rock.

In this instance, the crew were on the rock for just two days before the men began to entertain thoughts of cannibalism. The weather was extremely cold, the men suffered terribly from hunger and frostbite and they had been unable to start a fire. They survived on seaweed, two or three mussels a day per man, and water obtained from rain or snow or melted in cavities in the rock.

Having traversed Antarctica on foot with Sir Ranulph Fiennes, Mike Stroud knows only too well the hardships of trying to survive in freezing conditions:

> If the temperatures were so low that they could threaten their survival in one night without shelter and they were contending with the damp as well as the cold, as well as their relentless hunger, certainly their vulnerability would increase extremely rapidly. It would obviously also depend on exactly what clothing they had on, but I would reckon it would be a matter of days, rather than weeks, before they reached the limits of their capacity for survival.

At the end of December, a fourth member of the ship's company – a corpulent carpenter – died, and the thoughts of the stranded sailors began to turn to cannibalism. As in many of these cases, there is some discrepancy over who first suggested eating the carpenter's body, but once the subject was out in the open it took very little time for the group to decide to become cannibals.

Without further ado, the captain ordered that the carpenter's body be dismembered and the head, hands and feet thrown in the sea. He then instructed the men to skin, dress and quarter the corpse. The crew justified their actions thus: 'It was no Sin, since God was pleased to take him out of the World and that we had not laid violent hands upon him.'

This type of post hoc justification is common in cases when a particularly extreme course of action is taken, as James Thompson noted:

> Whenever we're faced with a clash of ideas, we have to find arguments and excuses in order to cope with that tension. In a situation of overcoming a taboo about eating human flesh, we have to say we had absolutely pressing need. They, the people, wouldn't have minded. They would have wanted us to survive.

Even in their starving state, three of the crew blanched at eating raw flesh, but after a day of soul-searching everyone began to eat strips of the meat, mixing it with seaweed to make it more palatable.

The captain rationed the meat until the ten survivors were rescued on 4 January 1711. Interestingly, when they finally reached London the sailors made no attempt to hide what they had done. None of the sailors was arrested for their cannibalism and, to this day, no law against cannibalism exists in the UK (this was confirmed as recently as 1998, when questions were asked in the House of Commons following television presenter Hugh Fearnley-Whittingstall's programme about placenta-eating). Indeed, the reputation of the captain of the *Nottingham Galley* was so enhanced that he was later made British consul in Flanders.

Fifty-four years later, on 24 October 1765, an American ship, *The Peggy*, sailed from the Azores with a cargo of wine and brandy bound for New York. *The Peggy* was sailed by a captain and a crew of eight, one of whom was a Negro slave. The ship carried barely enough provisions to sustain her on a normal voyage to New York, and strict rationing of food and water was ordered from the start.

On 29 October the ship was caught in a storm which lasted for several weeks. Tossed around like a rag doll, the ship was left permanently disabled. Adrift on the ocean, with no control over their fate, the crew set about drinking the supplies of wine and brandy on board. Riotously drunk, they could at least ignore the hopelessness of their plight.

On Christmas Day a ship was sighted and drew alongside *The Peggy*, but after some discussion with the drunken sailors the ship left hurriedly. The crew killed and ate their two pet pigeons, the ship's cat, barnacles scraped from the ship's side, and they also ate tobacco, lamp oil, candles and all the leather they could find, including that in the ship's pumps.

Despite their eclectic diet, by 13 January 1766 the entire crew was still drunkenly alive and resolved to draw lots to decide who should die to keep the others alive. The captain acquiesced, and the men left the captain's cabin to play their deadly game of chance. In fact, the lottery was nothing but a sham. The crew had already decided who was to make up their meal and, predictably, they informed the captain that the Negro had lost and that they had shot him through the head. One of the crew ate the victim's raw liver; some of the rest of the body was cooked, and the remainder was pickled. Only the head and fingers were thrown overboard. It was later claimed that the captain alone refused to eat any of the meat.

According to one contemporaneous account, the crewman who ate the liver of the Negro died 'in a state of raving madness', and the superstitious sailors feared that they, too, would become mad if they ate him, so they threw the body overboard. One of the myths surrounding cannibalism is that people who descend to eating human flesh have in some way become insane. In fact, the effects of food deprivation are more complex, as James Thompson pointed out:

> I think generally when we're in a well-fed state and we look at a whole lot of taboo acts like cannibalism we assume it could only happen among the mad. In fact, it can happen among very rational people in an extraordinarily difficult and extreme situation. It's rather like saying suicide occurs only when the balance of your mind is disturbed – it's an oversimplification. Hunger is a very powerful motivator. One is used in ordinary society to having food regularly. Even after five hours, people will find hunger quite unpleasant. Three, four days and one's mind changes considerably. All the experiments that have been done on depriving people of food show they become obsessed with food, and even a picture of food is enough to get them fantasizing about what a meal would be like. It's a very powerful effect,

and so it should be. Without food, we die. If you're starving and there's food available, even though it's human flesh, the rational thing is to eat it, if you can overcome the taboo and the squeamishness.

In the case of *The Peggy*, it was clear that the crew members were disorientated not only through hunger but also through excess alcohol, which almost certainly would have led to dehydration and the consumption of seawater, which can cause madness.

In addition, these hardened sailors would not have been encumbered by the same sense of squeamishness and sensitivity possessed by people today, with our insulation from any sense of the visceral, purchasers of packaged meat and processed meat products that we are.

The body of the Negro was carefully rationed among the crew of *The Peggy* until 26 January, and on 29 January the captain was once again petitioned to conduct a lottery. He reluctantly obliged, fearing that if he refused he would be the automatic loser. The loser was in fact a very popular sailor, and the crew decided to delay his execution until the following morning in order to commiserate with him. But after only a few hours – so the reports tell us – the man 'went deaf' and became 'a raving madman'.

As the fateful hour of the execution approached and a fire was prepared on deck to roast the corpse, a ship was sighted and all the crew were taken aboard. By the time the rescue boat reached Dartmouth on 2 March, only the captain and three crew remained – one of whom was the condemned man who had become 'a raving lunatic' (but who was later, miraculously, restored to perfect health).

As with the *Nottingham Galley*, the survivors were greeted with neither criticism nor surprise for their cannibalistic exploits.

It was considered that a 'fair' lottery had taken place, and the fact that a Negro slave had been killed and eaten, though 'regrettable', was regarded as an expedient course of action under the circumstances.

The eighteenth-century 'fashion' for maritime cannibalism *in extremis* continued well into the next century, with an episode immortalized in Géricault's painting *Radeau de la 'Méduse'*. The interesting thing about the disaster that befell the French frigate *Medusa*, which sailed from France for Senegal in June 1816, was the number of people involved. Unlike the small crews of the *Nottingham Galley* and *The Peggy*, 150 people managed to scramble on to a makeshift raft when the ship struck reefs extending from the African coast. Of these 150, 67 managed to survive the rough seas through the night and consoled themselves with quantities of wine the following day.

It took only until the fourth day for the sailors to begin to cut strips from the dead bodies and dry them for consumption. Some flying fish became entangled in the raft and were eaten, mixed with human flesh. By the seventeenth day, only fifteen men were left on the raft, the rest having been swept away or thrown off to conserve rations (the 'fair' means of drawing lots was once again deployed to choose those to be jettisoned). By the time the rescue craft reached land, just six men remained.

A full investigation by the French government was launched and found that the means by which people were thrown off the raft was, under the circumstances, entirely justifiable, and the investigators didn't even question the necessity of cannibalizing the dead. It was fast becoming an accepted hazard of maritime travel.

This is cannibalism in its purest form – unencumbered by symbolism or ritual of any kind, a straightforward reaction to the stark choice of life or death. Archaeologist Dr Timothy Taylor of

Bradford University, who has performed extensive studies of cannibalism in pre-history – recognizes how, at such times, centuries of Christian civilization are stripped away to reveal a basic behavioural reflex:

> There is an instinct to survive *in extremis* at any cost, and very few people ultimately have the resolve to choose to die when they could live. It's not unprecedented, but it's rare, and as people become weakened by hunger their thought processes change. Their brains change their mechanism and workings, and I suspect that it becomes easier to cannibalize and less easy to make a moral argument stick in one's mind and resist.

Certainly, those presiding over cannibalistic episodes in the eighteenth and nineteenth centuries did not adopt a moralistic approach to the perpetrators. It is only relatively recently – with the intellectual and social refinements of the twentieth century – that some have attempted to question the rationale or even the very existence of cannibalism.

For these 'deniers', the accounts of human flesh-eating by survivors of shipwrecks are, for the most part, based on legend and hearsay and are to be viewed with extreme scepticism. It is in this spirit that most regard the tale of cannibalism by the survivors of the Nantucket whaler *Essex*, which was immortalized as a chapter of Herman Melville's *Moby Dick*. But recently, director of the Egan Institute of Maritime Studies on Nantucket Island, Nathaniel Philbrick, has discovered the accounts of the survivors of this horrific episode.

Philbrick's evocative account of the events of January to March 1821 (when the two boatloads of *Essex* survivors drifted aimlessly on the Pacific Ocean) brings vividly to life the dilemmas of committing cannibalism and, in particular, captures the suffering and sorrow of the relatives of the dead as well as the perpetrators.

On 20 November 1820 the *Essex* was scouring the whaling grounds of the Pacific, about halfway between the Hawaiian and Galapagos Islands. A shoal was spotted and the whaleboats moved in for the kill. Three whales were quickly slain before a fourth rammed the *Essex* at full tilt; it was quickly apparent that the ship would not stay afloat for long. Before the ship sank, the crews of the whaleboats brought out casks of bread, fresh water, boat nails, a musket, two pistols, a bit of powder, and light sails and spars to outfit the lifeboats in order to make them seaworthy enough to reach land. Unfortunately, they were unable to recover the charts or navigation instruments from the ship. So equipped, they set off in three whaleboats on 22 November.

For the first few weeks they ate the bread, rinsed their mouths with seawater and drank their own urine (a common practice for shipwrecked sailors). For food, they relied on their scant provisions and the occasional flying fish dropping into a boat and being devoured raw. On 20 December, exactly a month after the *Essex* sank, the three boats, containing twenty men, landed on uninhabited Henderson Island. They exhausted what few resources they found there before continuing their perilous voyage east. By 20 January 1821 only two of the boats remained – the third had gone missing, presumed lost, in fierce storms – containing ten starving crew members. It was two long months since the *Essex* had gone down, and all the men were suffering from acute malnutrition, dehydration and sunburn. The boats were under the command of Captain George Pollard, who controlled the rationing of their meagre supplies. There was barely a pound of hard tack (dry bread or biscuits) left to share between the seamen, who were becoming increasingly desperate.

With the death of crew member Lawson Thomas – a black man – on 20 January, the dreaded spectre of cannibalism was raised. It was patently the only resource of food left to the sailors, and they set about butchering Thomas's body with maniacal zeal. Used to butchering sperm whale carcasses, the sailors made short shrift of the corpse, removing the head, hands, feet and skin and throwing them into the sea. Thomas's heart, liver and kidneys were also taken out, before joints of meat were hacked from the backbone, ribs and pelvis. A fire was lit on the bottom of the boat, on which the organs and meat were roasted before the men began to eat. The more they ate, the hungrier they became. Anthropologists and archaeologists studying the phenomenon of cannibalism estimate that the human body would provide about sixty-six pounds of edible meat but – having subsisted on survival rations for many weeks – Thomas's body may have provided as little as thirty pounds of 'lean, fibrous flesh'.

On 22 January another man, Charles Shorter – also black – died and was eaten. The fact that the black members of the group began to die off first was probably not a coincidence, as Philbrick noted: 'A recent study claims that American blacks tend to have less body fat than Caucasians.' The importance of body fat in long-term survival under starvation conditions has been demonstrated. Isaiah Sheppard became the third member of the crew to die and was eaten in seven days. Then, on 28 January, Samuel Reed – another black man – died and was eaten. That left William Bond as the last surviving black. As captain's steward, he had enjoyed a better diet than his shipmates had. The following night, the boat containing Bond and two other men disappeared in the dark. They were never seen again.

One and a half thousand miles from the coast of South America, Pollard and three inexperienced young sailors drifted in the final boat. On 6 February, having consumed the last morsel of Samuel Reed, the four began to draw lots to decide who should be the next to be killed and cooked. The lot fell to eighteen-year-old Owen Coffin, Pollard's young cousin, who acquiesced gently, speaking a final message to his mother before his death. A distraught Pollard had offered to take Coffin's place, but Coffin resolutely refused to let anyone come between him and his destiny. He was duly killed and eaten.

The boat from which Pollard's boat had been separated back in January, manned by Owen Chase, suffered a similar fate. When seaman Isaac Cole, after a series of convulsions, died, his body was consumed by the starving sailors. Chase later told how 'no language can paint the anguish of our souls in this dreadful dilemma'. On 18 February, Chase's boat was rescued by a passing ship, *The Indian*, whose captain was moved to tears by the sight of these desperate men and who later recorded how 'Chase and his companions didn't even have the strength to climb on board... the whole surface of their bodies was one entire ulcer'. They were carried on to the ship and restored by tapioca pudding.

On 23 February, Pollard's boat was rescued by *The Dauphin* of Nantucket. He did not reach home until 5 August. Word of the cannibalism preceded his arrival, and Philbrick poignantly described the reaction of the Nantucket community on his return:

When Pollard stepped on the wharf, surrounded by more than a thousand familiar faces, there was absolute quiet. People moved aside to let him pass. None said a word. Soon he was at the doorstep of his aunt, Nancy, Owen Coffin's mother. He bore the awful message to the mother as her son desired. Nancy Coffin had entrusted Pollard with her eldest son. Yet he had not only presided over the boy's execution but had eaten him. The idea that he was living as a consequence of her boy's death was too much to bear. A little over three months later, Pollard again set sail for the Pacific, as captain of another whaling ship. It struck a reef north-west of the Hawaiian Islands. His career was over. He became Nantucket's night watchman, a position on the lowest rung of the social ladder, but one the former captain is said to have performed most conscientiously for many years.

What becomes clear through these maritime disasters is that cannibalism *in extremis* is tolerated so long as killing to eat is not involved. Where killing to eat is involved, it is permissible only as long as lots have been drawn. What is also interesting is that, even *in extremis*, and even when it comes to action as desperate as cannibalism, some sense of social order and authority still applies. Even among men who are out of their minds with hunger and, in some cases, alcohol, it is the captain who must supervise the drawing of lots, and the lottery must be rigged so that either the blacks or the younger members of the party must be eaten first.

But lest we should think that cannibalism of this period was confined to the high seas, there have also been land expeditions in which cannibalism has played an equally significant part. One of these is the infamous Donner Party expedition of 1846, in which almost half the group of eighty-seven people died and many of their bodies were defiled in an orgy of cannibalism. This episode has recently been the subject of some in-depth and revealing analysis by anthropologist Donald Grayson at the

University of Washington and Jared Diamond, Professor of Psychology at the University of California Medical School.

On 31 July 1846 a number of wagon parties left Fort Bridger, Wyoming, bound for California. In this particular party were eighty-seven people in twenty-three wagons, made up of ten unrelated families and sixteen lone individuals, most of them well-to-do Midwestern farmers and townspeople who had met by chance and joined forces for protection. None had any real experience of the western mountains or the Indian tribes who lived in them. They became known as the Donner Party because they elected an elderly Illinois farmer named George Donner as their captain. Their first mistake was to depart from the trail to try to take a short cut through the Wasatch mountain range (a short cut recommended by a popular guidebook author of the time, Lansford Hastings). When they reached the steep, brush-covered Wasatch mountains, however, the terrain was so wild that to get across the range the men would have to build a wagon road. It took sixteen backbreaking days to cover just thirty-six miles, exerting an enormous toll on both people and animals alike.

When they finally crossed the mountains, they discovered that they had walked into hell. They were confronted by an eighty-mile stretch of merciless desert, running along the western side of the Great Salt Lake. To save themselves from death by thirst, some of the pioneers were forced to unhitch their wagons, rush ahead with their precious animals to the next spring and return to retrieve the wagons. The rush became a disorganized panic, as many of the animals died, wandered off or were killed by Indians. Four wagons and large quantities of supplies had to be abandoned. Not until 30 September – two full months after leaving Fort Bridger – did the Donner Party emerge from their fatal short cut to rejoin the California Trail. By 1 November they made it up to Truckee Lake on the eastern flank of the Sierra Nevada. Having been scorched in the desert, the exhausted party now faced a fierce snowstorm as they attempted to cross a 7,200-foot pass just west of the lake. Ahead of them lay a long winter at the lake with very little food.

Of the original party of eighty-seven, which had set out with such high hopes from Fort Bridger, seventy-nine made it to the lake. One, Luke Halloran, had died from tuberculosis. The other seven had died during a number of unfortunate incidents ranging from a knife fight when two teams of oxen became entangled to an accidental shooting during the cleaning of a pistol. One elderly man named Hardkoop was simply abandoned. The trapped pioneers lay freezing inside crude tents and cabins. They quickly exhausted what remained of their supplies and then killed and ate their pack animals. Finally, they boiled hides and blankets to make a glue-like soup. As people began to starve and panic set in, the group began to deeply resent each other and fight over the remaining scraps of food. On 16 December twenty-four-year-old Baylis Williams succumbed to starvation, and on that same day fifteen of the strongest people in the party (five women and ten men, including two Indians who had been sent from Sutter's Fort to assist the group) set out across the pass on home-made snowshoes and virtually without food to try to reach outside help.

In the appallingly cold and stormy conditions, it wasn't long before this group began to contemplate cannibalism. On the ninth day, with one of their number already dead from exhaustion, the remaining fourteen began to discuss how they could most fairly select who should be eaten. They debated drawing lots or letting two people shoot it out until one of them was dead. Both methods were rejected in favour of waiting for someone to die naturally. On Christmas Eve, as one of the group – a twenty-three-year-old named Antoine – slept in a heavy stupor, his arm accidentally fell into the fire. Another member of the group quickly lifted it out. When the arm fell in a second time, however, the rest of the group simply watched it burn. Antoine died, followed by Franklin Graves, Patrick Dolan and Lemuel Murphy. Their flesh was cut off and roasted by the others, whose only rule was that they should not eat the flesh of a relative. When the flesh of the corpses was finished, the group began to eat old shoes.

Once cannibalism had taken hold, the craving for human flesh could not be satiated. On 5 January, twenty-three-year-old Jay Fosdick died, only to be cut up and eaten by Mrs Foster despite the protests of Mrs Fosdick. Soon after, the frenzied Mr Foster chased down, shot and killed the two Indians to eat them. That left just seven of the original fifteen to stagger into the first white settlement in California, after a midwinter trek of thirty-three days through the snow. On 31 January 1847, the first rescue team set out to the sixty-six remaining members of the Donner Party, dying of cold and starvation beside the Truckee Lake. Two more teams followed in quick succession. When they finally reached the camp in early March, they found a group of haunted and bitter people, barely recognizable as the hopeful band that had set off from Fort Bridger six months previously.

The party at Truckee Lake had first resorted to cannibalism in late February. One of the group – Lewis Keseberg (who had earlier abandoned the elderly Hardkoop) – was accused of taking one of the children to bed, of strangling him and hanging the corpse on the wall before eating it. Keseberg, in his defence, claimed the child had died naturally. For his crime, Keseberg was left to wait for the fourth and final rescue team, due to arrive in mid-April. Waiting with him were four others of the group – the badly injured George Donner, his wife Tamsen, his four-year-old nephew Samuel and the elderly Lavinia Murphy.

When the final rescue team reached the lake on 17 April, they were met by a grisly scene. Keseberg alone was alive, surrounded by indescribable filth and mutilated corpses. George Donner's body lay with its skull split open to permit extraction of his brains. Three frozen ox legs lay in plain view almost uneaten beside a kettle of cut-up human flesh. Nearby sat two kettles of blood and a large pan full of fresh human liver and lungs. Keseberg alleged that his four companions had died natural deaths and was open about why he had preferred the human flesh to the ox meat. He explained that human liver and lungs tasted better and that human brains made good soup. In particular, Keseberg told his revolted interrogators, Tamsen Donner tasted the best, being well endowed with fat. In a bundle held by Keseberg, the rescuers found silk, jewellery, pistols and money that had belonged to George Donner. Keseberg was later accused by one of the rescuers of murder, but his guilt could never be proved and he sued successfully for defamation.

Out of eighty-seven Donner Party members, forty died: five before reaching Truckee Lake, twenty-two in the winter camp at the lake and thirteen (plus the two Indians) during or just after efforts to leave the lake. The question that Donald Grayson sought to resolve is why those particular forty.

> Most of the males, thirty out of fifty-three, died; most of the females, twenty-four out of thirty-four, survived. The death rate among the males was fifty-seven per cent, compared with thirty-four per cent among females. The worst toll was among the young and the old. Without

exception, everyone over the age of fifty died, as did most of the children below the age of five. Children and teenagers between the ages of five and nineteen fared better than adults in their prime, aged twenty to thirty-nine. Much of the vulnerability of the old and young under stress is simply a matter of insufficient physical strength: these people are less able to walk through deep snow. Babies have special problems – for every pound of body weight, a baby has twice an adult's surface area (i.e. twice the area across which body heat can escape). To maintain body temperature, babies have to significantly increase their metabolic rate when air temperature drops only a few degrees below body temperature, whereas adults can withstand a drop of twenty to thirty-five degrees relatively comfortably. And the Donner Party babies were at a crippling further disadvantage because they had so little food to fuel their metabolism. They literally froze to death.

A key question is why women fared so much better than men. Certainly, it was not down to any *noblesse oblige* or self-sacrifice, as there is no evidence that any special consideration was given to the women and babies on the trip. One contributing factor is that the men were busy killing each other, but that still leaves twenty-six out of thirty deaths unexplained. In fact, the reason why men began to die out on average two months earlier than women is down to basic physiology and metabolism. Women have greater fat reserves than men and their metabolic rate is 25 per cent lower than for an average-size man.

The final intriguing issue surrounds the unexpectedly high death toll of people in their prime, aged twenty to thirty-nine, made up almost entirely of men. Significantly, the majority of these men were not family men but bachelors, or, in a few cases, widowers. Research has shown that married people have lower death rates than single, widowed or divorced people. Regardless of age, sex or initial health status, socially isolated individuals have well over twice the death rate of socially connected people.

The tragedy of the Donner Party should have brought home to all that cannibalism is not the preserve of any particular society and cannot *in extremis* be warded off through any standard of morality or religious teaching, however ingrained. It is true that some people have chosen to die rather than to eat human flesh, but there are few cases in which that can be considered some kind of principled choice as opposed to ignorance or failure to find the strength of will necessary to throw off the taboo.

What was extraordinary from our own research is that the taboo of cannibalism seems to dominate all other considerations. Because of our notions of corporeal reverence, inextricably bound up as they are with religious belief and ritual, people appear to be more preoccupied with what happens to the body after death than before. Premeditated murder, for example, should be a far more powerful taboo than cannibalism, but it does not seem so. Certainly, from the mid-nineteenth century the taboo of cannibalism in the UK appeared to grow in stature. 'British sailors would never do such a thing!' (despite all evidence to the contrary) was the response to Dr John Rae on his return to England from the Canadian Arctic in 1854, with his findings from his investigation of the Franklin Expedition.

Led by veteran Arctic explorer Sir John Franklin, two ships and 129 hand-picked officers and men sailed from Greenland on 12 July 1845, seeking a navigable short-cut link between the Atlantic and Pacific. It was the most technologically advanced mission of the nineteenth century. The ships were revolutionary: iron-plated, locomotive-powered and steam-heated. They were equipped with desalinators, canned food – a recent innovation – the world's first cameras and other equally sophisticated gear. On 26 July two whaling ships in Baffin Bay spotted Franklin's ships. They were never seen again.

Over the next fourteen years, more than fifty expeditions scoured the Arctic in search of Franklin and his men. In 1859, on desolate King William Island in the heart of the Arctic archipelago, searchers found evidence of catastrophe: a mountain of abandoned equipment, two skeletons and a chilling message, signed by the expedition's second-in-command, Francis Crozier. The message reported that Franklin's ships, trapped in monstrous ice for nearly two years, had been deserted in April 1848. By the time the ships were abandoned, a total of twenty-four officers and men, including Franklin, were already dead. The message, however, left no clues as to what had caused their deaths or what had caused the remaining 105 members of the expedition to abandon their still-sound ships and to embark on a desperate 900-mile march inland in a vain attempt to reach safety. In the years that followed, the skeletal remains of twenty more crewmen were found scattered along the path of their desperate march. The rest of the party had vanished into the Arctic.

During Dr Rae's 1854 investigation of the Franklin Expedition, his examination of the evidence – from eyewitness accounts of the Inuit and his own observations of items from the ships – led him to conclude in his report to the British Admiralty that 'from the mutilated state of the corpses and the contents of the kettles, it is evident that our wretched countrymen had been driven to the last resource – cannibalism – as a means of prolonging existence.' The British public and much of the British

Admiralty refused to believe such a story, which was based entirely on the testimony of natives, and the fate of the tragic expedition remained shrouded in controversy and confusion. Then, in 1981, a research team led by Dr Owen Beattie discovered cut marks on a femur recovered from a Franklin site on King William Island. Even twenty years ago, there was resistance to the idea that British explorers could commit cannibalism. People came up with alternative explanations, claiming that the cut marks could have been caused by surgery to remove frostbitten limbs or from wounds sustained during attacks by the Inuit.

The discovery excited a new wave of interest in the expedition, and in 1992 a major new site clearly visited by the Franklin survivors was discovered in Erebus Bay on King William Island. The following year, a team of scientists led by archaeologist Ann Keenleyside and anthropologist Margaret Bertulli scoured the site, finding more than 200 artefacts, including iron nails, buttons, shoe leather and a broken clay pipe, and nearly 400 human bones and bone fragments. The analysis of these bones makes fascinating and revealing reading:

> Morphological observations (based on the presence of eight mandibles) indicated that the remains represented a minimum of eight individuals, while X-ray fluorescence revealed the presence of at least eleven individuals. Age estimates indicated that all of the individuals were under the age of fifty at the time of death. One individual was initially estimated to have been twelve to fifteen years of age on the basis of the stage of dental clarification of the third molars [probably one of the four cabin boys]. The most worthy aspect of the analyses was the discovery of cut marks on ninety-two bones, or approximately

a quarter of the total number of bones. In contrast to cuts typically made by stone tools, the observed cuts, examined under a scanning electron microscope, exhibited features characteristic of cuts made by blades, namely straight edges, a V-shaped cross section and a high depth-to-width ratio. The location of the cut marks is also consistent with de-fleshing or removal of muscle tissue. Evidence for decapitation is suggestive but not conclusive.

The evidence in support of the cannibalism theory is quite overwhelming. It also now appears – courtesy of Scott Cookman's *Ice Blink: The Tragic Fate of Sir John Franklin's Lost Polar Expedition* – that the reason the party abandoned their ships after nineteen months in pack ice was an invisible killer living in the ships' poorly canned provisions: botulism. Cookman claims that the man responsible was the Admiralty's canned food contractor, Stephen Goldner, whose ridiculously low bid won him the contract but also quite possibly made him a murderer.

While botulism claimed the lives of Sir John Franklin and twenty-three crew members, the survivors in their 900-mile death march inevitably descended to cannibalism. What is extraordinary is not that these men ate each other but that, in the face of overwhelming evidence, there should be so much resistance to the idea. It is as if people are personally insulted by the thought and fear that the reputation of English explorers will be tarnished for ever. There is also concern that the brave accomplishments of these men would be diminished in some way if they were found to have been cannibals. This whole mindset, believes psychologist James Thompson, derives from our view of each other:

The astounding thing is that we are a species that's so interested in other people. We have a love of faces, we create persons and that creation of persons is so strong that we do regard bodies as a very, very distinct form, as sacred. The whole art of burial means that the taboo was there, that we had fantasies about people still surviving in some way. So the moment you get burial, you get taboo about the person, the flesh. It isn't rational, but then creation of persons isn't all that rational. It's something we find very important. We respect the person, and so we also respect their body. The moment you get burials, you get evidence that people respect burial and bodies. You get the taboo. OK, rational point of view, you should eat the flesh, it's there. But realistically so strong is the impact of the individual person on everyone round you that you respect that body. You put in things for the afterlife, you protect it from wild beasts. You respect the body the way you respected the person.

But *in extremis*, such finer considerations of 'the person' or 'the body' no longer carry the same weight or meaning. The need to do whatever is necessary to survive consumes all energies, as man regresses into the animal at his core. The members of the Franklin Expedition endured unbelievable hardships, and no one can fault them for making every effort to survive. As Christina Toren, Professor of Anthropology at Brunel University, comments: 'It doesn't seem very strange to me at all. It's as explicable as anything else that humans do.'

A central element of the denial of cannibalism is that episodes such as the Franklin Expedition or the Donner Party can be explained away as isolated tragedies, harking back to a bygone era and based on evidence that – in some cases – was more anecdotal than absolute. This sort of episode, claim 'deniers' like William Arens, author of *Man-Eating Myth*, represents a historical aberration rather than a true indicator of human nature. What Arens and his co-thinkers ignore, however, is the improbability of cannibalism as a dissociated behavioural reflex that surfaces in humans only in times of severe stress. Two notorious incidents of survival cannibalism in 1972 – the principal participants of which lived to tell the tale – help to dispel this simplistic notion.

One was the case of German-born pilot Marten Hartwell, who in November 1972 was flying a pregnant Inuit woman, a nurse and a fourteen-year-old Inuit boy with acute appendicitis to a hospital in Yellowknife, northern Canada. The plane's instruments failed, and Hartwell came down too low and crashed into a hillside. The nurse was killed on impact, and the Inuit woman died a few hours later from a broken neck. Hartwell himself suffered two broken legs and a shattered kneecap; only the boy escaped unscathed.

Under Hartwell's instruction, the boy constructed a makeshift tent and set up rabbit traps. They caught no game, however, and lived for the next three weeks on small supplies of corned beef and sugar. On 30 November Hartwell noted in his diary: 'Still alive. David is going to die tomorrow and I two or three days later. No food, my legs don't carry me.' The following day Hartwell made his last attempt to subsist on natural provisions by dragging himself to a tree and trying to make soup from the lichen on the branches, but it was useless. Now, there was only one final food resource left: human flesh. Until his rescue on 9 December, Hartwell sustained himself on the flesh of the twenty-seven year-old nurse. He had survived for an incredible thirty-two days in the wilderness, on nine of which he had eaten human flesh. He later described the moment of breaking the taboo in the Channel 4 documentary *Survive*: 'The worst thing was to take the first bite. The horror of what I was doing didn't bother me after that.'

Unlike the sailors of the eighteenth and nineteenth centuries, Hartwell admitted to being constantly concerned about what society would think of him if he survived and he even thought he would be hanged for his actions. He later said that the moment he committed cannibalism was the moment he lost all faith in God. For Hartwell, the horror of cannibalism was made greater by the fact that it was a decision he took in total isolation (David, the boy, was prepared to die rather than eat human flesh), utterly tormented by the notion that even if he survived he would not escape society's condemnation and probable retribution.

At almost exactly the same time as Hartwell was wrestling with his conscience, however, another group of survivors high in the Andes was preparing to cannibalize their dead friends and relatives. Their collective actions would explode for ever the notion that modern civilized communities of the twentieth century were incapable of bestial behaviour.

NINE

Cannibal Killers – The Last Taboo

If cannibalism is society's ultimate taboo, then cannibal killers are the personification of this taboo at its very worst. The idea that someone could kill another person and eat his or her flesh is something that shocks and horrifies almost all of us.

For most people, the archetypal cannibal killer is Hannibal Lecter, the fictional creation of author Thomas Harris, made famous in the 1991 film *The Silence of the Lambs*. In the movie, Anthony Hopkins played the psychiatrist turned serial murderer, whom the police were using to track down another vicious killer. Lecter was highly intelligent, deeply cultured and magnetically charismatic – but, most memorably, he was also a cannibal.

The idea of a cannibal killer is, of course, nothing new. Folklore and literature have given us a number of famous precedents, from the giant in *Jack and the Beanstalk* to Bram Stoker's Dracula – even *Hansel and Gretel* is supposed to be based on a real-life instance of cannibalism in fourteenth-century Germany. But who were the real-life cannibal killers in history, ordinary people who have entered into the murderers' hall of infamy simply by virtue of being people-eaters?

We start by going back over four hundred years, to examine one of the first recorded cannibal killers, Sawney Beane. Beane was born within a few miles of Edinburgh towards the end of the sixteenth century. His parents worked in hedging and ditching, and it was no doubt intended that Sawney would later follow in their footsteps. But perhaps through a rebellious streak, or sheer laziness, he showed early on in life that he was not going to stick to the straight and narrow. As soon as he was old enough, Sawney left home, met and married a girl, and started out on his life of crime.

Sawney and his wife set up home in an isolated cave on the Galloway coast and started to rob passing travellers, of which there were many making their way between the remote villages in the region. To make sure that his victims would never be able to report and identify their attackers, Sawney killed them and buried their bodies. After a while, however, it became clear that highway robbery in rural Galloway was not as lucrative as the Beanes had hoped for. The fact was that in this impoverished, rather backward community, people simply did not carry much money about their person. And so Beane and his wife found it difficult to steal enough to buy their own food. Sawney hit upon a drastic but ultimately very pragmatic solution: they already had a ready supply of meat right under their noses – the flesh of the victims that they were murdering on a regular basis. Once they ambushed and killed their next victim, this time the Beanes brought the body back to their cave. After disembowelling and dismembering the body, the limbs and best portions of flesh were dried, salted and pickled, and then hung on hooks around the main part of the cave. And so it was that the Beanes became cannibals.

The Beanes' change of diet was therefore partly economically motivated, although clearly it was a move influenced and driven by their innately murderous habits. Certainly, the couple were not overly bothered by the squeamish nature of their new diet, nor did the taboo of flesh-eating ever seem to enter into their minds. Theirs was not a time of great poverty and famine, so the decision to enter into cannibalism was not taken out of desperation or starvation. As time went on, the Beanes' cannibalism slotted neatly into their daily existence, as if for them it was simply another way of hunting and gathering. With their regular supply of food, they felt more settled and decided to start a family. Sawney Beane's wife would eventually have some fourteen children, who would in turn incestuously bear her twenty-two grandchildren, all of whom were brought up as murderers and cannibals. They received no education, apart from basic speech patterns and, of course, how to kill and prepare humans for food.

The Beanes' cannibal practices continued for almost twenty-five years. Estimates vary as to how many people they killed, but Captain Charles Johnson, the local historian whose telling of the Sawney Beane story forms the basis for most people's subsequent accounts, writes: 'In the twenty-five years they continued their Butcheries, they had washed their Hands in the Blood of a thousand at least, Men and Women and Children.'

They were finally caught when an ambush went wrong. Members of the Beane clan attacked a young couple and dragged the woman away, killing and disembowelling her before her husband's eyes. But another group of travellers, passing nearby, managed to rescue the husband. He was swiftly taken to Glasgow, where he recounted the whole of the horrific story to the provost, who immediately ordered a small army to go out and search for the cannibal killers. Assisted by dozens of bloodhounds, the search party found the Beanes' lair after scouring the Galloway coastline. It was high tide, and the cave's entrance was completely waterlogged, so a few brave soldiers went ahead of the rest, using small burning torches to light their way. They all noticed the smell as soon as they were inside the cave – a terrible smell of death and decay – but nothing could have prepared the soldiers for what they were about to find. Charles Johnson describes the scene:

> They were all so shocked at what they beheld, that they were almost ready to sink into the Earth. Legs, Arms, Thighs, Hands, and Feet of Men, Women and Children were hung up in Rows, like Dried Beef. A great many Limbs lay in Pickle, and a great Mass of Money, both Gold and Silver, with Watches, Rings, Swords, Pistols, and a large Quantity of Cloaths, both Linnen and Wollen, and an infinite Number of other Things, which they had taken from those whom they had murdered, were thrown together in Heaps, or hung up against the Sides of the Den.

With an army of over 400 inside their lair, blocking every possible exit and escape route, this was the end for Sawney Beane. He and his family were swiftly arrested and marched to Edinburgh, where they were all executed without trial.

The story of Sawney Beane is one of the earliest recorded instances of cannibal murder, but unfortunately the seventeenth-century accounts do not tell us much more than the bare facts about his crimes. Two centuries later, when scientists became increasingly interested in the psychology of murderers, we find more substantial medical accounts and diagnoses of cannibal killers who get caught. And with these diagnoses, the sexual element in each crime becomes increasingly prominent.

Not until the second half of the nineteenth century, with the work of Baron Richard von Krafft-Ebing, do we begin to see the first wide-ranging accounts of sexually sadistic murder. German neuro-psychiatrist Krafft-Ebing's ground-breaking work, *Psychopathia Sexualis*, was one of the first studies into sexual aberrations and psychopathology. The book first appeared in 1886, in a German text with Latin where the situations described were deemed too provocative, and it brought about a total re-evaluation of European and American thinking about sex.

In *Psychopathia Sexualis*, Krafft-Ebing assembled a large number of case reports from all over Europe of people who engaged in unusual, often extremely violent forms of sexual behaviour. Many of these cases involved sadism or masochism; in fact, Krafft-Ebing was the first to coin the term 'sadism' for the disorder. He also wrote extensively about 'Lustmord', the German term for 'lust-murder', which means murder for pleasure. And according to Krafft-Ebing's studies, the ultimate step for a lust-murderer was the escalation to anthropophagy – murderous cannibalism.

During the course of compiling his research, Krafft-Ebing found several cases of lust-murderers who developed a taste for human flesh. One particularly notorious killer, Vincenzo Verzeni, fascinated Krafft-Ebing so greatly that he devoted a large part of his study to him. In keeping with the rest of *Psychopathia Sexualis*, Krafft-Ebing describes Verzeni's crimes in graphic detail. His first victim was a fourteen-year-old girl, Johanna Motta, who disappeared when she was walking between one village and another. As she did not return, her master set out to find her and discovered her body near the village, lying by a path in the fields. The girl's body had been severely mutilated – there were multiple abrasions on her legs, her intestines and genitals had been torn from the body, and a portion of flesh had been torn from the right calf.

No one suspected Verzeni of this crime, and about ten months later he struck again. This time it was a married woman named Frigeni, whom he again attacked in the open countryside. She was later found dead, lying naked in a field. There was severe marking around her neck where she had been strangled, numerous stab wounds and, most shockingly, her abdomen had been ripped open and her intestines were hanging out.

Verzeni was caught in August 1871, at the age of twenty-two, after he tried unsuccessfully to strangle his cousin, Maria Previtali. He was brought to court, where he was tried on suspicion of some twenty murders, all of which had involved severe mutilation and suspected cannibalism. Verzeni explained his crimes in a lengthy set of confessions, a large part of which Krafft-Ebing reproduces in *Psychopathia Sexualis*. These confessions give a disturbing insight into the mind of a nineteenth-century cannibal killer, and they also have resonances with some of today's cannibal cases:

> I had an unspeakable delight in strangling women, experiencing during the act erections and real sexual pleasure. The feeling of pleasure while strangling them was much greater than that which I experienced while masturbating. I took great delight in drinking Motta's blood... I took the clothing and intestines, because of the pleasure it gave me to smell and touch them. It never occurred to me to touch or look at the genitals or such things. It satisfied me to seize the women by the neck and suck their blood.

Verzeni explained that the abrasions on Johanna Motta's legs were caused by his teeth when he tried to drink her blood. He had also torn out a piece of flesh from her calf and taken it home with him, intending to roast and eat it. Verzeni actually asked to be kept confined in prison, knowing that if he remained at large he would not be able to resist his impulses. The court granted his wishes, sentencing him to life imprisonment.

Ultimately, Krafft-Ebing could not come up with any plausible explanation for Verzeni's bizarre behaviour. He may have had some form of brain damage, and he may well have been affected by events while growing up. Verzeni did explain that he arrived at his perverse acts at the age of twelve, after noticing that he experienced a peculiar feeling of pleasure while wringing the necks of chickens. What is certain, however, is that Verzeni's sadistic crimes and abnormal sexual impulses form many of the characteristics that we see in the modern cannibal killer. Fifty years later, Germany would produce not just one but three of the most infamous examples of the early twentieth century.

After suffering the immense psychological blow of defeat in the First World War, social and economic conditions in Germany in the early 1920s hit an all-time low. Inflation rates were catastrophically high, and the country was suffering from widespread unemployment and chronic food shortages. The atmosphere quickly turned into one of anarchy as law and order collapsed, and crime flourished everywhere. Germany was a country in chaos, and the all-pervasive social malaise provided the perfect breeding ground for a triumvirate of cannibal killers, all operating within just a few years of each other.

Karl Denke was one of the most respected citizens of the sleepy little town of Münsterberg, Upper Silesia, in what is now Ziębice, in north-west Poland. He served as the organ blower for his local church, and carried the cross at funerals of members of the local Evangelist commune. No one ever suspected that there might be anything more to Denke until his suicide in jail on the night of his arrest, when the police made a gruesome discovery at his one-bedroom apartment.

Denke was born in August 1870 to a middle-class farmer in a small village in Silesia. He did badly at school, and left at the age of twelve to become a gardener. When Denke was twenty-five years old, his father died, and he used his inheritance to buy a small farm and garden in Münsterberg. Farming was not his forte, and after a while Denke was forced to sell his land, and with the proceeds he bought a two-storey house with a garden. With Germany's defeat in the First World War, crippling inflation meant that Denke lost his savings and was forced to sell his house. He continued, however, to rent the same apartment on the ground floor. Due to his impeccable reputation, Denke had no problem in persuading the local police to give him a vending licence, and from then on he worked as a peddler, selling leather braces, belts, shoelaces, and also pickled 'boneless pork'.

At around 1.00pm on 21 December 1924, a young man ran into the Münsterberg police station, covered in blood, claiming that Karl Denke had just tried to kill him. The police, surprised that one of their most respected citizens was being accused of such a crime, nevertheless made their way to the apartment and arrested Denke. They brought him back to the station, where they left him locked up in a holding cell. That same night, at about 11.30pm, one of the officers decided to check up on Denke and found that he had hanged himself with his own handkerchief. The police, still unaware of what they were dealing with, went to search Denke's apartment the next day, where they found evidence of the true extent of his crimes. Around the main room were several containers, each filled with pickled human flesh;

there were piles of human bones ready for processing, and an apparatus for making soap. Hanging on the walls were dozens of belts, braces and shoelaces made from human skin. And on the table was the proof of Denke's large body count – personal documents belonging to his victims, and Denke's own ledger listing names, dates and the respective weights of each body he had pickled from 1921 onwards.

Since the true extent of Denke's crimes was only discovered after his suicide, there is unfortunately no way of knowing why Denke behaved as he did. He left behind plenty of evidence of his cannibalism, but no clues as to his motives. Fritz Haarmann, probably Germany's most prolific serial murderer, was caught alive, and we have far more information about his background and development into a cannibal killer.

Fritz Haarmann, the Butcher of Hanover, was convicted of murdering twenty-seven young boys, but it was rumoured that he was involved in many more deaths, probably well over fifty.

Just as the First World War was ending, Haarmann was freed from prison, where he had just spent the previous five years serving time for fraud and theft. He was already thirty-nine years old and had spent most of his life either behind bars or drifting around Germany, stealing and selling on goods. He soon found work in the makeshift market next to Hanover's main railway station, joined a meat-smuggling racket, and within six months had his own business as a meat hawker.

This market at the station also became the place where Haarmann would meet most of his victims over the next five years. The place had become a magnet for the homeless youths and teenagers who arrived in Hanover every day, most of whom had run away from home. Haarmann developed a routine, where he would chat to one of the youths and invite him to accompany him to his apartment, promising him a good meal or the possibility of working for him.

His first victim was seventeen year-old Friedel Roth, who vanished on 27 September 1918. The police investigating Roth's disappearance actually went to Haarmann's apartment to question him, where they caught him in bed with an underage boy. Haarmann was promptly arrested and served another nine months in prison. Four years later, when in custody, Haarmann bragged that the head of the missing boy Roth had been in his apartment at the time the police arrested him, wrapped in newspaper and hidden behind the stove. If they had only found it then, they might have saved Hanover from the ghastly bloodbath that ensued.

After his second stint in prison, Haarmann met and fell in love with a young runaway, Hans Grans. At twenty years old, Grans was some twenty-four years younger than Haarmann, but just as evil and even more manipulative. Although Grans never got involved in the actual murders, he would select victims and order their killings, often simply because he wanted their clothes. Haarmann's killing spree began in earnest. Over the next four years he seduced dozens of youths at the market and took them back to the apartment. There, he would sodomize the young boys before killing them by tearing their throats out with his teeth. He then had sex with the dead bodies, and also drank their blood. Afterwards, he and Grans would drag the body up to the attic, where they dismembered the corpse and sliced it up, transferring the flesh to buckets. They threw the useless portions into the River Leine but took the rest of the flesh back to the market, where they sold it, along with the victims' clothes. In these times of food shortages, the two murderers never found it hard to sell their pails of meat – Haarmann's prices were the lowest, and he simply told hungry customers it was horse meat.

In May 1924 a child's skull from which all the flesh had been removed with a sharp instrument was washed ashore by the River Leine. This gruesome discovery prompted the authorities to dredge the Leine for further human remains. The results were shocking – they found more than 500 human bones, many with the same telltale cut marks on them.

As a convicted child molester, Haarmann became the prime suspect in these murders, and the police put him under surveillance. Soon afterwards, they caught him molesting a young boy at the railway station. Haarmann was arrested and locked up in custody, as the police went to search his apartment for evidence. There, they found the bloodstained attic, as well as piles of clothes taken from many of the victims. Haarmann eventually gave a full confession, implicating Grans in all the murders.

The trial began on 4 December 1924. Haarmann was charged with the murder of twenty-seven teenage boys, but this was believed to be an underestimate. Throughout the trial, Haarmann behaved like a showman. His much-wanted moment of fame had finally come, and he was going to make the most of it. He mugged continuously for the gallery and interrupted proceedings constantly, often making sick jokes at the expense of his victims' relatives. With the confession and overwhelming circumstantial evidence, the court did not take long to find Haarmann guilty of twenty-four of the twenty-seven murders. Two psychiatrists declared that he was mentally sound, and Haarmann was beheaded. Grans was given a life sentence, but this was later commuted to twelve years' imprisonment.

The police officers and psychiatrists who questioned Haarmann found in his background several clues about his development into a fully fledged cannibal killer. He was born the youngest of six children on 25 October 1879. Fritz's mother

Johanna treated her son differently from other mothers, encouraging him to play with dolls, and generally pampering him and spoiling him. His father, Olle, was a violent alcoholic, who spent most nights out drinking and chasing other women. He also beat Fritz frequently, the result of which was that Fritz hated his father from a very early age.

Later, as a teenager, Haarmann was sent to a mental institution after molesting small children. He escaped to join the army, where the routine and order suited his troubled mind. However, after just over a year Haarmann collapsed on a training exercise and spent four months in military hospital. The doctors diagnosed a 'mental deficiency', and he was expelled from the army. Not long afterwards, Haarmann began his career of theft, sex attacks and cannibal murder.

The details about Germany's other infamous cannibal killer are again rather sketchy. Georg Karl Grossmann, another meat peddler, lived in Berlin in the early years after the First World War. Like Haarmann, Grossmann may have also had convictions for acts of a sexually sadistic nature; it is said that some of these convictions included bestiality and paedophilia. Grossmann's motives for cannibalism appear to be primarily economic. He picked up his victims – usually itinerant women – at Berlin's railway station and took them back to his flat to kill them and sell their meat at local markets. In 1921 neighbours in his tenement block heard screams coming from Grossmann's apartment. The police were promptly called, and when they broke into the room they found Grossmann in the process of butchering a freshly killed girl. Like Denke, Grossmann hanged himself in jail.

Given the lack of substantial data we have on Grossmann and Denke, it is difficult to make a detailed comparison of the three German cannibals of the 1920s. At first glance it would appear that a combination of dire economic circumstances and their unbalanced minds pushed Grossmann and Denke into cannibalism. However, there may well have been other psychological or even biological factors that tipped them over the edge. For instance, we cannot rule out that their cannibalism was sexually motivated, just as it was in the case of Fritz Haarmann.

Not long after the three German cannibals committed their vile acts, on the other side of the Atlantic Ocean another cannibal killer would horrify and disgust the whole of New York with a much-publicized case of grisly murder.

It all began on 3 June 1928, when a ten year-old girl, Grace Budd, was mysteriously kidnapped from her home New York City. The man who took Grace had introduced himself to her parents, pretending to be a wealthy farm-owner who could offer their son Edward a job in the countryside. Delia and Albert Budd met this friendly old man a couple of times and felt they could trust him. And so, when he told them that his sister was having a children's party one afternoon, the Budds allowed him to take young Gracie away. They thought it would be a lovely treat for their daughter. The Budds waited for their Gracie to return that evening, but she never did. The next morning, they sent Edward down to the police station to report their daughter missing. The search was now on. But every lead the police followed up turned out to be nothing: the old man had given a fake name, the farm did not exist, and his sister's address had been invented. Little Grace Budd had disappeared, and nothing would be heard of her for another six years.

On 12 November 1934 Delia Budd received a strange-looking letter. The letter, unsigned, started off in gruesome fashion. The letter's author described a 'friend', who went to China in 1894 as a deckhand. There, it continued, 'so great was the suffering among the very poor that all children under twelve were sold for food in order to keep others from starving... You could go in any shop and ask for steak... Part of the naked body of a boy or girl would be brought out and just what you wanted cut from it.' The letter explained that this 'friend' came back to the USA with a taste for human flesh, and not long after his return he stole two boys, one aged seven and one eleven, and killed and ate both of them.

Even such a gruesome beginning could not have prepared Delia Budd for what was to follow. The mystery letter-writer explained that he was so fascinated by his friend's description of eating the two young boys that he made up his mind to try human flesh too. He then started to describe how he had kidnapped Grace back in June 1928. There was no doubt that this letter was from the seemingly sweet old man who had visited the Budds in 1928. The note continued: 'Grace sat in my lap and kissed me. I made up my mind to eat her.' Grace was taken to an empty house outside New York City, where he strangled her to death, cut her up into small pieces, and took parts of her back to eat at his home. As a final insult, the writer boasted that her flesh was 'sweet and tender', and that it took nine days 'to eat her entire body'.

At first, the police were not sure what to make of this revolting letter. It seemed too outlandish to be true. But one detective decided to follow it up, after spotting a distinctive hexagonal emblem on the back of the envelope – an emblem that belonged to a small Manhattan company. Further investigations led them to Albert Fish, an old man living alone in a New York boarding house.

While Fish was being taken to the police station, detectives searched his apartment. Nothing remarkable turned up, except that they did find a large number of newspaper cuttings about

Fritz Haarmann, the cannibal killer from Hanover. When Edward Budd arrived at the police station, he instantly recognized Fish as the man who had abducted Grace. Fish confessed at once.

In lengthy interviews with the police, Fish admitted to several other murders: a mentally handicapped boy in New York in 1919, and another boy in Washington in the same year. He also gave a graphic description of his murder of four-year-old William Gaffney, telling the police that he had made a stew out of the boy's ears, nose and belly, with onions, carrots, turnips and celery. Fish took enormous pleasure in telling these stories, the defence psychiatrist Dr Fredric Wertham later revealed. 'He spoke in a matter-of-fact way,' said Dr Wertham, 'like a housewife describing her favourite methods of cooking.' Dr Wertham's interviews with Albert Fish revealed many more dark sides to his character. 'There is no known perversion that he did not practise and practise frequently,' Dr Wertham revealed. Fish had often indulged in at least eighteen sexual perversions, including coprophagy (eating of faeces), exhibitionism, fetishism, sado-masochism, undinism (sexual acts involving urination) and, of course, cannibalism.

Research into Fish's background revealed that his father had died when Albert was only five years old, and he was sent to an orphanage, where he was savagely beaten all the time. However, Fish told his psychiatrist that when he was being caned or belted at school, he actually enjoyed it. This masochism continued throughout his life. As a young man, Fish had managed to start a family. Some of his children, now grown up, testified at the trial that their father had got his children to beat him as they were growing up. Fish himself told Dr Wertham that he enjoyed inserting needles into his body, and an X-ray later confirmed this, showing twenty-nine needles lodged in his pelvic region. Finally, there were reports that Fish was also a religious maniac. His children told the court that their father would often climb up a nearby hill and, naked, scream at the moon: 'I am Christ! I am Christ!'

The defence used all this evidence to suggest that Fish was insane. However, the public were baying for blood, and even Fish himself said that he did not think he was insane, telling reporters, 'I'm not insane. I'm just queer. I don't understand myself.' A unanimous jury found Fish sane and therefore guilty, and he was executed in January 1936 in the electric chair.

The final two characters in our trawl through the history of cannibal killers are Edward Gein and Edmund Kemper. Both men were serial murderers who ate parts of their victims, and their cases share a number of traits in common. Most important, for both Gein and Kemper, their cannibalism was again a way of feeding their darkest sexual desires.

Ed Gein is best known for having inspired at least two cinematic villains – Norman Bates in *Psycho* and Buffalo Bill, the serial killer who tries to make a suit of human skin in *The Silence of the Lambs*. Gein was born in 1906 in an isolated farmhouse just outside the small settlement of Plainfield, Wisconsin, and lived in the same house until his arrest at the age of fifty-one. For most of his life, Gein was dominated by his mother, Augusta. She was a fanatically religious woman, who repeatedly warned young Edward about the dangers of immoral and loose women. She had deliberately chosen the isolated farmstead outside Plainfield in order to keep her son away from the evil influences of other people. Ed Gein grew up idolizing his mother, and when she died in 1945 his way of life changed dramatically.

Left alone in the big old house, Gein started buying pornography and books about medical experiments and anatomy. He was particularly fascinated by the Nazis' experiments on concentration-camp inmates during the Second World War. Gein found that he was sexually aroused by images of autopsies and dead bodies. Not long afterwards, the books and magazines ceased to be enough, and Gein began robbing graves to fulfil his necrophiliac needs. Gein visited local cemeteries in the dead of night, stole freshly buried bodies and took them home, where his perversions reached new dimensions of horror. He ate parts of the corpses and made waistcoats of human skin, wearing them next to his body. It was not long before grave robbing turned into murder.

Officially, Gein killed two women, but the police believed that he murdered many more. Certainly, when they searched the old house and grounds, they found body parts belonging to a further eight women, although it was impossible to ascertain whether these came from graves that Gein had robbed or from his murder victims.

The police caught Gein very easily after the second recorded murder: his victim, Bernice Worden, ran a shop, and Gein had left his signature in the receipt book on the day he murdered her. After arresting him, Plainfield police officers went to the lonely farmhouse to search for evidence. At first, they found only rubbish and decomposing food amid the unimaginable squalor, but in the kitchen they discovered the headless corpse of Bernice Worden. She had been slit open and completely gutted. Upstairs, in Gein's bedroom, they found his collection of human remains, including skulls on his bedposts and a suit made from human skin.

Back at the station, the police now turned to Gein to find out what had happened to all his victims. They interrogated him for hours, during which he never showed any sign of remorse or emotion. In fact, as Gein described the horrors he had practised over many years, he spoke very matter-of-factly, even cheerfully at times. He had no concept of the enormity of his crimes. Gein was interviewed by a number of psychologists and psychiatrists. They ran a barrage of psychological tests on him, and concluded that he was schizophrenic and a sexual psychopath. He told the psychiatrists that as a child he had witnessed his mother killing a pig, slitting its stomach open and ripping out the entrails with her bare hands. This memory had profoundly affected him, and certainly the image bears striking comparison with what Gein did to his victims' bodies forty years later.

Generally, it was concluded that Gein's condition had been brought about by his upbringing and by the unhealthy relationship he had had with his mother. His feelings towards women were a complete contradiction: he was sexually attracted to them but also tried to dispel these emotions because of what his mother had taught him. This love–hate tangle of conflicting desires eventually developed into a full-blown psychosis, which tipped Ed Gein over the edge. Gein appeared in court charged with the two murders, but his plea of not guilty by reason of insanity was backed up by the doctors. In early January 1958 a judge committed him to the state mental hospital, and he spent the rest of his life in psychiatric institutions. Gein died in 1984 and was buried next to his mother in an unmarked grave in Plainfield cemetery.

Fifteen years after Edward Gein's depraved crimes shocked Wisconsin, another cannibal killer terrorized young college girls in Santa Cruz, California. Like Gein, Edmund Kemper was driven by an unhealthy love–hate relationship with his mother. But in Kemper's case his mother would mark not only the start of his murderous rampage but also its savage conclusion.

Santa Cruz in the early 1970s was a place of relative innocence. For the students of the University of Santa Cruz, the easiest and preferred form of transport between campus and their apartments on the coast was to hitchhike. This was still the era of the flower-power generation, and so California's youth were blissfully unaware of any of the potential dangers of accepting a lift from a total stranger. It was in this climate that Ed Kemper, the Co-Ed Killer of Santa Cruz, flourished.

Perhaps surprisingly for a serial killer who remained undetected for so long, Edmund Emil Kemper was one of the oddest-looking characters in the whole of Santa Cruz, standing six feet, nine inches tall, powerfully built and weighing over twenty stone. He was also highly intelligent and, despite his strange appearance, charming and adept at putting his victims at ease. Kemper was given the moniker of the Co-Ed Killer because until the very end of his spree all his victims were co-eds, the American term for a female university undergraduate. With the majority of the Santa Cruz student population hitchhiking everywhere, it was easy for Kemper to cruise the roads around the university, offering rides to single girls. Once he got them into his pick-up truck, the seemingly innocent ride would turn into bloody murder.

When it came to killing his victims, Kemper's preferred method was a combination of strangulation and frenzied stabbing. For Kemper, the act of stabbing alone could bring him to orgasm – a common feature among sexually sadistic killers. Most sexual sadists' preferred *modus operandi* is repeatedly stabbing or strangling someone to death – as opposed to shooting them cleanly and quickly – because by prolonging the actual death throes of the victim, the killer can continue the attack until they reach ejaculation.

After the first couple of murders, however, Kemper became less interested in the killing and more interested in getting his thrills from what followed afterwards. Like Ed Gein and Fritz

Haarmann before him, Kemper was a necrophile, and he particularly enjoyed decapitating his victims and having sex with the headless corpses. He also performed sex acts on the severed heads, and drove around with them in his car for days afterwards. In this way, the heads served as a kind of 'trophy' from the murders – items that would help Kemper to relive the actual killing and become sexually aroused again.

In the twisted mind of Ed Kemper, the ultimate way of prolonging, preserving and reliving the sexual thrill of his murders was cannibalism. Kemper would take his dead victims back to his apartment in Alameda, and with the corpse still malleable, before the onset of rigor mortis, he would strip the victim naked and pose their body in the bath, making them look as if they were still alive and taking Polaroid photographs of them. After that, he dismembered the bodies, removing the head, hands and limbs, before dividing up the remainder of the flesh and storing most of it in the freezer. With the last portion of human flesh prepared, he was ready for the final stage in his ritual.

Kemper later revealed to psychiatrists that he had a whole series of recipes for cooking human meat. He took enormous trouble preparing these meals, even laying the table the same way each time. Once the table was set, Kemper would place the Polaroid photographs of the victim next to his meal. As he ate, he would look at the photographs, which would bring him to orgasm again. In this way Kemper was using cannibalism as a way of prolonging his sexual arousal. And by freezing enough meat to last him a month, he could repeat the experience many times over.

Kemper's series of murders reached their bloody climax on Easter Sunday, 21 April 1973. By now he was totally out of control and ready to carry out the crime he had been dreaming about for many years. At five o'clock in the morning, Kemper sneaked into his mother's bedroom and killed her with a hammer and his favourite knife. Once she was dead, he decapitated her and cut out her larynx, throwing it down the waste disposal unit, explaining later, 'It seemed appropriate, as much as she'd bitched and screamed and yelled at me over all the years.' With blood lust still running high, Kemper then telephoned one of his mother's best friends, Sarah Hallett, inviting her to come to a 'surprise dinner.' When Mrs Hallett arrived, he strangled her to death too.

After sexually attacking the corpses of his mother and Sarah Hallett, Kemper slept that night in his mother's bed. He finally felt satisfied. For the next three days, Kemper went on the run, hoping for a massive manhunt and nationwide publicity. To his dismay, nothing happened, so Kemper telephoned the police and turned himself in. After a lengthy trial, the jury found Kemper to be sane and guilty of all eight counts of first-degree murder, and he was sentenced to life imprisonment.

For Ed Kemper, the motive for cannibalism was again sexual, manifesting itself in his uniquely bizarre ritual. But what could possibly lie behind such behaviour? Like Ed Gein, Kemper grew up in odd circumstances, and his relationship with his mother was troubled from the very beginning. Born in December 1948, he suffered severe psychological disturbance from an early age. As a young child, he would chop the heads and hands off his sisters' dolls, and at the age of thirteen he cut the family cat up into pieces. Kemper's parents separated when he was seven, and his mother, Clarnell Kemper, brought him up. In custody, Kemper told his psychiatrists that his mother frequently punished him, and that when he was eight she banished him from his bedroom into the cellar, accessible only via a trap door in the kitchen floor, because his vast size was making his sisters feel uncomfortable. It was during these periods locked in the cellar that

Kemper began to formulate his dark plans of revenge, mutilation, sadism and sex.

By the time Kemper was thirteen, Clarnell was finding him increasingly difficult to live with, and he was sent to live with his grandparents on a ranch in northern California. Kemper, who was by now deeply disturbed, objected to this 'punishment', and transferred his murderous fantasies to his grandmother. On 27 August 1963 Kemper shot and stabbed his grandparents to death in a fit of rage. He was fifteen years old. The courts ordered that Kemper be detained in Atascadero maximum security mental hospital, where he spent the next four years, becoming a model prisoner. IQ tests showed that he was one of the brightest inmates there, and Kemper worked at the psychology laboratory, where he helped to administer psychological tests. In 1969, at the age of twenty-one, the California Youth Authority considered him cured and released him back into the care of his mother. It would only be a few years before Kemper killed again.

If we examine Kemper's life history, we can make a start at identifying different factors that may have contributed to his violent behaviour. His troubled relationship with his mother obviously played a part in his attitude towards women, and his cruelty to animals as a child was a forerunner of his violence in adult life – something frequently found in other psychopaths. However, of the dozens of psychologists who have interviewed and examined Kemper over the years (and there have been many), none has really been able to classify, diagnose and treat Kemper satisfactorily. When he was at Atascadero helping out in the psychology laboratory, he read up on all the standard psycho-logical tests, such as the Minnesota Multi-Phasic Personality Inventory, and learned every possible combination of answers. So when he was arrested in 1973, no doctors were able to perform psychological tests on Kemper satisfactorily because he knew exactly which way to answer to confuse the results.

Now confined in the California Medical Faculty in Vacaville, Edmund Kemper still remains an enigma. With his unique combination of sexual perversions, he remains both undiagnosable and untreatable. However, in his sadism, his troubled childhood and his sexual disorders, Kemper does share a number of traits with many of the other cannibal killers that history has produced.

Kemper was given eight consecutive life sentences in 1973. He will never have any opportunity for parole. The Co-Ed Killer was finally caged, and the people of Santa Cruz could rest easy. But elsewhere in the world, it would not be long before another cannibal killer would emerge to commit this most gruesome of crimes.

TEN

The Real
Hannibal Lecters

In April 1992, a year after *The Silence of the Lambs* broke box-office records, details of the crimes of the world's worst cannibal killer, Andrei Chikatilo, were released to the world. Just two months earlier, Milwaukee cannibal Jeffrey Dahmer was sentenced to life imprisonment for murdering seventeen gay men; he admitted preserving his victims' body parts, and cooking and eating their flesh. In February 1991 Arthur Shawcross was convicted of murdering eleven prostitutes in Rochester, New York; he says he ate the sexual organs of four of his victims. Meanwhile, in Japan, another convicted cannibal killer, Issei Sagawa, lives free in a flat outside Tokyo, despite having killed and eaten a Dutch student in Paris back in 1981.

If Hannibal Lecter is the fictional representation of the cannibal killer, these four men are the reality behind the fiction. But what kind of individual becomes a real-life Hannibal Lecter? We went on a journey into the lives and backgrounds of these four cannibal killers in search of signs and clues that could help to explain their aberrant behaviour.

With its mixture of drab Soviet-era tower blocks and crumbling historical buildings, the city of Rostov-on-Don does not give off any immediate indications of its sinister alter ego: an unfortunate reputation as the serial killer capital of the former Soviet Union, gained during the savage killing spree of Andrei Chikatilo. It was around Rostov that the world's worst cannibal killer murdered the majority of his fifty-three victims over a twelve-year period. When the police eventually caught Chikatilo, the gruesome details of his crimes were made public in a long and harrowing trial, which took people into a dark world of sadism and murder few would ever have imagined possible.

Chikatilo was born in 1936 in the small village of Yablochnoye in the Ukraine. His family, in common with the rest of the inhabitants of the Ukraine, were still suffering from the terrible famine artificially induced by Stalin in 1932–33. They could well remember how bad the famine had been at its peak: many starving villagers had turned to cannibalism, eating relatives who had died. Furthermore, rumours abounded that marauding gangs of cannibals were kidnapping children, killing them and selling their meat at local markets. As Andrei Chikatilo grew up, his mother told him that his older brother Stephan had been taken away and murdered by one of these cannibal gangs. Whether true or not, the story certainly had a profound effect on Chikatilo, and he was imprinted with nightmares about cannibalism from an early age.

Andrei Chikatilo's childhood was not a happy one. His family was extremely poor, and frequently struggled to find enough money for food and warm clothing. Chikatilo was also a chronic bed-wetter, right up to the age of twelve. This caused immense problems with the rest of his family, particularly with his mother. Because they had so little money, the whole Chikatilo family slept together on a wooden platform called the divan. When Andrei Chikatilo wet the bed, everyone else knew about it, and his mother Anna, who was particularly fiery and domineering, would frequently fly into wild rages at her son about this.

With the onset of puberty, Chikatilo's bed-wetting stopped but he developed an equally embarrassing problem. He discovered that he was prone to extremely premature ejaculation, often before he achieved an erection. And while the other boys at school were seducing and having sex with the girls, Chikatilo's few experiences with girls were nearly all traumatic. When he was sixteen years old, a friend of his younger sister's came to the Chikatilo hut. Chikatilo was the only person at home, and he invited the girl in to wait for his sister. The girl was only about ten or eleven years old, but Chikatilo suddenly felt a sudden and overpowering desire to rape her. He grabbed her and pushed her to the ground, but in struggling with her he ejaculated.

After his troubled adolescence, Chikatilo seemed to find respite in studying. He went to university and became a teacher at a local school. Despite his chronic shyness and sexual problems, he got married, in 1963, to a miner's daughter called Feodosia. Against all odds, theirs was a reasonably successful marriage at the beginning. They even managed to produce two children, although because of Chikatilo's impotence problems, in order to conceive he had to ejaculate on his wife and then push the semen inside her.

Eventually, Chikatilo found work as a teacher, and he and his new family settled down in Novoshakhtinsk, near Rostov-on-Don. But after only a few years, Chikatilo was caught molesting some of the girls at the school, and he was asked quietly to look for alternative employment.

He found another teaching job in 1978, this time at a mining school in Shakhty. While the rest of his family temporarily stayed behind in Novoshakhtinsk, Chikatilo went ahead to start the new job. Although the school provided Chikatilo with a flat for himself and his family, Chikatilo secretly bought a run-down little hut in the slum area on the other side of Shakhty. Deliberately and intentionally, Chikatilo was creating his own secret world away from his normal everyday existence, a world that no one was to discover until his capture twelve years later. While the rest of his family settled in to their new home in the mining school's flat, Chikatilo brought prostitutes, runaway teenagers and then little girls to his secret shack, in a bid to overcome his impotence.

In December that year, the hut on the outskirts of Shakhty became the place where Chikatilo first discovered the true nature of his own terrible desires. Chikatilo persuaded a nine-year-old girl, Lena Zakotnova, to come with him to his little hut. Twelve years later, Chikatilo confessed what happened next:

As soon as I turned on the lights and closed the door, I fell on her. The girl was frightened and cried out. I shut her mouth with my hands. I couldn't get an erection and I couldn't get my penis into her vagina. The desire to have an orgasm overwhelmed all else, and I wanted to do it by any means. Her cries excited me further. Lying on her and moving in imitation of the sex act, I pulled out my knife and started to stab her. I climaxed, as if it had happened during a natural sex act. I started to put the sperm into her vagina by hand.

Chikatilo had discovered, almost by accident, that the act of stabbing, attacking and killing got him aroused. From this point forwards, there was to be no turning back. For the next three years, whenever he was alone, Chikatilo thought of nothing else but the urge to relive this experience with Lena Zakotnova. He would even cut short business trips and return home, rather than face the temptation to find a victim and kill again. But in autumn 1981 he succumbed once more. This time it was back in Novoshakhtinsk, where he spotted a runaway girl, Larisa Tkachenko, sitting in a bus shelter. Chikatilo approached her, and after a brief conversation the teenager offered to have sex with Chikatilo in exchange for a little money.

Chikatilo took Larisa Tkachenko into some nearby woods and immediately jumped on her. Remembering what got him so aroused back in the hut in Shakhty, Chikatilo strangled the girl violently and bit into her neck with his teeth, drinking her blood and smearing it on his face. He sunk his teeth into her breasts, swallowed her nipples, and also mutilated her genitals. It was at this moment that Chikatilo first discovered that the flesh and blood of his victims also brought him to ejaculation.

After the murder of Larisa Tkachenko, Chikatilo started to kill on a regular basis. That same year, he left the teaching profession and started work as a supplies administrator for a construction firm. His new job involved travelling around the Soviet Union sourcing and collecting replacement supplies for his company, Rostovnerud. It would serve as a convenient cover for finding and killing his victims when he was travelling on 'business trips'.

Over the next eleven years Chikatilo murdered at least fifty-one more women and children. Almost all of his victims were runaways or vagrants, and in his confessions later Chikatilo expressed his disgust at these kinds of people, calling them 'déclassé elements... always pestering people for one thing or another'. But Chikatilo's motives were only partly driven by some kind of misplaced desire to rid the streets of these 'anti-social elements'. It became very apparent from the state of the victims' bodies that there was something far more disturbing about his behaviour, something that could only be associated with dark sexual perversions.

Chikatilo was satisfying his deepest sexual desires, and, as the murders continued, like all sadistic killers he began to search for variation. After the earlier more frenzied stabbing attacks, he started using his knife more precisely, inflicting shallower wounds to prolong the victims' suffering. He also started cutting off boys' genitals and excising the uterus from his female victims, chewing and eating them to attain new heights of sexual pleasure. His wife also told police that Chikatilo had carried a pot and pans with him on his 'business trips', and police found traces of campfires near some of the victims, which suggested that Chikatilo had also tried cooking his victims' sex organs.

Eventually, the police caught up with Chikatilo. The arrest that the whole of Rostov had been hoping for came on 20 November 1990. Chikatilo was brought in for questioning, and the police soon matched his business trips to some of the murder cases they had been investigating. The police brought in a Rostov psychiatrist, Alexandr Bukhanovsky, who helped coax a full confession out of Chikatilo. As it turned out, Chikatilo seemed keen to unburden himself of the massive psychological load he had been carrying for so many years.

The police charged Chikatilo with thirty-six murders, but he surprised them by confessing to another nineteen. For the next eighteen months, he was comprehensively questioned by the police investigators about every single one of his crimes, as well as many other unsolved murders. Chikatilo told his investigators: 'The more I've thought about it, the more I've come to the conclusion that I suffer from some kind of sickness. It was as if something directed me, something outside me, when I committed these murders.' Pre-empting an insanity defence, the police also sent Chikatilo to the Serbsky Psychiatric Institute in Moscow, where a young psychiatrist, Andrei Tkachenko, would examine Chikatilo for two months.

Andrei Chikatilo's trial began on 14 April 1992 in Rostov-on-Don's main court and lasted over six months. The trial has since become memorable for the cage in which Chikatilo was kept during proceedings. Feigning insanity, Chikatilo often played up to the court from his cage: exposing his penis, singing the communist anthem, the Internationale, and at one point unbuttoning his shirt and saying, 'It's time for me to give birth!' But the presiding judge ignored Chikatilo's rants, and on 15 October 1992 he found Chikatilo guilty and sane of all but one of the fifty-three murders.

Chikatilo was imprisoned in Mosow and left to await execution. When his punishment was finally meted out to him, it was all done in the prescribed Russian manner. On 16 February 1994 two soldiers simply arrived unannounced at Chikatilo's cell early that morning, and then led him down to the execution room, where one of them put a pistol to the back of his head and killed him with a single shot. The notorious cannibal killer of Rostov-on-Don was dead.

Three years before Chikatilo's execution, another cannibal killer in America, Arthur Shawcross, was caught. Shawcross was dubbed the Genesee River Killer, because all his murders took place close to the main river that runs through Rochester, New York. Now in prison, he prefers to be known as a real-life Hannibal Lecter. We went to interview him for the television series to find out what made him develop into a cannibal killer.

Arthur Shawcross's eleven murders in Rochester took place between February 1988 and January 1990. Nine of his victims were prostitutes, and they were all killed either by strangulation or by a blow to the head. Most of the bodies had also been severely mutilated after death.

When the police eventually caught Shawcross, they discovered that he had actually been in prison before. Back in 1972 in Watertown, upstate New York, Shawcross had been convicted of the rape and manslaughter of an eight-year-old girl, Karen Ann Hill. He also confessed in prison to murdering another child, ten-year-old boy Jack Blake, but he was never charged with this crime. Shawcross had been sentenced to twenty-five years in prison, but the parole board granted him early release in March 1987. Eleven months later, he committed his first murder in Rochester. This was obviously a source of acute embarrassment for the Rochester police. Incredibly, during the whole of their three-year hunt for the Genesee River Killer, no one on the police's task force uncovered the fact that a known sex offender and child killer who was still on parole was living in their midst.

It was in Shawcross's lengthy confessions that the ghastly truth about what he had done to his victims finally emerged. He told police that he liked to go back to his victims after killing them, and that he became sexually aroused either by looking at their dead bodies or by mutilating the corpses. With two of the victims, he had cut out their vaginas and eaten them. He also revealed that in 1972 he had cut out Jack Blake's heart and genitals and eaten them. The police were dealing with not only a sex murderer but a sex murderer who was also a cannibal.

Shawcross himself is keen to pin much of the blame for his murders – both in 1972 and in Rochester – on his experiences in Vietnam, explaining, 'I was trained to kill. I was not trained to stop. Even today that bothers me.' Vietnam is also the place where Shawcross first tried out cannibalism. According to

Shawcross, he frequently went on patrols into enemy areas by himself, on search-and-destroy missions where he was given licence to destroy everything. In one particular incident, Shawcross says that he surprised two Vietcong women in the jungle. He managed to kill the first woman and then tied the second one to a tree and forced her to watch while he cut up and cooked her dead comrade's body:

> I made a little campfire there, and I took the leg, the right leg from that woman's body, from the knee to the hip, took the skin off, took the cords out and took the fat off and it was only – what? – dead leg around anyway. And I had crushed rock salt in one of my oil pouches, and I sprinkled water on it, and I'm staring at this other girl because I don't know if she speaks English or whatever, broken English, and I'm putting the rock salt on it, and I'm sitting there cooking over a fire, you know. And when I bit into it, looking at... staring this other girl in the eye, she just urinated right there, you know.

There is disagreement on whether Shawcross's claims of cannibalism are true or a weird form of bravado. The autopsies of the bodies retrieved from the river were so decomposed that the evidence of cannibalism is inconclusive. But either way, the cannibalism has become part of the legend Shawcross has created. Dr Jonathan Pincus of Georgetown University is the psychiatrist who has most recently questioned Shawcross about his cannibalism. He remains fairly convinced that Shawcross is telling the truth:

I'm not sure why someone would claim to do that if they hadn't done it. Now whether it occurred as often as he said it did, whether it occurred at all, it's obviously something that gives him satisfaction to talk about, to think about and to pose about. Let's say he didn't do it; let's say he's just fantasizing the whole thing or lying about it. It really doesn't matter. Obviously, he wants people to think that he was a cannibal and he ate these victims – it represents his mastery over these women he killed. It represents his complete control and makes him seem important and unusual and, I guess in his own mind, competent.

Arthur Shawcross was born in 1945 to a US Marine and a teenage mother. He claims that from the outset his life was blighted: his most controversial claim is that he was abused as a child. His defence team asked criminal psychiatrist Dorothy Otnow Lewis to testify in court that Shawcross was insane. Lewis spent several hours conducting interviews with Shawcross, in which she hypnotized him, and supposedly 'uncovered' evidence that Shawcross's mother had abused him when he was a young boy.

Rochester psychiatrist Dr Richard Kraus compiled an extensive report on Arthur Shawcross for the murder trial in which he attempted to find out what made Shawcross become a serial killer. Kraus does not believe any of the allegations of child abuse:

When I first met Shawcross – and I was one of the earliest psychiatrists to start seeing him – I'd ask him about these things as part of a routine evaluation about early life. And I was looking for abuse and so on. Nothing! Nothing at all! Besides, when I saw the records from when he was seven and eight years old, the records describe him as a boy 'well cared for'. And that speaks volumes to this whole issue of whether he was abused.

The other thing, too, was that in my going over the history with Shawcross now, step by step through his life, at no time did he ever make any reference to abuse until much later, and by that time he'd been so contaminated by all the people questioning him and cross-questioning him that at the end, at the end of the year, he was telling me: 'Well, I think I had sex with my mother.' I mean, it was just absurd! And I think he was beginning to try to portray himself as really crazy, when in fact he wasn't.

Kraus looked back into Shawcross's childhood and found out that, far from being abused, Shawcross had actually had quite a pleasant upbringing. Shawcross's family lived in Brownville, a small settlement outside Watertown, New York. In an era when paper mills were continually shutting down, Brownville's two big mills still ran twenty-four-hour shifts, and the townsfolk enjoyed a modest level of prosperity. Arthur's grandparents lived nearby, as did many of his cousins, and by all accounts the community was friendly and supportive, where a young boy could enjoy a very happy childhood.

However, as Kraus went through Shawcross's medical history, he found more and more that the psychiatrists who treated him all gave up in the end: they simply dismissed Shawcross as 'different', 'odd' and 'untreatable'. His childhood had been pretty unremarkable. The fact was, Shawcross's medical and school reports showed that he hadn't become 'odd' as he grew up, suggesting that childhood experiences had shaped him for the worst. Rather, he had always been 'different', from a very early age.

What was more, Shawcross had suffered traumatic head injuries on a number of occasions. At one time at high school he was hit by a discus on the side of his head at point-blank range, and when he was eighteen he was hit by a sledgehammer while working on a building site. On both occasions he was knocked out and concussed. Could he have sustained brain damage from these two incidents? Kraus organized a number of tests on Shawcross, including brain scans, genetic and biochemical tests, the results of which we will discuss in the next chapter.

Until 1991 the city of Milwaukee's biggest claim to fame was probably its beer. But then the appalling crimes of Jeffrey Dahmer were made public all over the world. Milwaukee suddenly became world famous for spawning America's worst cannibal serial killer.

On a sticky summer night on 22 July 1991, two police officers were driving along North 25th Street, a residential street in one of Milwaukee's rougher areas, when they almost ran over a half-naked black man wearing a pair of handcuffs. The man told them that some 'freak' had placed the handcuffs on him, and could they please remove them. The two police officers wandered over to Apartment 213, Oxford Buildings, expecting to have to deal with a routine domestic fight.

The man who let the police in to Apartment 213 was Jeffrey Dahmer. He seemed a clean-cut, polite young man, and the apartment he lived in was surprisingly neat and tidy for that neighbourhood. Dahmer assured the officers there was nothing to worry about. As he looked for the key to the handcuffs, one of the officers spotted a large knife lying beneath the bed. In the top drawer of a chest, he could see piles of Polaroid photographs of what looked like naked men. But when the officer looked closer, he realized that many of these pictures were of dismembered body parts, severed heads and decomposing torsos. Some of the photographs were of Dahmer himself, engaging in sex acts with the body parts.

The two officers moved to arrest Dahmer, and after a brief struggle they had him in handcuffs pinned to the ground. While one police officer called for backup, the other started to look around the apartment. He opened the fridge and saw on the bottom shelf a cardboard box containing the severed head of a black man, facing upwards. The ghastly odyssey into the perverted world of Jeffrey Dahmer was about to begin.

Over the next few days, Milwaukee police officers and forensic examiners went over every inch of Dahmer's apartment, removing a vast collection of grisly finds. What they took away included: chemicals for preserving human body parts; dried genitals and hands; seven bleached human skulls and a complete skeleton; a fifty-seven-gallon blue plastic drum with three human torsos in various stages of dismemberment and decomposition; and a free-standing freezer cabinet containing three more heads as well as zip-locked bags of human flesh.

At the same time, Jeffrey Dahmer was just at the beginning of his long and detailed confession, in which he would admit to seventeen murders over a period of thirteen years. His first victim was hitchhiker Steven Hicks, whom Dahmer had picked up near his parents' house in June 1978. Dahmer was just eighteen years old. He invited the young man back to his home and the two of them drank beer and smoked some marijuana together. But then things got out of hand. 'The guy wanted to leave,' Dahmer told the police thirteen years later, 'and I didn't want him to.' Dahmer became angry and battered the hitchhiker to death with a barbell.

The hitchhiker now lay limp and dead on the floor. Dahmer undressed the man, stroked his chest and masturbated over the corpse. The next day, overcome by fear and panic, he moved the corpse to the 'crawlspace' underneath the house and dismembered the body, putting the parts into three rubbish bags. At the same time he paused to slit open the belly – he wanted to examine the organs inside. After completing the dismemberment, he stuffed the rubbish bags down a drainage pipe at the back of the house, covering them with earth.

Dahmer's bizarre obsessions had now developed into murder, and he would never be able to return to normality afterwards. For the next nine years he desperately tried to fight his urges, but the battle was one he lost steadily. He had started drinking heavily while still in high school, but his alcohol problems became much worse. He enrolled at university but was thrown out shortly afterwards, partly because of his drinking. He enlisted in the army, serving for almost two years in Germany, but the army's regular supply of heavily subsidized alcohol again led to his being discharged early. The army did, however, train Dahmer as a medic for six months, and this training ironically gave him skills that he would put to use when he started killing again.

After his early discharge from the army, Dahmer lived in Florida for a few months before returning to his family in September 1981. He moved in with his grandmother in West Allis, Wisconsin, but things got even worse. His drinking continued, and then Dahmer was arrested for exhibitionism at a local state fair. Dahmer's behaviour was embarrassing his family, and he decided to make a fresh go of things. He started going to church and reading the Bible with his grandmother. Dahmer admired his grandmother's faith, one he wished he could share. He also felt guilty about his homosexual thoughts and fantasies. Both his father and grandmother were devout churchgoers – his father, Lionel, was a Lutheran who practised a particularly austere brand of Protestantism – and for a while Jeffrey Dahmer truly believed that religion would lead him out of his obsessions.

After a while, however, his interest in religion started to wear off, and the old urges came back to Jeffrey Dahmer. He stole a mannequin from a department store and slept with it, imagining it was a real person. He even went to the local cemetery with the intention of digging up a corpse and taking it home. And then he began submitting to his homosexual desires. He started frequenting gay bathhouses in Milwaukee, where it was easy to meet and have sex with other men. But what Dahmer really desired was for the other man to keep still. He later explained: 'I trained myself to view people as objects of potential pleasure instead of people, instead of seeing them as complete human beings.' And to this end he started drugging potential partners with sleeping pills, causing them to fall unconscious. With a partner now asleep and still, Dahmer would lie next to him, fondling him and masturbating himself, and also lay his head on the other man's chest to listen to his heartbeat. After a while, the bathhouses received complaints about Dahmer, and the management revoked his membership.

Dahmer's struggles against his dark side came to an abrupt end on 16 November 1987. He picked up Steven Tuomi at the 219 Club, a popular gay disco in downtown Milwaukee. The two men returned to the Ambassador Hotel, a guesthouse frequented mainly by gay men. Dahmer was already very drunk, and became even drunker. What happened next is unclear, but the next morning he woke up with a corpse next to him; Tuomi had been strangled. Dahmer would later express remorse about this killing, saying that he had not intended to murder Tuomi. However, this was the event that precipitated Dahmer's final bloody killing spree. He was to kill another fifteen men in just three years. And he would not be able to stop killing, right up until that sticky night when two police officers stepped into his apartment on 22 July 1991.

Dahmer's killing spree began in earnest. He killed three more men at his grandmother's house, and then found his own apartment in Milwaukee where he could kill even more regularly. 'For a long time, it was just once every two months,' he said. 'Near the end it was once every week... Just really got completely out of control.' Typically, Dahmer would invite his victims back to his flat, where he would drug them. And when they had fallen asleep, Dahmer could do what he wanted with them. But once the drug wore off, Dahmer resorted to other methods to keep his victims 'asleep', usually strangling them with his bare hands. And when the victim was dead, Dahmer's sexual desires would be unleashed. He would have sex with the corpse and masturbate on the body. He dissected the bodies in different ways, taking Polaroid photographs of the process. He stored different body parts, keeping them in the freezer or preserving them with chemicals.

And then, with about his sixth or seventh victim, Dahmer turned to cannibalism. 'It started out as experimentation,' he said, 'because it made me feel like they were more a part of me.' He told police detectives that he ate hearts, liver and thighs. He even bought an adapter for his gas stove so that he could char-broil the meat. Dahmer even had a favourite part of the body, the bicep, which he said tasted just like 'filet mignon'. When the police opened up his freezer back at the main administration building, they found individually wrapped portions of heart, thigh and bicep, some of which had already been tenderized and had the fat trimmed from them.

On 27 January 1992 the trial of Jeffrey Dahmer began in Milwaukee. With Dahmer's full confession, it was only ever going to be a trial about whether or not Dahmer was insane when committing his crimes. A long line of expert psychiatrists testified for both defence and prosecution, but in the end the jury's verdict was really a foregone conclusion. Faced with the details of such a gruesome crime, and surrounded by weeping relatives of the victims, it was hardly surprising that their final verdict was to find Dahmer guilty and sane in all seventeen counts of murder. He was sentenced to over nine hundred years in prison, for the state of Wisconsin had no death penalty. Two and a half years later, another prison inmate bludgeoned Dahmer to death. In a final irony, Dahmer was killed by a barbell, just as his first victim had been murdered all those years before.

There are no immediately obvious clues in Jeffrey Dahmer's childhood of what might have caused him to turn into a cannibal killer. He had a seemingly normal childhood, living with his research chemist father, mother and younger brother in an upper-middle-class neighbourhood in Bath township, Ohio. If one looks at the home movies filmed by Dahmer's father Lionel, the whole family look happy together. But in reality Lionel Dahmer and his wife Joyce had a very troubled marriage. Joyce suffered from depression and was addicted to painkillers, and both she and Lionel argued frequently. Police were called to the house more than once, and a divorce was granted on 24 July 1978, after each of the parents charged the other with 'extreme cruelty and gross neglect'.

During this childhood, Jeffrey Dahmer retreated into his own world, becoming progressively shyer. He developed a fascination, however, with dead animals and would pick up road kills, dissect them and pickle their bones in jars of formaldehyde. The scientifically minded Lionel Dahmer was actually pleased to see his son take up this interest, and even thought that this might be the first steps towards a career in science or anatomy.

At thirteen, Dahmer realized he was gay, a cause of great concern for him because his father was such a strict Lutheran. He told police interviewers that by the time he was sixteen, he was already having strong sexual fantasies, most of which involved his having total control over his partner. As we have already discovered, Dahmer started drinking heavily when he was still in high school, and heavy drinking was later to become both his escape from and the fuel for the realization of his gruesome fantasies. It was only a few years before the fateful encounter with the hitchhiker and Dahmer's first step towards becoming a cannibal killer.

Issei Sagawa is extraordinary among cannibal killers. One afternoon in Paris in 1981, he invited a girl he had befriended back to his flat, shot her and began to eat her. But while all other known cannibal killers are either in jail or dead, Issei Sagawa lives free in a small flat just outside Tokyo. We flew to Tokyo for an exclusive interview with the only convicted cannibal killer living at liberty.

Sagawa was born in Tokyo in 1949 to very wealthy parents. By his own admission, he has been obsessed with cannibalism from a very early age. When he was three years old, his parents held a New Year party where his father and his uncle Mitsuo played a game that strongly affected the young Issei. Uncle Mitsuo was a flesh-eating giant who wanted to gobble up Issei and his brother, while their father was a brave knight who tried to defend the children. But the game ended with the cannibal giant devouring the knight, and then carrying off the brothers to his cooking pot. As criminologist Colin Wilson explains, this had a profound effect on the child Sagawa:

> I'm sure this is the answer to why it affected Issei so deeply – these games made him probably scream with a sort of pleasurable fear. And having acquired a taste for that thrill, Issei then turns to fairy stories that include brutality and sadism and begins to enjoy them. You can also see that it's beginning to spread across his life like a kind of stain.
>
> And as Issei grows older, the games and fairy stories have this effect on him, because he has nothing else to focus on. Now anything you focus your whole attention on acquires a kind of unhealthy significance for you. If you could concentrate your mind totally on anything at all for a quarter of an hour, you would remember it for the rest of your life. It would stick. That's one of the basic laws of psychology, and it's certainly true as far as Issei is concerned. From then on there was an association in his mind with eating and horror and pain.

Sagawa became obsessed with the idea of cannibalism, reading about it in fairy tales and comic books. He even tried to confess his secret desires to his brother, as he explained:

> When I was sleeping with my brother I tried to tell him that when I saw a beautiful girl I wanted to eat her. But my brother didn't understand. He laughed, so I was very

ashamed. I felt very ashamed, and I thought I would
never tell another person.

Sagawa went to Wako University in Tokyo to study English literature. It was here that he first tried to act out his cannibal
fantasy. He broke into a German woman's apartment while she
was sleeping, intending to knock her unconscious and take a
bite out of her. But the woman woke up and raised the alarm.
As a result, Sagawa started seeing a psychiatrist, who declared
that Sagawa was 'extremely dangerous'. But the incident was
hushed up, and in the late 1970s Sagawa, with the support of
his wealthy father, went to live in Paris to study for his PhD at
the Sorbonne.

Sagawa was almost thirty by the time he arrived in Paris, and
deep down he must have felt that time was running out for him
to realize his cannibal dream. He started seeing prostitutes in
Paris frequently, and on a couple of occasions tried to kill them
and eat them. He even bought a rifle, intending to use it
to kill one of the prostitutes. And every day his obsession grew
stronger, Sagawa told us:

Always I want, every evening, every night, that I should
realize my fantasy on that night. Always in the sunset,
after the sunset, always I thought the same thing. This
is very, very hard. During the day, I was studying, I was
writing a paper, but when it was dark, the obsession
arrived and I went outside my apartment to look for
prostitutes. Then when I have them in the house, in my
room, when they use the bidet, I tried to shoot but I
couldn't, really couldn't. It's not the sense of morality or
something. I don't think so. I was scared.

The obstacle between Sagawa and his lifelong desire was the killing. On 11 June 1981 he finally overcame this obstacle. He invited a Dutch student whom he had met, Renee Hartevelt, to his apartment, where she had agreed to give him lessons in German. When she arrived, he asked her to sit down and read out some poetry. As she was doing this, Sagawa walked around behind her and shot her in the back of the head. Sagawa described the whole incident to us:

> This day it's very hot, very sunny day and, Renee, she looks very healthy, and I felt a sunbeam penetrated in her body, and me, I feel very weak, and I want the energy of her. Even the sunbeams. I took the gun and aim and I fire. And she fell down on the table. Too much blood, her face all completely pale. I thought I have to call the police or the ambulance, really, but suddenly I realized for my fantasy I killed her.
>
> I carry the body to the bathroom and I began to cut. I choose a little, little fork, I pick, I try to pick but I couldn't. Finally I take the big knife and push. Fat is very like yellow corn, and cut, cut, cut, and finally I could find the red one. I cut and I put the red meat in the mouth.

With eating came the sexual release that Sagawa had been craving. He had sex with the corpse before proceeding to dismember the body. With an electric carving knife he carefully removed strips of flesh to store in his fridge. Some pieces he ate raw, others he fried with salt, pepper and mustard. This would continue for another four days. One of Sagawa's neighbours reported hearing him howling and banging the walls during one of these nights. But by 15 June Sagawa needed to find a way of disposing of the rest of the corpse. He bought two enormous suitcases and filled them with body parts, hoping to dump them in a lake in the Bois de Boulogne. Not surprisingly, the sight of a diminutive Japanese man dragging two large suitcases attracted lots of attention. Sagawa took fright and ran off, leaving the suitcases, which were found to contain human remains. The police soon tracked Sagawa down at his flat near the Sorbonne.

Sagawa was arrested and committed for trial. But in 1983 the presiding judge decided that Sagawa was mentally incompetent to stand trial, that criminal charges should be dropped because Sagawa was in a 'state of dementia' at the time of the murder, and that he should be placed in a secure mental hospital indefinitely. And so Sagawa was sent to an asylum just outside Paris, where doctors labelled him 'an untreatable psychotic'.

Twenty-two months later, Sagawa was suddenly sent back to Japan. The authorities in Paris decided that there was no point in the French taxpayer spending millions of francs trying to treat someone who was, in their words, 'untreatable'. He was to be treated by Japanese doctors, and he entered the Matsuzawa Hospital in Tokyo.

Implicitly, for the French as well as for the Japanese, his hospitalization was to be for a lifetime, but on his return to Japan, Sagawa found that he had become a celebrity. Crowds of journalists were waiting for him when he flew in, and the media interest continued when he was at the hospital: photographers waited opposite his bedroom window, hoping to get photographs of him with long lenses. The doctors became more and more angry at the constant press attention – one doctor even thought Sagawa had used the cannibalism as an excuse to be declared insane, stating, 'I think he is sane and guilty.'

The Japanese police felt the same, and they wanted to reopen the case and try Sagawa for murder. They tried to get Sagawa's dossier from Paris, but the French refused to hand it over – if Sagawa was found guilty, this would amount to an open criticism of the French justice system.

On 15 September 1985 the hospital superintendent decided to discharge Issei Sagawa. Matsuzawa Hospital had had enough of holding Japan's notorious cannibal killer. Sagawa changed his name and moved to a small flat close to his parents.

Then, in August 1989, a child serial killer, Tsutomu Miyazaki, was caught in Japan. A local TV station contacted Sagawa to see if he could offer any expert comment. Shortly afterwards, Sagawa was offered other work by the media. This started to snowball until he was even reviewing restaurants and writing columns in a pornographic magazine. By the mid-1990s Issei Sagawa the Cannibal Killer had become Issei Sagawa the Cannibal Celebrity. He started appearing in pornographic films, some of which even featured pastiches of the murder he'd committed in 1981. At the same time, he has also published over eight books – all of which deal with his obsession with cannibalism, often in graphic detail.

Four cannibal killers – two dead, one in prison, and one a minor celebrity. The acts of these individuals are so repulsive that it is hard to look beyond the savagery of their crimes in search of explanation. We have already looked for possible clues in each of their childhoods, but can science and medicine also provide us with answers? In the next chapter, we examine some of the latest scientific research into what makes a psychopathic killer.

ELEVEN
Nature vs Nurture

> Ladies and gentlemen, in this case, you're going to hear
> about things you probably didn't know existed in the real
> world. In this case, you're going to hear about sexual
> conduct before death, during death, and after death. Will
> you be so disgusted by that you won't be able to listen?

This was how Jeffrey Dahmer's defence attorney began his opening speech in the trial of his notorious client. And so it was that over the next three weeks a courtroom of jurors, lawyers, expert witnesses, victims' relatives, journalists and a packed public gallery were to listen to the hideous facts behind each one of Dahmer's disturbing murders. The trials of Jeffrey Dahmer, Andrei Chikatilo and Arthur Shawcross all unfolded the very same way. In each case, jurors and/or judges, victims' relatives and members of the public were taken into the perverted worlds of these three cannibal killers. In Chikatilo's trial, the graphic horror was so much that one of the soldiers standing guard actually fainted. And after Dahmer's trial, several of the jurors needed psychological counselling after sifting through vast amounts of the grisly details of what Dahmer did to his victims.

The ghastliness of these cannibal killers' acts unfortunately takes us further away from trying to comprehend their aberrant behaviour. Are they simply evil, perverted individuals, who choose to go out, kill and cannibalize their victims just for the fun of it? Are they in fact in some way damaged by external, socio-environmental factors around them? Or is there another explanation for the genesis of the cannibal killer? We have already cast a cursory glance into each of these cannibal killers' childhoods and backgrounds in the last chapter. But what were the most significant events and experiences in their early lives, events that might have contributed to their later development into cannibal murderers?

As discussed in the previous chapter, Andrei Chikatilo was haunted from an early age by the idea that his brother Stephan had been kidnapped and killed by a gang of cannibals. But it is equally important to trace the course of Chikatilo's childhood, during which he came to discover that he was sexually aroused by violent thoughts and acts. The psychiatrist who examined Chikatilo in Moscow, Andrei Tkachenko, explained to us:

Chikatilo lived in occupied territory, so together with thoughts of the brother who had been eaten, his head was filled with memories, at least as he tells it, of the victims of the bombings he witnessed. There were bodies torn apart, blood and so on and so forth. At the time, there was a sense of fear, and later this sense of fear and this series of emotions were of course transformed. In adolescence he started to resort to certain types of fantasies, fantasies with themes that featured sadistic, aggressive experiences. For example, he loved books about the partisans, and in his fantasies he imagined himself as a member of a partisan brigade who, on the orders of his commander, takes a German prisoner for interrogation and humiliates him in all sorts of ways – beats him, tortures him and so on. So this taste for aggressive tendencies, including sadistic ones, could already be seen.

As we have seen, Chikatilo's childhood was coloured by the awkward relationship he had with his mother. Anna Chikatilo was a fierce, domineering woman with a cruel and nasty temper. After Andrei Chikatilo's sentence, even his sister Tatyana found it hard to say a good word about their mother, telling a newspaper interviewer: 'We were very poor and we were hungry. My parents worked day and night and got nothing for it. My father was kind despite it all. But my mother was very harsh and rude. I suppose it was because of the difficulties of her life. But she only yelled at us and bawled us out. She never had a kind word.'

The fact that Chikatilo wet his bed until the age of twelve, a bed that he shared with his mother, also drove her into terrible rages. Andrei Tkachenko could only imagine how this period might have affected Chikatilo – his mother's foul temper, her strong words, and the blows that would rain down on her weak son. Chikatilo was also teased and bullied mercilessly at school, and this, too, played a part in developing his feelings towards other people. These childhood experiences undoubtedly played a part in shaping Andrei Chikatilo, and turning him into the awkward, solitary character he became, beset by feelings of humiliation and inadequacy. However, for psychiatrist Andrei Tkachenko, the fact that Chikatilo had a difficult childhood could not be the only cause of his development into a cannibal killer. Tkachenko explained:

You see, would every boy who lived through the occupation, every boy who was told frightening stories, remember such early childhood memories with such emotion? No, of course not. So here a particular mental background must have determined the way these memories were ingrained and preserved, and their emotional significance for Chikatilo's subsequent development. There can be no doubt that in this case social factors had a huge significance. There is no way they could not have any significance. But the thing is that in this case they were probably secondary. Secondary because, let us say, this boy was already developing along defective lines, as a consequence of certain deficits which he already had, and had had from birth.

Unlike Andrei Chikatilo, Jeffrey Dahmer was born into a comfortable, middle-class family who lived in relative rural tranquillity in Ohio. At first glance, Dahmer's childhood was a happy one. But several events in his childhood may have proved significantly formative for the young boy's development. Author Brian Masters, who studied and wrote about the case at length, interviewed Dahmer as well as his father and stepmother. Masters had this to say about Dahmer's upbringing:

His parents were attentive to him in their manner, but their manner was – how can I put it? – diluted. In his father's case it was diluted by two things. First of all he was a very busy man; he was hardly ever at home. He spent the week in another state working and came home at weekends. Secondly, he was also himself a withdrawn character, not a demonstrative, outgoing, loquacious man but a quiet, subdued, controlled man, not the sort of person who would throw his hands around his son and cuddle him. His mother was more demonstrative, but all her demonstrations have been reserved for herself. She had become a hypochondriac. She was taking pills for everything all day long, and pills to go to sleep at night as well. She was always lying in bed during the afternoon [and] the morning – any excuse to lie down and feel ill... The degree of regard she had for herself excluded the possibility of maternal regard for her son. Or so it appeared. So the boy in fact grew up with perfectly normal parents on the outside, but parents who were in some degree removed from what one would expect an affectionate life to contain.

As Dahmer grew up, his parents' once-happy marriage started to crumble. The strain of Joyce Dahmer's worsening drug addiction and Lionel Dahmer's absence from the family home took their toll, and Jeffrey's parents argued frequently. This unhappy atmosphere at home simply forced Jeffrey Dahmer into his own private world, a world of fantasies that revolved around dissecting dead animals and playing with their bones. During his teenage years, alcohol began to play a major part in Dahmer's life. At the age of fourteen he was already drinking heavily, and alcohol would later be the agent that bypassed his inhibitions and fuelled his aggressive sexual urges.

Summer 1978 was the period when Lionel and Joyce Dahmer's marriage reached its absolute nadir. Although they had been arguing and fighting for many years, it was not until now – when Jeffrey was already eighteen – that they finally moved towards getting divorced. During the acrimonious divorce negotiations, Lionel and Joyce accused each other of neglect and cruelty, and Lionel alleged that Joyce was suffering from 'extreme mental illness'. Lionel moved out of the family home into a motel in a neighbouring township, and when Joyce moved away, taking Jeffrey's younger brother David with her, Jeffrey Dahmer was left alone in the house. It was shortly after this that Jeffrey Dahmer met and murdered the first of his seventeen victims, hitchhiker Steven Hicks.

But why was Jeffrey Dahmer so introverted and why did he become so obsessively interested in dissecting dead animals, to such an extent that when he reached puberty he found that the dead animals' viscera aroused him sexually? Plenty of other boys are shy and reclusive, and occupy themselves with odd, sometimes gruesome pastimes, but none of them grow up to be cannibal killers.

Issei Sagawa was born to extremely wealthy parents and, again, like Dahmer, his childhood had the outward appearance of being happy and contented. But perhaps the most significant fact about Sagawa's early years is that he was born very small and weak. He was a premature baby, so small that his father could hold him in the palm of one hand. And as Sagawa grew older, his size and frailty affected him profoundly. He admitted to us:

When I was born, I was very small, very ugly, so I think my mother had a sense of guilt or shame. For Japanese, shame is almost the same thing as guilt. I was very weak. I was short... I always wanted to be more strong, more big, and so, in that sense, I feel different. I got sick very often... [and] I was not so happy at school, especially when I was a high school student. Sometimes they [the other students] said something that hurt me: 'You are very small' or short or thin, something like that. It hurt me very, very profoundly.

Sagawa believes that this inferiority complex, his awareness of being weaker and smaller – for he is markedly smaller than most Japanese men and women – is the reason why he is attracted to tall, Western women, as opposed to Japanese women:

> Because I'm short and small, I admire tall and beautiful women. Maybe I like their strength, and also their beauty... In the case of Japanese women, I feel they are like my own daughter or sister, and so I don't have [any] sexual desire for them. I prefer [young] white girls.

We have already seen how the cannibal giant game that Sagawa played with his uncle Mitsuo had a profound effect on the young child's thoughts and fantasies. Some writers have also speculated that other cultural influences may lie behind Sagawa's aberrant behaviour. In *Cannibal Killers*, Moira Martingale points out that the Japanese, more than most nationalities, have demonstrated a peculiar appetite for the bizarre, especially if there is a macabre element of suffering to spice up the entertainment value. Examples include the hugely popular *Endurance* game shows, and also the life and work of Yukio Mishima, one of the most successful Japanese writers of all time. This fascination for the unusual may go some way towards explaining the celebrity status Sagawa has gained in the Japanese media.

However, many babies – Japanese or not – are born premature and weak. And many young children are profoundly affected by fairy tales and childhood games. But there is only one Issei Sagawa. Is there another explanation for his development into a cannibal killer?

Our fourth cannibal killer, Arthur Shawcross, also enjoyed a relatively happy childhood. His parents' marriage was a good one, and both his father and mother tried to bring their son up as best they could. Although Shawcross tried to claim that he had been abused by his mother, these allegations were not only denied by his entire family but have also been roundly rebutted by psychiatrist Richard Kraus. Kraus wrote about Shawcross's childhood in a report he prepared for the Wayne County defence team:

> In his [Shawcross's] case, there was no predisposing family history of alcoholism, violence, criminality, or psychiatric disorder and no evidence of parental abuse, neglect, abandonment or cruelty. However, at age seven years, this '...bright, well-dressed, neat...' child (as he was then described) was beginning to exhibit solitary aggressive conduct, disordered behaviours which set him apart from his family, alienated him from his peers, and probably contributed to his becoming a loner.

When Shawcross was seven years old, Kraus reported, he was referred to a mental health clinic after hitting other schoolchildren with an iron bar on a school bus. A couple of years later, he was caught stealing money from a teacher's purse. The problems at school continued into his teenage years, and Shawcross left at the age of fifteen. Later, a police background investigation contacted people who remembered him as a child and teenager. The investigation received responses that pointed towards a consistent theme: 'Not too bright... different-acting... kind of strange... a loner... aggressive... quick-tempered... known for fast mood changes...'

Six months after quitting school, Shawcross was arrested for burgling a local shop and placed on eighteen months' probation. Two years later he committed another burglary shortly before he left for his thirteen-month tour of duty in Vietnam. And after his return from Vietnam in 1969, he burgled a petrol station and committed three arsons. This time, Shawcross received a custodial sentence, spending five months in prison. Just over a year later, in May 1972, he became a suspect in the disappearance of Jack Blake. Then, in September that year, Arthur Shawcross was charged with the rape and murder of Karen Ann Hill, and was subsequently convicted and sentenced to twenty-five years in prison. Fifteen years later he was released on parole, and within eleven months the Genesee River murders had begun.

Unlike the other cannibal killers we examined, Arthur Shawcross's childhood is probably the most typical of the average serial killer. His progression from anti-social behaviour in the classroom at a young age, to petty crime, burglary and arson, and finally to rape and murder, is a progression that psychiatrists have found in many other sadistic killers. Many studies have suggested that this model of behaviour is usually found in killers who grew up in broken homes, or who were severely abused as a child, or whose parents punished them violently. But by all accounts, Arthur Shawcross had experienced none of these, and yet from a very young age he was profoundly disturbed, with anti-social and violent tendencies. Is there another explanation for Arthur Shawcross's violence?

Ultimately, it appears that we cannot simply look to socio-environmental factors when examining the reasons why these four individuals developed into cannibal killers. As we have seen, not every Ukrainian child grew up with dark dreams of cannibalism; Issei Sagawa was not the only Japanese child to be weak and tiny; and Jeffrey Dahmer wasn't the only boy whose parents divorced acrimoniously.

Could the answer lie elsewhere, in the realm of biology? Are there biochemical or neurological causes that might perhaps have predisposed these four individuals to behave as they did? The search for biological causes of criminal behaviour is a field that has always been wrought with controversy, which is due in particular to the long-standing debate whether our behaviour is driven by socio-environmental (nurture) or biological (nature) causes. Are we 'blank slates' ultimately defined by social and cultural forces, or are we genetically predetermined organisms with prescribed roles to play? Is our behaviour malleable and perfectible, or is it constrained and resistant to change? Are we inherently gentle and altruistic, or are we aggressive, even violent beings, barely civilized by our culture? And more specifically, are the violent criminals in our society 'born' or 'made' – a product of their biology or their environment?

We looked into the medical history of all four cannibal killers, searching for significant evidence of biological abnormalities or dysfunctions. Could science and medicine provide an alternative explanation for the cannibal killer?

Over the last decade, ground-breaking psychiatric research has suggested that biological factors also play a significant role in influencing criminal behaviour. Although socio-environmental factors certainly have a major influence in defining an individual's personality, this research has increasingly shown that biology has a demonstrable effect, either in conjunction with environmental factors, or on its own, predetermining the individual to act and behave in a certain way.

One of the leading researchers in this field is Adrian Raine, a British-born clinical neuroscientist based at the University of Southern California. Raine has worked extensively with psychopathic murderers, looking at possible biological explanations for their behaviour. Because so much of Raine's work has involved examining psychopaths, it is important to run through what is known as the 'psychopathy checklist', first devised by Robert Hare in 1980. Hare's checklist is a set of specific personality traits that characterize the psychopathic individual. These traits include glib and superficial personalities; appearing egocentric and grandiose; a lack of remorse or guilt; a lack of fear; a lack of empathy for other people; and generally blunted, shallow emotions. On a more behavioural level, traits that can account for psychopaths' social deviance include: impulsive reactions; poor behaviour controls; a need for excitement and arousal; lack of responsibility; behaviour problems early on in life; and anti-social behaviour as an adult.

At first glance, one can already see that all our four canni-bal killers exhibit at least some of the features associated with the psychopathic personality. Andrei Chikatilo did not exhibit remorse for any of his fifty-five victims; Jeffrey Dahmer came across as incredibly glib to everyone who met him; Arthur Shawcross again felt no guilt or remorse, and had behavioural problems from a young age; and when he describes his crime, Issei Sagawa displays a noticeable lack of empathy for his victim. But how do the features on the 'psychopathy checklist' work to make a psychopathic individual more predisposed to violence and murder? Adrian Raine explains:

A psychopathic individual is an individual with blunted emotions. One of the defining characteristics is that they lack a conscience. They don't feel bad when they have done something wrong. Most of us will feel bad when we do wrong, and we'd know it, we'd feel guilty. Psychopaths simply lack that emotion. Psychopaths therefore have a completely different emotional make-up from normal people. They lack fear, and so they don't worry about being counterattacked by the person they are attacking, nor do they fear the consequences of their actions, such as prison. And this emotional blunting and lack of empathy means that they are able to 'de-personalize' more easily. This is especially important when it comes to mutilating a victim, cutting up and even cannibalizing them – if you don't relate to other people as persons, as human beings, then of course it is far easier to perform such horrific acts on them without feeling the basic emotions of empathy or disgust.

A common behavioural feature of the psychopathic individual is that they are 'stimulation-seekers'. For a psychopath, normal living is not enough, so they crave excitement and stimulation. And physiological correlates of 'stimulation-seeking' can be measured in clinical tests: low heart rate, low sweat rate and slow brainwave activity. Since the early 1980s, Adrian Raine has been running a series of tests on schoolchildren and following them up when they reach adult life to see which ones have turned into violent offenders:

Our studies found that schoolchildren with low physiological arousal at age fifteen are more likely to become criminal, violent offenders by age twenty-nine. These were schoolboys that we took measures of arousal on at age fifteen and followed it up for over fourteen years. Similarly, on the island of Mauritius, we took over 1,800 children aged three, measured physiological arousal and followed them up, and found that the young children with low physiological arousal were much more likely to become aggressive and anti-social at age eleven. So we have certainly established a link between stimulation-seeking and later anti-social and aggressive behaviour.

Adrian Raine explains why this stimulation-seeking might even lead a psychopath to cannibalism:

> If we turn to cannibalism, it's very difficult to understand why people eat other people's flesh. But we do know that, at one level, breaking boundaries in life, rule-breaking, is linked to low physiological arousal, which we think predisposes to stimulation-seeking. If you view cannibalism as a form of stimulation-seeking, as doing something bizarre, strange and unusual for a kick, then there could be a link here between low physiological arousal, stimulation-seeking and these bizarre acts of eating flesh.

But why do some individuals grow up to become psychopaths? Again, we are dealing with the question of nature vs. nurture. Are they products of their environment? Have they been moulded by bad parenting or broken homes? As we have seen, this can only give us part of the picture. Adrian Raine's clinical research has thrown up startling results that suggest that a variety of biological factors is involved in causing and driving psychopathic behaviour, factors that often work alongside socio-environmental factors to mould and drive the violent offender.

One example of this is the link between birth complications and maternal rejection. Raine and his researchers conducted a study of over 4,300 live male births in Copenhagen, Denmark, in a one-year period. They measured complications at the time of the birth, such as forceps delivery, breach birth, placental abnormalities, pre-eclampsia and anoxia (lack of oxygen to the foetus, which can cause brain damage to the baby). During the first year of the babies' lives, they interviewed the mothers to determine whether or not there was any maternal rejection of the child. This was measured in three ways: firstly, if the mother did not want the pregnancy; secondly, if she had made an attempt to abort the foetus but failed; and thirdly, if the child was institutionalized for at least four months in its infant life, because this kind of detachment caused major disruption to the mother-infant bonding process, which has been shown to lead to psychopathic personalities later in life.

In this way, Raine's researchers were collating a combination of biological measures – birth complications that lead to brain damage – plus a social variable – maternal rejection of the child, which can result in a lack of emotionality and impersonality. They followed up the babies until they were eighteen years old and found that the individuals with this combination of birth complications plus maternal rejection were the most likely people to become violent offenders in adult life.

In researching Issei Sagawa's medical history, we managed to track down a copy of his psychiatric report, compiled by French doctors after his arrest and hospitalization. The psychiatrists examined Sagawa's mother's pregnancy, as well as the birth itself. Both the pregnancy and Sagawa's birth and early infant life met the above criteria almost exactly. During the time that Sagawa's mother was pregnant with him, she almost miscarried at three months. Later on, the doctors recommended an abortion because of poor uterus growth, and there was eclampsia late on in the pregnancy. There were also complications during the birth, including anoxia. And after Sagawa was born, he spent much of the first two years of his life in hospital, suffering from a number of medical complaints, which meant he was often separated from his mother at the crucial bonding stage.

Looking more specifically into the medical history of our other cannibal killers, we find there are other possible medical explanations for their bizarre behaviour. Confronted with little evidence of socio-environmental factors causing Shawcross's delinquency and rages, psychiatrist Richard Kraus sent off blood and urine samples from Shawcross to be tested for any biochemical abnormalities. The results were striking.

Firstly, Shawcross was born with an extra Y-chromosome, making him XYY. Most people are born with two chromosomes: women are XX, and men are XY. Arthur Shawcross's extra male chromosome is an abnormality generally associated with making the individual slightly retarded, but it has been linked to violent, anti-social behaviour, although not specifically to violent offending.

Secondly, a biochemical analysis showed that Shawcross's urine contained abnormally high levels of a chemical marker known as kryptopyrrole, which translates as 'hidden fiery oil'. Over the course of his research, Kraus found out that excessive levels of kryptopyrroles contributed to a rare condition called pyroluria, and Shawcross had more than ten times the normal levels. A small number of researchers are currently studying the effects of biochemical imbalances and their associations on the causes of violent behaviour. Psychiatrists such as William Walsh at the Carl Pfeiffer Treatment Center in Chicago have found that deficiencies in certain key vitamins and minerals can lead to unstable and even violent behaviour. According to their research, kryptopyrroles strip the bloodstream of both vitamin B6 and zinc, which can ultimately lead to depression, mood swings and sudden rages, irresponsibility and impulsiveness, and delayed adult behaviour – all Shawcross hallmarks. Although the validity of this kind of research into biochemical causes of violence is still highly disputed by many other psychiatrists, Richard Kraus felt that this kryptopyrrole disorder plus Shawcross's chromosomal abnormality were moving him closer to finding the causes of Shawcross's violent behaviour:

> This seemed to be, to me, the key in beginning to move towards an explanation of Arthur Shawcross. I felt that the genetic abnormality, which is associated with violence, was one piece of it. This was now a second piece, a kryptopyrrole disorder that has been written about extensively. It's just so buried in literature it's not easy to find, but I was able to dig it out. So these were two major risk factors that I felt, and do feel to this day, predisposed this man towards very violent behaviour.

But Shawcross also had suffered a number of head injuries during adolescence and early adult life, and there was a strong suspicion that he might be suffering from brain damage. At sixteen, he suffered a right skull fracture and cerebral concussion when a discus hit him at close range on the school athletics field. Then, when he was twenty, Shawcross was working on a building site when he was struck by a sledgehammer and again sustained concussion. In that same year he was also involved in a car crash, in which he was again concussed. And in the following year he fell from a ladder while employed on a construction job, again hitting his head. With Shawcross having such a history of head trauma, Kraus wasted no time in arranging for brain scans to be carried out on the killer, the results of which showed significant damage to parts of the brain.

Georgetown Professor Jonathan Pincus is one of the most respected neurologists examining the causes of violent crime. A few years after Shawcross was tried and sentenced, Pincus re-examined him. He was hoping to see if, by using the latest neurological research, he could ascribe Shawcross's violent behaviour to specific structures of the brain that were damaged. Pincus conducted magnetic resonance imaging (MRI) brain scans and electroencephalograms (EEG) on Shawcross, which revealed the full extent of the brain damage. MRI is an imaging technique which can show up physical traces of damage to different parts of the brain, while an EEG records the brain's electrical activity. The MRI scans revealed lesions on the left frontal lobe of the brain and an abnormality in the right anterior temporal lobe. The frontal lobes are part of the brain's frontal cortex, a large part of the brain that sits above the eyes immediately behind the fore-head. The temporal lobes are next to the frontal lobes, on the side of the brain around each ear.

By finding scars on Shawcross's forehead and checking the notes in his medical history, Pincus could be fairly certain that one or more of the head injuries that Shawcross had suffered earlier in life had caused this damage. However, many people can have such lesions and yet suffer nothing more than a few mild migraines. But in Shawcross's case, Pincus could prove that these lesions were causing poor functioning in the frontal and tempo-ral lobes, because EEGs revealed unusual electrical activity coming from that part of the brain. Pincus explained what this kind of brain damage could do to an individual:

> That particular part of the temporal lobe has a great deal
> to do with atavistic behaviour, instinctual behaviour,
> primitive behaviour – fighting, anger, sex, violence,

running away – and it's supposedly the site of the id –
the psychiatric concept of a primitive instinctual being
within the brain. And the frontal lobe is supposed to put
a lid on that to keep the id under control. Now, if there's
not much to control, then loss of control doesn't do any
harm. We've all had a drink or so at a cocktail party and
experienced a slight sense of loss of control, and it's not
unpleasant, but with somebody who has a lesion on the
frontal lobe it's very much like being a little drunk all the
time. Their censoring devices, their capacity to inhibit
urges and impulses is defective.

Jonathan Pincus believes that Shawcross's impulsive, violent rages
can be partly explained by the damage that he sustained to the
frontal lobe, and that these impulsive rages might have released
primitive and atavistic behaviour, generated in the damaged
temporal lobe. Could Arthur Shawcross's damaged brain structures
therefore have released a modern version of the most horrific of
primitive behaviours, the desire to cannibalize his victims?

Shawcross is not the only cannibal killer to suffer from brain
abnormalities. When Andrei Tkachenko examined Chikatilo, he
discovered that the Russian cannibal killer suffered from hydro-
cephalus at birth – an accumulation of fluid in the brain – which
can make the head enlarge and can cause mental handicap.
Tkachenko conducted neurological tests to see if there was
further brain damage: 'We discovered in our research that
Chikatilo had a whole range of neurological symptoms, which
indicated that he had certain brain defects related to development before and during birth. In particular, using functional
imaging, we found that he showed signs of dysfunction in the
front sections of the right side of the brain.'

Furthermore, Issei Sagawa's psychiatric report revealed that, in a brain scan carried out on 23 November 1981 by a Dr D. Fredy, the results showed 'insufficient density' in the frontal lobe, and that there were 'expanded cerebrum fissures' in the same area of the brain, indicating that there was more spinal fluid than brain in parts of the frontal lobe.

So Shawcross, Chikatilo and Sagawa have all been found to have abnormalities in the frontal region of the brain. For Adrian Raine, the fact that three of these cannibal killers have poor frontal functioning comes as no surprise – it correlates several key brain imaging studies that Raine has carried out on impulsive murderers, looking at their frontal functioning, and comparing it with normal people.

Raine used an imaging technology called Positron Emission Tomography (PET), a type of 'functional' brain imaging that does not simply look at the brain's structures but also measures physical activity in different regions of the brain, including the prefrontal cortex. In Raine's first brain imaging study of murderers in 1994, twenty-two murderers who had pleaded not guilty by reason of insanity were compared with twenty-two non-murderers who matched the murderers in sex and age. With PET scans, the subjects are given a task to perform over thirty minutes, a cognitive task that 'challenges' or activates the part of the brain suspected to be dysfunctional. Afterwards, PET can measure how much or how little activity the cognitive task generates in the subjects' brains. In the case of the twenty-two murderers, Raine used the continuous performance task, a standard visual task known to activate the frontal region of the brain.

The results of the study are remarkable. Comparing the brain scan of a normal individual used as a control with the brain scan of a murderer, there are very noticeable differences in brain activity in the prefrontal cortex area. The normal subject shows much activation in this area, while the murderer shows little. Adrian Raine revealed why these results are so significant:

> At the top of the brain scan you'll see a distinct lack of activation in the prefrontal cortex. So these impulsive and violent murderers have a deficiency in the function of the prefrontal region of the brain. And the significance of that is that it's the prefrontal cortex that's involved in regulating and controlling behaviour. We all feel angry and aggressive at times, but most of us don't translate those aggressive feelings into violent acts. Why do some people become physically violent and aggressive? It's because they don't have a well-functioning prefrontal cortex that acts to control, inhibit and stop their aggressive behaviours and feelings, leading them to act them out, committing violent, murderous acts.
>
> The prefrontal cortex is a bit like the emergency brake on a car: when a car runs out of control we pull on the emergency brake to stop it. So when our behaviour runs out of control, when we're beginning to feel angry and aggressive and we want to lash out, what stops us doing that is our prefrontal cortex. The prefrontal cortex of the brain is a bit like the guardian angel of our behaviour. It stops us [performing] anti-social, aggressive, outrageous acts. And it's this part of the brain that our brain imaging studies have shown differs in psychopathic individuals.

The brain is an incredibly complex organ, and scientists like Adrian Raine are still only just beginning to understand how different structures within the brain may contribute to violent and murderous behaviour. Since his 1994 study, Raine has conducted several other studies, including one with twice as many murderers, which replicated his findings. He has also examined the interaction between damage to the frontal cortex and socio-environmental factors, testing both murderers who grew up in deprived broken homes and murderers who grew up in happy, stable environments. In these tests, Raine found that the murderers from stable environments had even poorer prefrontal functioning than the other murderers, suggesting that when socio-environmental factors play little part, then biological factors are an even more important part of the equation.

Raine's research is controversial and causes yet more disagreements in the eternal debate over nature vs nurture. However, his personal views are that it is neither nature nor nurture that governs behaviour, but both. Raine calls for a 'bio-social approach', where nature and nurture interact together. Just as a broken home may make a prefrontally damaged child even more predisposed to violence, someone born with high physiological arousal levels may be more likely to be led astray by his or her school peers. This interaction between nature and nurture can also be seen in Shawcross, Sagawa and Chikatilo. However, as we have seen, no two psychopaths – let alone cannibal killers – will share the same set of interacting factors, as Adrian Raine explained:

> One of the problems with this whole field is that there are no one-to-one connections. So there are some psychopaths who do have meaningful relationships. There are some psychopaths who do have some sense of conscience. So unfortunately it's not like a medical disor-

der or illness, where everyone with tuberculosis has a certain set of symptoms. I believe the violent offender is a complex jigsaw puzzle. He's made up of lots of different pieces. We're only just beginning to turn over and discover separate pieces of the jigsaw puzzle: birth complications, maternal rejection, low physiological arousal, brain damage. The next step is to take these pieces and be able to find out how they get put together to go to create the violent criminal psychopathic individual.

But if poor brain functioning and socio-environmental factors played a part in leading Chikatilo, Shawcross and Sagawa towards being cannibal killers, what can be said about Jeffrey Dahmer?

We interviewed Fred Berlin, one of the world's experts in paraphilia – sexual perversions of an extreme nature. Berlin was also one of the expert witnesses at Dahmer's trial, and he spent several hours interviewing Dahmer about his crimes. For Berlin, the key to understanding Jeffrey Dahmer is not that he was simply psychopathic but that he was driven by utterly abnormal sexual urges, namely necrophilia, which gradually took over his entire life:

> When I met with Jeffrey Dahmer, he had already killed a number of people, and the issue was how to understand what he had done. Now, he wasn't generally an anti-social person; he wasn't generally criminal. In most other spheres of his life he behaved in a responsible and even productive manner. What I learned through interviewing Jeffrey Dahmer is that his behaviour wasn't a reflection of character, or temperament, or intellect. It was a reflection of the privacy of his sexual make-up and

how he was driven, driven by intense recurrent fantasies and urges about having sex with dead bodies, to the point where he ultimately succumbed to these temptations and admitted to himself that he just didn't know how to resist acting upon them.

At the trial, of course, Dahmer was found sane and guilty of the murders, and the general consensus was that Dahmer was simply evil. Berlin disagrees with this, believing that Dahmer was actually a very ill person, in his words, 'a broken mind in need of repair.' And at the root of this illness lay Dahmer's sexual urges, which Berlin believes must also be at least in part biologically driven:

Sex is, in a sense, just another sort of biological appetite, and just as some people may have difficulties with overeating, some people may have difficulties because of cravings for drugs or alcohol, there are some individuals whose sexual drive is sufficiently intense that without proper treatment they may not be able through willpower alone to control their behaviour in a consistently appropriate fashion.

Towards the end of his killing spree, Dahmer's already bizarre behaviour became even more disturbed. In an attempt to create human zombies, he experimented with drilling holes in his half-conscious victims' skulls. He wanted to keep them as submissive unresponsive slaves, to satisfy his peculiar sexual tastes. Dahmer also started wearing yellow contact lenses when he went out to the Milwaukee gay bars and clubs, thinking that this might give him some kind of 'special power'. And finally, he made plans to construct a shrine with an altar made from a black table in his apartment, on which he was going to place twelve of his victims' skulls, with two complete skeletons at each end.

Dahmer's behaviour during the last year of his murder spree differed greatly from previous years. For Berlin, this is even more evidence that Dahmer was profoundly mentally ill, as he began to show signs of psychosis:

> Eventually, after fighting this for several years, he had lost the battle. That's when his thinking began to become progressively more disturbed. It was almost a religious conversion in reverse. He began to think, 'Perhaps this is my destiny, then, to kill. I haven't been able to stop doing it. Perhaps there is a devil; perhaps this is the work of the devil. Perhaps if I build a temple out of the sacred remains of my victims, the devil will reveal himself.' I believe at the end, Jeffrey Dahmer was very close to being psychotic. In psychotic mental illnesses, people lose the ability to reason rationally. That ability becomes substantially impaired. In the extreme form they become delusional, that there is no amount of rational explanation that can bring them to their senses.

Unfortunately, Dahmer's arrest and trial took place before PET technology became advanced enough to allow researchers like Adrian Raine to start their brain imaging work. Nor was there any chance of scanning his brain after the trial, for Dahmer was killed by another inmate in prison. Research into abnormal sexual make-ups is also quite a way behind neuro-psychiatric work such as Adrian Raine's, as Fred Berlin reveals:

When I interviewed Jeffrey Dahmer, I was probably where physicians were a hundred years ago when they interviewed and observed someone with epilepsy. You could look at them, you could know that something was terribly wrong, but science and research had not yet developed to the point where we had a full appreciation of what was causing it.

Ultimately, Jeffrey Dahmer remains the most enigmatic of our four cannibal killers. Neither socio-environmental factors nor biological dysfunction can fully explain his unique psychology and cannibalistic urges. But there was one intriguing final remark that Dahmer made to one of the psychologists testifying at his trial. When asked in the psychiatric interview about his cannibalism, Dahmer replied: 'Maybe I was born too late. Maybe I should have been an Aztec.'

This striking observation takes us back to many of the other instances of cannibalism that we have visited over the previous chapters. How different are individual cannibal killers like Jeffrey Dahmer from entire civilizations such as the Aztecs? Was the cannibalism of Dahmer, Chikatilo, Sagawa and Shawcross something unprecedented, or are they simply following on a human tradition, buried deep in our 'primitive' past? In the final chapter, we will trace this thread in order to find out how thin and perhaps inauthentic the veneer of modern liberal civilization really is.

TWELVE

The Taboo Within Us All

From Jeffrey Dahmer's shrine in Milwaukee to the shell of a Uruguayan aircraft high in the Chilean Andes; from Fijian cannibal sacrifice to Issei Sagawa's mutilation and consumption of his victim; from starving Leningraders to Aztec zealots; and from the ritualized killing of the Iron Age to the political genocide during China's cultural revolution – it is clear that cannibalism is a widespread phenomenon that can take many shapes and forms.

And yet many people would prefer to believe that cannibalism only ever existed on some remote South Sea Island, as part of a long-extinct civilization, or in the depraved world of an aberrant sadistic psychopath. As we have seen, however, this is far from the truth. Cannibalism as a feature of human behaviour is something that has taken place throughout history, in every continent on our planet. The Victorians may have revelled in their comical images of missionaries being boiled in pots, comforted by the knowledge that 'civilized' Western man would never have engaged in such 'savage' practices. But little did they realize that archaeological discoveries would later show that the tradition of cannibalism was also practised by our ancestors in the Western world. It is, of course, ironic that Eton College, the breeding ground for the 'civilized' English Establishment and one of the last bastions of the English class system, should turn out to be where archaeologists found bones that hint at a darker, more primitive human past.

Cannibalism wasn't simply the preserve of our prehistoric ancestors, though. Closer to our time, over the last two hundred years, and even in the last couple of decades, we find that *in extremis* it is far easier than many people imagine for ordinary human beings to resort to eating other dead human beings. For sailors travelling through uncharted territory in search of new worlds, or the North-West Passage, cannibalism became so common that it was known as 'the custom of the sea'. In our modern world of satellite telephones, global positioning systems and digital cameras transmitting pictures from Mount Everest, the thought that we might ever end up in such a position makes cannibalism for most people simply unimaginable. And yet people like Marten Hartwell, and the survivors of the 1972 Andes crash resorted to cannibalism and lived to tell the tale. We may flinch at the thought of it, but who can say whether they would do it or not, without being in that position themselves?

For most of us, however, cannibalism remains far beyond the fringes of our lives. Archaeological discoveries tell us only about the extremely distant past, and it is unlikely that we will ever be in a situation where we might end up isolated and stranded for a long period. But at the same time, we choose to ignore the fact that there are things we do in our modern lives that are not so very far removed from cannibalistic practices. Placenta-eating, for instance, is more widespread than many of us would care to think – so much so that Channel 4's cookery series *TV Dinners* featured placenta pâté on one of its programmes in 1998. (The programme generated hundreds of complaints from viewers afterwards.) Most new mothers choose not to take home their placenta and put it in the kitchen freezer, but hospitals in England and Ireland have admitted selling discarded placentas to French pharmaceutical firms, who use the human tissue in various prescription medicines taken by thousands of people. Not forgetting the gruesome stories of foetus-eating in modern-day China and Hong Kong.

The thought of ingesting human flesh or drinking blood may fill us with disgust, but organ transplants and blood transfusions are now an accepted part of standard medical practice. Perhaps when it has to do with medicine, we accept cannibalism more readily, forgetting that some treatments actually constitute taking in another's person's flesh and blood. This was also the case in the sixteenth and seventeenth centuries, when New World explorers were aghast at the sight of natives eating other human beings, while conveniently forgetting (or simply not knowing) that many Europeans were practising 'medicinal cannibalism', with 'mummy', a substance obtained either from Egypt or from local executed criminals and consisting of flesh, blood, hearts and skull fragments, being touted as a 'universal' cure.

Cannibalism remains a lot closer to our lives than many of us might have imagined. And yet there appears to be one glaring exception: cannibal killers, the murderous few who choose to kill and then consume their victims. How different are these aberrant individuals from us? Are they simply so ill and damaged that their behaviour bears no comparison with any part of normal life, or are there still links to other aspects of human behaviour, possibly less commonly associated with the sexual psychopathy of these real-life Hannibal Lecters?

To be a cannibal obviously requires an unusual degree of violence and savagery in order to cope with the butchery it entails. Today, few of us can imagine this kind of violence, with so little experience of war, conflict and even street-fighting, let alone dismembering another person's body. We may see these kinds of images in the cinema, although we're usually grateful when the camera pans away at the last moment, sparing us a close-up of the gore. In our cosy modern existence, it's very hard to imagine that we, too, could ever be involved in this kind of extreme behaviour. But for people who feel so far removed from savagery, we live in a very violent world. In the twentieth century alone, it has been estimated that over 180 million people died as a result of war, murder and aggression. And much of this violence and aggression was not simply the inevitable result of war, soldiers killing other soldiers, but something far more sinister and shocking.

During their twelve years in power in Germany from 1933 to 1945, the Nazis killed over five million Jews, not to mention Poles, Russians and gypsies. The vast majority of these deaths were brought about in execution camps set up and operated in Poland and the Baltic states during the Second World War. As the Nazis decided what form their so-called 'final solution' to the 'Jewish question' was going to take, they built crematoria that were then converted into gassing facilities, with the capability of murdering thousands of people and disposing of their remains quickly and efficiently. At Auschwitz-Birkenau, the largest and most notorious of the execution camps, two of the four gas chambers were able to process over 6,000 victims per day, and in this way millions of Jews were systematically slaughtered in just a few years. The scale of these operations and the administrative structure supporting them required the employment and co-operation of thousands of individuals. Although it is possible that a few psychopaths and sadists may have welcomed the opportunities such work afforded them, the majority of those employed in the camps must, by definition, be regarded as ordinary human beings.

Post-war Germany saw many trials of concentration camp guards, firing squad leaders operating on the Eastern Front and even gassing engineers from crematoria firms, and in each case the same observation could be made. The perpetrators were neither aberrant sadists nor psychopathic outcasts from society: they were ordinary men and women who had suddenly descended into savagery, and this, too, in Germany, one of the most cultured nations in history.

Lest we think that the Holocaust was the only example of man's latent inhumanity rising to the surface, there are, unfortunately, many other examples. We should also cite the examples of the ordinary Americans who performed a variety of inhuman acts during the Vietnam War, from medieval-style raping and pillaging to the infamous My Lai massacre. And this kind of savagery can be found all over the world — Argentinian or Chilean murder squads, renegade police officers killing street children in Rio or Mexico City, tit-for-tat terrorist executions by either side in Northern Ireland (not to mention the comparable measures taken by the British troops and special forces), and most recently the shocking ethnic cleansing in Rwanda, Bosnia and Kosovo.

Does this mean there are sadistic impulses buried deep within us all that, given the right circumstances, can control us? What many psychologists and researchers into violence now argue is that the question is not whether we all have these impulses, but how effective our inhibitory mechanisms are at keeping a lid on potentially aggressive behaviour.

In his seminal study *On Aggression*, zoologist Konrad Lorenz argues that inhibitory mechanisms are actually more poorly developed in humans than in animals. Although, Lorenz explains, other species obviously do fight among themselves occasionally, it's actually a rare occurence compared with the frequency with which human beings attack and kill each other. In particular, heavily armed carnivores, such as lions, possess sufficiently reliable inhibitions to stop random acts of rage, such as killing another species member for no reason, because this in turn prevents the self-destruction of the species.

The consensus is that there are probably impulses towards sadistic cruelty lurking within every human psyche, but that some of us are better at keeping control of these urges than others. In the cases of serial killers and murderers, their inhibitory mechanisms may function particularly poorly because of biological defects or troubled childhoods. In the case of officials or camp guards involved in carrying out the Nazis' final solution, there are probably other psychological factors at work, because not every German was necessarily born to be an evil executioner. Hannah Arendt, in her study of Adolf Eichmann, the logistical planner and co-ordinator of the final solution, concluded that Nazis like Eichmann are not necessarily monsters, but people whose inhibitions have been stripped away by historical processes and aspects of group psychology. Others have suggested that man has an inherent capacity to lose his humanity when subordinating his individuality to an institutional structure. The point is, however, that aggressive and destructive impulses are ubiquitous, and that they form an integral part of human nature, just as surely as generous, creative and loving impulses do.

Even if we all have a latent aggressive streak within our character, this still doesn't fully explain cannibalism. Aggressive impulses can take all sorts of forms, from shouting at somebody right up to murder. Some may therefore deduce that, although we are all capable of aggression and violence, only the aberrant few will ever progress to killing, and, of those murderous few, a fraction of those might go on to commit appalling acts such as cannibalism. But again, history has taught us that behaviour such as cannibalism – if not worse – can be committed by the most ordinary people.

During the Bosnian War in 1993, ordinary Croat soldiers allegedly made weeping mothers hold their babies while they shot their infants dead. Heinrich Himmler's SS teams, known as 'Einsatzgruppen', went all over the Baltic states and White Russia executing hundreds of Jews and burying them in mass pits. And the guards at Auschwitz-Birkenau, again 'normal' German soldiers, had to send thousands of Jewish men, women and children to their deaths in gas chambers. These 'ordinary' Germans at the camps were not therefore psychopaths, specially selected for these grisly tasks. On the contrary, most of them would normally have found it terribly difficult to go through with the experience of rounding up large groups of terrified, screaming women and children, sending them to their deaths, and then supervising the disposal of the bodies afterwards. This is why measures were adopted to break the prisoners down as individuals, to depersonalize them until they appeared subhuman.

For example, dysentery was rife in the camps, and lavatory facilities were grossly inadequate. What was more, during the working day permission was often refused for inmates to use the latrines. The result was that prisoners were frequently covered in their own excrement and smelled repulsive. Writer Gitta Sereny interviewed Franz Stangl, the commandant of the Treblinka execution camp, and asked him why such humiliation was employed, since prisoners were going to be killed in any case. Stangl replied: 'To condition those who actually had to carry out the policies: to make it possible to do what they did.'

The more human beings are perceived as alien, or subhuman, the easier it becomes to inflict harm on them, or to slaughter them. Psychopathic individuals operate in a similar way: because they don't see other individuals as we see them, they don't feel the same empathy for those individuals' pain and suffering when they commit acts of violence toward them. Psychopaths could be born with a lack of empathy, or develop it in childhood, but in this instance, depersonalization was deliberately cultivated in the 'ordinary' concentration camp guards. It shows, however, that we all would have it in us to close down our empathy towards other human beings and commit unimaginable acts of brutality.

This process of depersonalizing the victim is also a common feature in cannibalism. If the victim is no longer considered human, then cannibalism suddenly becomes much more justifiable, and in fact easier to understand. Anthropologists discovered that many 'primitive' tribes considered people who were not members of their own particular tribe as not human. In fact, in the language of many of these tribes the word for their own particular tribe was synonymous with 'man'. So from their viewpoint it was not, strictly speaking, cannibalism if they ate the fallen warriors of an enemy tribe, because that enemy was not even 'man'. In 1999, journalist Richard Lloyd Parry reported outbreaks of cannibalism in Indonesia between the Dayaks of Borneo and their sworn enemies, settlers from the island of Madura. A Catholic Dayak teacher explained the cannibalism to Lloyd Parry: 'In the eyes of Dayaks, when people do not respect our traditional law, they become enemies, and we don't consider our enemies to be human any more. They become animals in our eyes. And the Dayaks eat animals.' Russian peasants in the Volga region during famines had a completely different attitude to eating their dead, because of what their Orthodox religion taught them to think about the afterlife. And the survivors of the Andes crash also found that they began to develop a different attitude towards their dead friends, seeing them more as meat that would help them to survive.

The depersonalization of the victims of cannibalism continues right up to the point where the victims are not simply subhuman, or animals, but become a product, ready to be processed from its original form and rendered into meat. In a similar way, the Nazis turned their 'final solution' to the 'Jewish question' into a veritable industry, from requisitioning vast numbers of trains to carry the Jews eastwards; organizing complicated timetables (which they stuck to throughout the war); working out how many humans the execution camps like Auschwitz-Birkenau and Treblinka could 'process'; and then extracting the necessary 'product' at the end – gold from the victims' teeth, hair to fill pillows and upholster chairs, and body fat to fuel the crematoria ovens. For the Nazis did not use the Holocaust solely as a means of mass extermination. Millions of Jews were worked to death in labour camps, unwittingly helping the German war effort, and the final irony is that, with this mass of free labour and the 'by-products' of the extermination process, the Nazis actually profited from the Holocaust.

The idea that a human being can become a product, something to be processed and rendered, just as the Nazis did with the Jews, is something we find mirrored in many of our cannibal cases. The Aztecs created a whole civilization based around blood sacrifice, and, like the Nazis, the Aztecs also made sure that no part of the body was put to waste. In the case of the

Aztecs, a priest would sacrifice the victims on top of one of their temples or sacrificial platforms, and remove the still-beating heart, offering it to their gods. Immediately, the body would be thrown down the steep temple steps, where it would roll towards the priest's assistants, waiting at the bottom. Then, the body would be spirited away to rooms below the temple, where other people would have the job of draining the blood. After that, more helpers would portion off the flesh to be given to various nobles, and the bones would be taken away, to be used as kitchen utensils or musical instruments.

The survivors of the Andes air crash also turned their cannibalism into a form of processing. The two medical students in the rugby team would do the dismembering, while Fito and Eduardo Strauch had the job of taking the meat off the bones. Others would then divide up the meat into portions and put it out to dry on the aeroplane's fuselage. The same could also be said about Alexander Zapiantsev, who murdered Valdemar Suzik in order to get some meat for himself, and also to sell around the other hostels in the Lenin district. And, finally, as Jeffrey Dahmer carried out his bizarre rituals with his victims' bodies – bleaching their skulls, preserving body parts and portioning off select cuts of meat – he, too, was processing his victims.

The manner in which the Nazis carried out the systematic extermination of European Jews, and the way in which thousands of ordinary German people so willingly complied in this genocide, tells us a great deal about human nature. It reveals that the capacity to commit foul, bestial acts is well within the capabilities of us all. And if man is still capable of such vile crimes against humanity, and this in the twentieth century, why, then, not cannibalism? If cannibalism is well within us all, however, why do we still try to ignore it? What is perhaps most surprising is not that cannibalism has proved to be so widespread, but that we as Westerners have such a problem confronting and dealing with it.

Why, precisely, is there such a taboo about cannibalism? A taboo generally implies that something is 'unclean' and 'forbidden' or, conversely, that it is 'sacred' and 'consecrated'. Ironically, the word 'taboo' comes from one of the regions most associated with cannibalism – Polynesia. Captain Cook first noted the term during his 1771 visit to Tonga, where he saw that Polynesian life and society were based on a complicated system of taboos – food taboos, for instance, that restricted the diet of pregnant women, or prohibitions about talking to or touching chiefs or members of other high social classes. Cook introduced the term into the English language, and it achieved widespread currency.

And how does something actually become taboo? Sigmund Freud famously discussed the topic in his 1913 work, *Totem and Taboo*. Freud noted that a taboo had about it a sense of something unapproachable, and it is principally expressed in prohibitions and restrictions. However, taboo restrictions, explained Freud, are distinct from religious or moral prohibitions:

> They are not based upon any divine ordinance, but may be said to impose themselves on their own account. They differ from moral prohibitions in that they fall into no system that declares quite generally that certain abstinence must be observed and gives reason for that necessity. Taboo prohibitions have no grounds and are of unknown origin. Though they are unintelligible to *us*, to those who are dominated by them they are taken as a matter of course.

Perhaps most intriguingly, Freud also saw an explanation for the apparently irrational nature of taboos, suggesting that they were generated by ambivalent social attitudes. From this, Freud concluded that taboos represent forbidden actions for which there nevertheless existed a strong unconscious inclination. Freud directly applied this viewpoint to the most universal of all taboos, incest, suggesting that there are incestuous urges within us all, buried within our subconscious. Could Freud's theory also partly explain our taboo about cannibalism – that it reflects primitive bestial urges and unconscious inclinations buried within us all?

There are other, more readily acceptable, reasons for the taboo of cannibalism, however. Much of it has to do with how we see and treat other people, both during life and after death. To cannibalize another human being obviously requires dismemberment, de-fleshing and all the other grisly things that need to be done in order to render a body as meat. But more than any other species, human beings are fascinated by other people, continuing even after they are dead. In particular, our culture has developed elaborate funerary rites. We dress up our dead, sometimes even making them up before placing them into beautifully crafted coffins to protect them from worms and wildlife. The thought of turning the dead body of another person into meat is so far removed from the highly respectful, almost reverential way in which we treat our dead that it isn't surprising we maintain such a taboo.

The cannibalism taboo is also about eating, but in this instance the rationale behind it is less immediately justifiable. Throughout the world, different cultures and religions operate rules about a variety of foods. As we have seen earlier, the Chinese are famous for their wide-ranging diet, which includes eating dog, monkey and bear – all taboo foods in the West. Another taboo food – horse meat – is eaten throughout France, but nowhere else in Europe or the West. Hindus worship cows, and so have a taboo about beef, while Jews will not eat pork or shellfish. In the light of the variety of taboos that exist all around the world, are the cannibal practices of the Polynesians just an example of an eating practice that happens to be forbidden in other cultures?

As for the taboo which exists today – stronger than ever despite relaxation of restrictions on many other prohibitions in our culture – the reason we shy away from the thought of cannibalism may also have much to do with the distinct lack of the 'visceral' in our society. We live in a hospital culture, insulated from the reality of death and burial, and few of us have ever seen a corpse. We also live in a culture where the sources of our food are hidden and obfuscated – most of us no longer buy meat from a butcher's counter, chopped up beside other carcasses. Instead, we prefer plastic-packaged chicken breasts, or frozen burgers. Little wonder, then, that cannibalism – with its inherent viscerality – shocks and appals us so fundamentally.

Ultimately, there is, it should be said, a great deal of confusion and hypocrisy in both our eating habits and the way in which we deal with our dead. We may eat meat, but we try to conceal its origins. We dress death up to avoid confronting it head-on. And this squeamishness has made aspects of our two most basic functions – eating and dying – into taboos. On the one hand, it makes most of us even less willing to even entertain the thought of cannibalism; on the other hand it could be partly responsible for creating the cannibal killers in our society. Their response to the hypocrisy of this 'visceral insularity' in society is to break the taboo in the most extreme way – by committing cannibalism.

As long as we have a taboo, you will have those who break it, so in that sense the cases of Chikatilo, Shawcross, Dahmer and Sagawa are not unprecedented. Every society has its taboo-breakers. What is perhaps more revealing is how that society chooses to react to and deal with the transgressor – and the taboo itself. When the Andes survivors chose to eat the flesh of their dead friends, they were caught between two of the strongest taboos in their Catholic culture. If they chose not to break the taboo of cannibalism, would they then be committing suicide – also unforgivable in the eyes of the Catholic Church – by choosing not to eat when there was sustenance available? One of the ways in which they overcame this was by turning to God, likening their cannibalism to one of the central tenets of the Christian doctrine: Holy Communion.

Cannibalism is inextricably linked to the Christian rite of Holy Communion. Just as the Fijians and Aztecs had their own sets of religious rituals, for the last 2,000 years, Christians in the Western world have had Holy Communion. The rite of the Eucharist commemorates the action of Jesus at the Last Supper with His disciples, when he gave them bread, saying, 'This is my body', and wine, saying, 'This is my blood'. All Christians see Holy Communion as a memorial action in which, by eating bread and drinking wine (or, for some Protestants, grape juice), the Church recalls what Jesus Christ was, said and did. But according to the Eucharistic doctrine of Roman Catholicism, the elements of bread and wine are also 'transubstantiated' into the body and blood of Christ, their physical substance is actually changed. So when the Catholic communicant takes the wafer and the wine, it is not enough that he should *believe* he is eating the flesh and drinking the blood of Christ – the wafer and wine are, at the moment of Holy Communion, literally the body of Christ. So is the Christian, particularly the Catholic, communicant therefore a cannibal?

In the press conference after the Andes air crash survivors returned home to Uruguay, trainee lawyer Pancho Delgado explained to the world's media: 'When the moment came when we did not have any more food, or anything of that kind, we thought to ourselves that if Jesus at His Last Supper had shared His flesh and blood with His apostles, then it was a sign to us that we should do the same – take the flesh and blood as an intimate communion between us all.' It is, of course, significant that even strict Catholics such as the Andes survivors could acknowledge their religion's close ties with cannibalism. The resonance that cannibalism has with the rite of the Eucharist was something European missionaries noticed when they first tried to convert Fiji to Christianity. Anthropologist Christina Toren can understand why the Fijians found the idea of Holy Communion very easy to accept, having themselves practised cannibalism for generations:

> I don't actually think the Fijians would particularly have had any problem with Christ offering Himself, for example, metaphorically in bread and wine and so on. They wouldn't have found anything paradoxical or particularly strange about it. I think the metaphors would have been quite plain to them.

Perhaps significantly, Toren reports, even in Fiji today there is an abundance of Last Supper imagery in Fijian churches and Christian homes.

Even in the acts of cannibal killers like Jeffrey Dahmer and Issei Sagawa, there are identifiable echoes of ritual and religion. Dahmer explained his cannibal habit to one psychiatrist, saying:

'I suppose in an odd way it made me feel as if they were even more a part of me.' The idea that eating part of a god would make him part of oneself dates back to pagan religions – by eating the body of his deity, the worshipper would assimilate his deity's power and divinity. Christianity in fact inherited this basic tenet of paganism, and when Christ exhorted His disciples to eat His flesh and drink His blood, He was merely following a precedent.

In Europe's most Catholic countries, Spain and Italy, Christian iconography and imagery are frequently very visceral. Images abound of Christ impaled on a cross, saints penetrated by arrows or disembowelled, and bloody representations of the sacred heart. There are churches in Italy where the altars or walls are covered with body parts – model representations of feet, hands, noses, which are offered by the faithful to their God, hoping that He will heal them or give them some of His power. The shrine of St Anthony in the basilica at Padua contains dozens of photographs of people mutilated or damaged in road accidents, with letters thanking the saint for his protection in their times of need. In the nave of the same church is another chapel where one can view the saint's larynx, tongue and jawbone.

One of the central beliefs of the Christian doctrine is how civilized and different man is in comparison with, say, the animal kingdom. And yet our history has been punctuated by thousands of wars and conflicts of an extremely violent nature, and the dominant religion in the Western world has at its core a rite with unmistakable cannibalistic overtones. People may protest that the media is now filled with graphic images, both real and imagined, but if you look back through our history and culture it is clear that man has always had a fascination with the gory and the visceral. Even that most sacred of institutions, religion, has had a part to play in this. We consider ourselves to be the most civilized of all species, but under closer scrutiny the veneer of our so-called liberal culture turns out to be paper-thin. When the conquistadors took over South America, they were actually more bloodthirsty than the Indians they attacked. Ironically, they were also the first Europeans to discover New World cannibalism – the archetype of deeply 'uncivilized' behaviour.

Bartholomé de las Casas, a sixteenth-century chronicler of the conquest of South America, wrote in 1552 that 'the Indians had a greater disposition toward civility than the European people', reporting some of the Spanish atrocities:

> For greed of gold, ornaments were torn from neck and ear, and as the masked burglar threatens his victim until he reveals the hiding place of this store, the Indians were subjected to the most cruel tortures to compel the disclosure of mines which never existed and the location of gold in streams and fields in which the Almighty has never planted it... The courtiers rode proudly through the streets of the New Isabella, their horses terrifying the poor Indians while their riders shook their plumed heads and waved their glistening swords. As they rode along, their lances were passed into women and children, and no greater pastime was practised by them then wagering as to a cavalier's ability to completely cleave a man with one dextrous blow of his sword. A score would fall before one would drop in the divided parts essential to winning the wager... Fortunes were lost on the ability of a swordsman to run an Indian through the body at a designated spot. Children were snatched from their mothers' arms and dashed against the rocks as they passed. Other children they threw into the water that the

mothers might witness their drowning struggles. Babes were snatched from their mothers' breasts, and a brave Spaniard's strength was tested by his ability to tear an infant into two pieces by pulling apart its tiny legs... I have been an eyewitness of all these cruelties, and an infinite number of others which I pass over in silence.

And yet these were the conquistadors who would later claim to have 'civilized' the Americas. Four hundred years later, the Holocaust shows how one of the most civilized and cultured nations in the world, Germany, could descend into murder and savage cruelty on a massive scale.

Despite our history and reputation as the most cruel, violent and destructive race on the planet, human beings still like to think of themselves as civilized, finding it next to impossible to confront the taboo of cannibalism. In 1999, when Richard Lloyd Parry finally stumbled across the evidence of cannibalism that he was looking for, he was surprised by his own reactions, writing that 'The most devastating thing about cannibalism and head-hunting is not the fear and the blood, but the terrible, profound banality.' Yet despite its essential banality, cannibalism does remain one of our culture's most abhorrent taboos.

Our heightened disgust at cannibalism does reveal rather more about us than we would perhaps like. Beneath the hypocrisy and implausibility of the taboo, the mixed-up meanings of food, and away from the constructed ideals of Christian doctrines, a hitherto hidden side of humanity is revealed. Despite our cherished notions of civilization, passivity and humanity, man is innately violent, cruel and capable of anything – even cannibalism.

Bibliography

Books

Arendt, Hannah, *Eichmann in Jerusalem: A Report on the Banality of Evil* (London: Penguin, 1976)

Arens, William, *Man-Eating Myth: Anthropology and Anthropophagy* (New York: Oxford University Press, 1980)

Askenasy, Hans, *Cannibalism from Sacrifice to Survival* (New York: Prometheus Books, 1994)

Barker, Francis; Hulme, Peter and Iversen, Margaret (ed), *Cannibalism and the Colonial World* (Cambridge: Cambridge University Press, 1998)

Becker, Jasper, *Hungry Ghosts: Mao's Secret Famine* (Boston: Henry Holt, 1998)

Bloom, I. and Fogel, J.A. (ed), *Meeting of Minds. Intellectual and Religious Interaction in East Asian Traditions of Thought* (New York: Columbia University Press, 1997)

Brown, Paula and Tuzin, Donald (ed), *The Ethnography of Cannibalism* (Washington: Society for Psychological Anthropology, 1983)

Casas, Bartolomé de las, *In Defence of the Indians* (DeKalb: Northern Illinois University Press, 1992)

Cheney, Margaret, *Why? The Serial Killer in America* (Saratoga: R&E Publishers, 1992)

Clunie, Fergus, *Yalo I Viti: A Fiji Museum Catalogue* (Suva: Fiji Museum, 1986)

Conquest, Robert, *Harvest of Sorrow: Soviet Collectivization and the Terror Famine* (New York: Oxford University Press, 1986)

Cookman, Scott, *Ice Blink: The Tragic Fate of Sir John Franklin's Lost Polar Expedition* (New York: John Wiley & Sons Inc, 2000)

Cullen, Robert, *The Killer Department* (London: Orion, 1994)

Cunliffe, Barry (ed), *The Oxford Illustrated Prehistory of Europe* (Oxford: Oxford University Press, 1994)

Cunliffe, Barry, *Iron Age Communities in Britain* (London: Routledge, 1991)

Cunliffe, Barry, *The Ancient Celts* (Oxford: Oxford University Press, 1997)

Diamond, Jared, *Guns, Germs and Steel* (London: Vintage, 1998)

Elgar, M.A. and Crespi, B.J., *Cannibalism, Ecology and Evolution Among Diverse Taxa* (New York: Oxford University Press, 1992)

Ellis, Stephen, *The Mask of Anarchy* (London: C. Hurst & Co, 1999)

Endicott, William, *Wrecked Among Cannibals in the Fijis* (Salem: Marine Research Society, 1923)

Erskine, John E., *Journal of a Cruise Among the Islands of The Western Pacific* (London: John Murray, 1853)

Figes, Orlando, *A People's Tragedy: The Russian Revolution 1891–1924* (London: Pimlico, 1996)

Freud, Sigmund, *Totem and Taboo* (London: Ark, 1983)

Goldman, Laurence R., *The Anthropology of Cannibalism* (Connecticut: Bergin & Garvey, 1999)

Goodall, Jane, *Chimpanzees of Gombe, Patterns of Behaviour* (Cambridge, MA: Harvard University Press, 1986)

Green, Miranda (ed), *The Celtic World* (London: Routledge,1996)

Gwilt, A. and Haselgrove, C. (ed), *Reconstructing Iron Age Societies* (Exeter: Short Run Press, 1997)

Hare, Robert, *Without Conscience: The Disturbing World of the Psychopaths Among Us* (New York: The Guilford Press, 1993)

Harris, M., *Good to Eat, Riddles of Food and Culture* (London: Allen and Unwin, 1986)

Hedges, John W., *Tomb of the Eagles* (Oxford: Historical Associates Ltd, 1992)

Hook, R.H. (ed), *Fantasy and Symbol: Studies in Anthropological Interpretation* (London: Academic Press, 1979)

Imthurn, E. and Wharton, L. (ed), *The Journal of William Lockerby, Sandalwood Trader in the Fijian Islands During the Years 1808–9* (London: Hakluyt Society, 1922)

Johnson, Captain Charles, *A General History of the Lives and Adventures of the Most Famous Highwaymen, Murderers, Street-Robbers, &c.* (London: J. Janeway, 1734)

Keck, Verena (ed), *Common Worlds and Single Lives: Constituting Knowledge in Pacific Societies* (London: Berg, 1998)

Krafft-Ebing, Richard von, *Aberrations of Sexual Life: The Psychopathia Sexualis* (London: Panther, 1965)

Lady, A., *Life in Feejee: Five Years Among the Cannibals* (Suva: Fiji Museum, 1983)

Lessing, Theodor, *Monsters of Weimar* (London: Nemesis, 1993)

Lestringant, Frank, *Cannibals: The Discovery and Representation of the Cannibals from Columbus to Jules Verne* (Cambridge: Polity Press, 1997)

Lewis, Dorothy Otnow, *Guilty by Reason of Insanity: A Psychiatrist Explores the Minds of Killers* (London: Arrow Books, 1999)

Lorenz, Konrad, *On Aggression* (London: Methuen, 1966)

Lourie, Richard, *Hunting the Devil: The Pursuit, Capture and Confession of the Most Savage Serial Killer in History* (New York: HarperCollins, 1993)

Marriner, Brian, *Cannibalism: The Last Taboo!* (London: Random House, 1997)

Martingale, Moira, *Cannibal Killers: The History of Impossible Murderers* (New York: Carroll & Graf, 1994)

Masters, Brian, *The Shrine of Jeffrey Dahmer* (London: Coronet, 1993)

Merrifield, Ralph, *The Archaeology of Ritual and Magic* (London: B.T. Batsford, 1987)

Norris, Joel, *Arthur Shawcross: The Genesee River Killer* (New York: Pinnacle Books, 1992)

Olsen, Jack, *The Misbegotten Son: The True Story of Arthur J. Shawcross* (London: Headline, 1993)

Parker Pearson, Mike, *The Archaeology of Death and Burial* (Frome: Butler and Tanner, 1999)

Petrinovich, Lewis, *The Cannibal Within* (New York: Aldine de Gruyter, 2000)

Philbrick, Nathaniel, *In the Heart of the Sea* (London: HarperCollins, 2000)

Raine, Adrian, *et al*, *Biosocial Bases of Violence* (New York: Plenum, 1997)

Raleigh, Donald J., *A Russian Civil War Diary: Alexander Babine in Saratov, 1917–1922* (London: Duke University Press, 1988)

Read, Piers Paul, *Alive!* (London: Avon, 1992)

Ross, Anne, *Pagan Celtic Britain* (Chicago: Academy Chicago Publishers, 1996)

Roth, J. and Hooper, S. (ed), *The Fiji Journals of Baron Anatole von Hugel, 1875–1877* (Suva: Fiji Museum in association with Cambridge University Museum, 1992)

Salisbury, Harrison E., *The 900 Days: The Siege of Leningrad* (London: Macmillan, 2000)

Salmond, Anne, *Two Worlds: First Meetings Between Maori and Europeans 1642–1772* (Auckland: Viking, 1991)

Salmond, Anne, *Between Worlds: Early Exchanges Between Maori and Europeans 1773-1815* (Honolulu: University of Hawaii Press, 1997)

Schultz, Albert J., *The Diaries and Correspondence of David Cargill 1832-1843* (Canberra: Australian National University Press, 1977)

Sereny, Gitta, *Into That Darkness: From Mercy Killing to Mass Murder* (London: Pimlico, 1995)

Sheridan, Alison (ed), *Heaven and Hell and Other Worlds of the Dead* (Scotland: National Museums of Scotland, 2000)

Stewart, George Rippey, *Ordeal by Hunger: The Story of the Donner Party* (Boston: Houghton Mifflin Co, 1992)

Storr, Anthony, *Human Destructiveness: The Roots of Genocide and Human Cruelty* (London: Routledge, 1991)

Stroud, Mike, *Survival of the Fittest* (London: Jonathan Cape, 1998)

Tannahill, Reay, *Flesh and Blood: The History of the Cannibal Complex* (London: Abacus, 1996)

Townsend, Richard, *The Aztecs* (London: Thames and Hudson, 1992)

Turner, Christy, and Turner, Jacqueline, *Man Corn: Cannibalism and Violence in the Prehistoric American Southwest* (Salt Lake City: University of Utah Press, 1999)

Warner, Mariner, *Managing Monsters: Six Myths of Our Time* (London: Vintage, 1994)

Waterhouse, Joseph, *The King and People of Fiji* (London: Wesleyan Conference Office, 1866)

Wertham, Frederic, *The Show of Violence* (London: Victor Gollancz, 1949)

White, Tim D., *Prehistoric Cannibalism at Mancos* (Oxford: Princeton University Press, 1992)

Wilson, Colin, *The Mammoth Book of Murder* (London: Constable Robinson, 2000)

Williams, Thomas, *Fiji and the Fijians, The Islands and their Inhabitants,* Vol 1, 1858 (Suva: Fiji Museum, 1982)

Wilkes, Charles, *Narrative of the United States Exploring Expedition,* Vol III (Suva: Fiji Museum, 1985)

Woodward, Ann, *English Heritage Book of Shrines and Sacrifice* (London: B.T. Batsford, 1992)

Xun, Lu, *Diary of a Madman and Other Stories* (Honolulu: University of Hawaii Press, 1990)

Yi, Zheng, *A Scarlet Memorial: Tales of Cannibalism in Modern China* (New York: Westview Press, 1998)

Articles

Arens, William, 'Eating people isn't right', *New Scientist* (20 September, 1979)

Bahn, Paul G., 'Is cannibalism too much to swallow?', *New Scientist* (27 April, 1991)

Bahn, Paul G., 'Ancestral cannibalism gives us food for thought', *New Scientist* (11 April, 1992)

Bahn, Paul G., 'Atapuerca's double contribution to the cannibalism debate', *Journal Of Iberian Archaeology*, Vol 1 (1999)

Berlin, Fred S., 'Jeffrey Dahmer: was he ill? Was he impaired? Insanity revisited', *American Journal of Forensic Psychiatry*, Vol 15, No 1 (1994/95)

Billman, Brian R., *et al*, 'Cannibalism, warfare, and drought in the Mesa Verde region during the twelfth century AD', *American Antiquity*, Vol 65, No 1 (2000)

Billman, Brian R., *et al*, 'Response to critique of the claim of cannibalism at Cowboy Wash', *American Antiquity*, Vol 65, No 2 (2000)

Breskun, N.B., *et al*, 'Some procedural specifics in the identification of dismembered human body parts and meat products', *Expert Practice* (Kemerovo State Medical Academy, 1997)

Brittain, R.P., 'The sadistic murderer', *Medicine, Science and the Law*, 10 (1970)

Chen, Thomas S.N. and Chen, Peter S.Y., 'Medical cannibalism in China', *The Pharos* (Spring, 1998)

Clunie, Fergus, 'Rokotui Dreketi's human skull Yaqona cup?', *Domodomo*, Vol 2 (1987)

Clunie, Fergus, 'Daveniyaqona: a sacred Yaqona dish from Fiji', *Tribal Art* (1996)

Clunie, Fergus, 'Fijian Weapons and Warfare', *Fiji Times and Herald* (1977)

DeGusta, David, 'Cannibalism and mortuary ritual: bioarchaeological evidence from Vunda', *International Journal of Osteoarchaeology*, No 10 (2000)

DeGusta, David, 'Fijian cannibalism: osteological evidence from Navatu', *American Journal of Physical Anthropology*, No 110 (1999)

Denison, Simon, 'Burial in water "normal rite" for 1000 years: skeletons, animal skulls and other Iron Age offerings found in Thames', *British Archaeology*, No 53, (June 2000)

Diamond, Jared, 'Living through the Donner Party', *Discover Magazine* (March, 1992)

Diamond, Jared, 'Archaeology: talk of cannibalism', *Nature*, (7 September, 2000)

Fernandez-Jalvo, Yolanda, 'Human cannibalism in the early Pleistocene of Europe', *Journal of Human Evolution*, No 37 (1999)

Grant, Edward S., 'Something verging on criminality', *New Democrat* (21 October, 1995)

Green, Miranda, 'Humans as ritual victims in the later prehistory of Western Europe', *Oxford Journal of Archaeology*, Vol 17, No 2 (Oxford: Blackwell, 1998)

Hallett, Robin, 'Cannibalism in Liberia: a historical survey from the nineteenth century to 1997' (2000)

Hillson, Simon, 'Editorial: cannibalism and violence', *International Journal of Osteoarchaeology*, Special Issue, Vol 10, (2000)

Hurlbut, S.A., 'The taphonomy of cannibalism: a review of anthropogenic bone modification in the American Southwest', *International Journal of Osteoarchaeology*, Special Issue, Vol 10 (2000)

Keenleyside, Anne, *et al*, 'The final days of the Franklin expedition: new skeletal evidence', *Arctic — Journal of The Arctic Institute of North America*, Vol 50, No 1 (University of Calgary, March, 1997)

Kraus, Richard T., 'An enigmatic personality: case report of a serial killer', *Journal of Orthomolecular Medicine*, Vol 10, No 1 (1995)

Lloyd Parry, Richard, 'What young men do', *Granta*, Vol 62 (Summer, 1998)

Murphy, E.M. and Mallory, J.P., 'Herodotus and the cannibals', *Antiquity*, Vol 74 (June, 2000)

Novak, Shannon A. and Kollman, Dana D., 'Perimortem processing of human remains among the Great Basin Fremont', *International Journal of Osteoarchaeology*, No 10 (2000)

Obeyesekere, Gananeth, '"British cannibals": contemplation of an event in the death and resurrection of James Cook, explorer', *Critical Inquiry*, Vol 18, (Summer, 1992)

Philps, Alan, 'Nasty enough to eat', *Daily Telegraph* (4 January, 1997)

Pickering, Michael P., 'Food for thought: an alternative to cannibalism in the Neolithic', *Australian Archaeology*, No 28, (June, 1989)

Preston, Douglas, 'Cannibals of the Canyon', *The New Yorker* (30 November, 1998)

Raine, A., *et al*, 'Selective reductions in prefrontal glucose metabolism in murderers', *Biological Psychiatry*, Vol 36, No 6 (1994)

Raine, A., *et al*, 'Brain abnormalities in murderers indicated by positron emission tomography', *Biological Psychiatry*, Vol 42, No 6 (1997)

Raine, A., *et al*, 'Interaction between birth complications and early maternal rejection in predisposing individuals to adult violence: specificity to serious, early-onset violence', *American Journal of Psychiatry*, Vol 154, No 9 (September, 1997)

Raine, A., *et al*, 'Low resting heart rate at age 3 years predisposes to aggression at age 11 years: evidence from the Mauritius Child Health Project', *Journal American Academy of Child and Adolescent Psychiatry*, Vol 36, No 10 (October, 1997)

Raine, A., *et al*, 'Prefrontal glucose deficits in murderers lacking psychosocial deprivation', *Neuropsychiatry, Neuropsychology, and Behavioral Neurology*, Vol 11, No 1 (1998)

Raine, A., *et al*, 'Fearlessness, stimulation-seeking, and large body size at age 3 years as early predispositions to childhood aggression, at age 11 years', *Archives of General Psychiatry*, Vol 55, No 8 (August, 1998)

Richards, M.P. and Hodges R.E.M., 'Gough's Cave and Sun Hole Cave human stable isotope values indicate a high animal protein diet in the British upper Paleolithic', *Journal of Archaeological Science*, Vol 27, No 1–3 (2000)

Rykovtseva, Yelena, 'Cannibals return to Russia: human flesh being sold on the streets', *Moscow News* (25 Aug–1 September, 1996, No 34)

Smith, Joan, 'People eaters', *Granta*, Vol 52 (1995)

Smith, T., 'Is cannibalism a myth?', *British Medical Journal*, Vol 308, No 923 (2 April, 1994)

Spenneman, Dirk H.R., 'Saulaca: Fijian sail needles' *Domodomo*, Vol 4, No 2 (1986)

Spenneman, Dirk H.R., 'A human bone thatching needle from Vanuabalavu Island, Fiji', *Domodomo*, Vol 5, No 1&2 (1987)

Spenneman, Dirk H.R., 'Cannibalism in Fiji: the analysis of butchering marks on human bones and the historical record', *Domodomo*, Vol 5, No 1&2 (1987)

Turner, Christy G., 'Cannibalism in Chaco Canyon', *American Journal of Physical Anthropology*, No 91 (1993)

Villa, Paola, 'Cannibalism in prehistoric Europe', *Evolutionary Anthropology*, Vol 1, No 3 (1992)

Villa, Paola, 'Cannibalism in the Neolithic', *Science*, Vol 233 (25 July, 1986)

Whitell, Giles, 'Butchered friend was in banquet', *The Times* (3 August, 2000)

Index